Food for Your Thoughts and Strength for Your Spirit

LAURIE D. FISHER

This book is in honor of my late parents, Edward and Maria Fresquez, who endured much in their life's journey and have gone on to glory before us. It delights my heart to know that you are eternally with our Father God, and that I will see you again.

To my children, Toni and Mario, and his wife, Kylie; my grand-daughter, Jasmine, and her husband, Andrew; my grandsons, Malachi and Zaccai; my granddaughters, Shania, Robin, Alaysia, Arcadia, Amy; and my great-grandchildren Eva'Lise, Noah, Moses, and soon-to-be great-grandson. You are all my absolute joy and delight!

Special thanks to my wonderful husband, Glenn Fisher, who has truly been a true example of Christ's love to me by loving me as Christ has loved the church and who prays for me and always encourages and continues to draw out the best in me. Thank you, sweetheart, for believing in what God has placed on the inside of me for the sake of blessing others. I have the utmost respect for you, and I love and honor you.

FOREWORD

I loved it! I was so blessed by this devotional from the very first page. Every day, you get a fresh word to inspire you and challenge you to become a better you. One awesome feature is the practicality of the devotions—short, precise, and engaging. You can actually relate to the practical scenarios of everyday emotions, and you find yourself engaged in not yet another devotional but a thought-provoking self-analysis, leading to healthy cleansing of the heart and soul. God's love and spirit gently guiding one to purge oneself of all impurities of a contaminated mind and heart.

Laurie is an awesome personal friend of many years, and her husband, Glenn, goes back even more years in friendship. She is a woman after God's own heart, and her obedience to God in writing this devotional is a benefit to all who are blessed to read it. Expecting many more wonderful devotionals and books from Laurie. This is just a beginning of what will be!

Ernestina (Ernie) Garcia

Ernestina (Ernie) Garcia is a missionary in Mexico for thirty years. She is the pastor of Iglesia Fuego a las Naciones in Pachuca, Hidalgo, Mexico. She is an International Woman's Conference speaker and a television and radio host. She is the wife of evangelist Jerry Garcia for thirty-seven years. They have four daughters and seven grandchildren.

∾ ACKNOWLEDGMENT ∾

Special acknowledgment to my precious aunt, Odessa Dawson, who has inspired me. Thank you for always speaking encouraging words into my life. I love you dearly.

All glory, honor, and praise to my Father God, and my Lord and Savior, Jesus Christ, who is my treasured relationship above all! Thank you for your love and saving grace which saved me and transferred me out of the kingdom of darkness and into the kingdom of your marvelous light and for always being there to see me through every troubling situation that I have ever been through. You are my Rock on which I can stand on, rely on, and trust in; and I thank you for giving to me the precious Holy Spirit who is my help, my comfort, my standby, and my greatest teacher that always leads me and guides me into all truth!

We live in a world where there is so much negativity all around us, and we are far too often affected by what is going on around us. The passion for this devotion was birthed out of the encouragement from others who found inspiration from the scriptures and sayings that have been posted on my social media account for over a year. I never realized that this was my motivational gift in regards to the scripture Romans 12:8, which says, "If you have the grace-gift of encouragement, then use it often to encourage others."

All of God's gifts are given to us by grace. It is his ability in us that works through us, and it is not of ourselves lest we should boast. My prayer for you is that you find your motivational grace gift through this scripture, Romans 12:6–8, and use it to serve God by serving others and be one who builds God's kingdom here upon this earth.

> God's marvelous grace imparts to each one of us varying gifts and ministries that are uniquely ours. So if God has given you the grace-gift of prophecy, you must activate your gift by using the proportion of faith you have to prophesy. If your grace-gift is serving, then thrive in serving others well. If you have the grace-gift of teaching, then be actively teaching and training others. If you have the grace-gift of encouragement, then use it often to encourage others. If you have the grace-gift of giving to meet the needs of others, then may you prosper in your generosity with-

out any fanfare. If you have the gift of leadership, be passionate about your leadership. And if you have the gift of showing compassion, then flourish in your cheerful display of compassion. (Rom. 12:6–8, TPT)

This devotional, although simplistic, is designed to bring about a consistency of daily time, focusing on a personal relationship with the Lord and building a life of foundational truth through the Word of God (the Bible) which is his will for your life. Unlike other devotionals that begin in the month of January, you can begin reading this devotional any time of the year on any Sunday, which is the beginning of the week with the ending of the week being on a Saturday. The scriptures in this devotional have not been typed out for you with the purpose of getting you to a place where you will read the scripture for yourself. I would like to make the suggestion to have three different translations of the Bible for you to read so that the depth of each translation would minister to you personally.

May your life be enriched in every way as you make yourself ready to receive from God what it is that he has for you each day as you read through every scripture, word of encouragement, and prayer in Jesus' name!

In his love,
Laurie D. Fisher

Sunday, Day 1

(1)We have all heard the saying, "You don't have to reinvent the wheel." What that means is we don't have to do something in a drastically new way, often unnecessarily. We can say that is true of prayer. We do not have to reinvent prayer as prayer is setting yourself in *agreement* with God's Word. When we pray according to God's Word, we know that we are praying his perfect will and that he hears us, and we have whatever we have petitioned him for. That is his perfect will for us, and it does not get any better than that. Set yourself in *agreement with God.

Read Scripture:

1 John 5:14–15

Prayer:

Heavenly Father, I come before you now, thanking you that prayer is not something that is done by form or fashion, but it is when I set myself in agreement with your Word, which is your perfect will for me. As an act of my will and with the help of the Holy Spirit, I will take time to read and study your Word until it becomes

---

* Agreement—the state of being in one accord or in a harmonious relationship.

alive in my Spirit man so that when I come to you asking you for anything, I am in one accord with you and I've got your Word on it. Thank you that your Word will never return unto you void, but it will accomplish those things in my life that you have purposed for me. In Jesus' name, I pray, amen.

Notes:

_____

_____

_____

_____

_____

_____

_____

_____

_____

Monday, Day 2

(2) In the broken times of our life, we often question God as to why. Why are we going through this or that? Many times, we may think that God does not understand; but on the contrary, he most certainly does understand. He sent his Son, Jesus, and Jesus knows what you are going through for he himself was broken for us by his body on the way to the cross. He was despised, rejected, humbled, and broken. *Brokenness* led Jesus into humility so that God could raise him up and exalt him. The *brokenness that you are experiencing releases you into humility so that God can raise you up in humility to be used for his glory. Don't resist the process of brokenness that you are experiencing, but know that it has God's given purpose.

Read Scripture:

1 Peter 5:6

Prayer:

Heavenly Father, I come before you in my brokenness; and in godly sorrow, I repent for the spirit of self-pride, self-importance, and self-love. Please forgive me now. I thank you for your forgiveness

---

* *Brokenness*—subdued totally; humbled, quiet and a broken spirit, and repentant.

as I receive it now. As an act of my will, I surrender myself under your mighty hand, and to your plan and purpose for my life. Thank you that Jesus was my example—as he was rejected, beaten, broken—and he gave his life for me, and you raised him up and exalted him to sit with you at your right hand. This brokenness that I am going through breaks the spirit of pride and releases me into humility. I will not resist it but yield to the process, knowing that it will produce exactly what you intended for me, humility and readiness to fulfill your purpose. For this, I thank you. In Jesus' name. Amen.

Notes:

_____

_____

_____

_____

_____

_____

_____

_____

_____

_____

Tuesday, Day 3

(3) When we have done these things pertaining to God's Word, then with it is a promise from God. He says that you will be blessed, and the blessings will overtake you. These blessings will be in the fruit of your body physically, in your finances financially, and the increase and fruitfulness in blessings in everything that you do. *Hearken* to his Word today. Observe and obey his Word and then carry it out in your life, and with it, expect his promise to be fulfilled. *Hearken, *observe†, and *do‡.

Read Scripture:

Deuteronomy 28:1–8

Prayer:

Father God, I come to you now, thanking you for speaking to me today about your many blessings that you have promised me when I hear and obey your Word by walking it out in my life. I admit that this is something that I cannot do on my own without the help

---

*   Hearken—to listen attentively.
†   Observe—to comply with.
‡   Do—to carry it out.

15

of the Holy Spirit, so I am asking for your help, Holy Spirit. As an act of my will, I submit my will to you, Holy Spirit. I make the decision to take the time to hear, listen, read, study, meditate, and profess the Word of God, and observing the Word of God by training myself and bringing myself in agreement with it so that I can execute and live it to the full extent that God desires of me. In Jesus' name, I pray. Amen.

Notes:

_____

_____

_____

_____

_____

_____

_____

_____

_____

_____

Wednesday, Day 4

(4) As with any battle, any soldier of war will confirm that there are those who get wounded and need care for their deep wounds. There are *wounded* souls amongst us. They are sitting in the church pews every Sunday. The question is: are you one of them? If so, God wants to heal your heart and minister to your *wounded soul. You know that you have a wounded soul when others' words or actions cause you to react. Do not be ashamed to admit that you are *wounded for in doing so, healing can begin. Don't be afraid to reach out to your church leaders for guidance in the process. There is help for you.

Read Scripture:

Psalm 147:3

Prayer:

Heavenly Father, I want to thank you for showing me the condition of my heart and that there is no shame in admitting that my soul is wounded. I repent and ask you to forgive me for holding on to these hurt feelings, and I thank you for your forgiveness now. As an act of my will, I stand in faith, forgiving those who have hurt me.

---

* *Wounded*—feeling emotional pain. Hurt feelings.

Lord, I give you all of my hurts by laying them at your feet. I ask you to heal the sorrow of my heart as I give it to you now and I receive inner healing in my soul. Thank you for your love and healing power which heals my heart and my wounded soul, and makes me whole. In Jesus' name. Amen.

Notes:

_____

_____

_____

_____

_____

_____

_____

_____

Thursday, Day 5

(5) In this world that we live in, we are going to face trouble on every side. The trouble that we face can leave us feeling distressed or *afflicted* with great pain, anxiety, or sorrow and at times, confused mentally; and we are tempted to give up hope which can leave us in despair if we allow it. There is a treasure on the inside of you, and his name is Jesus. You can draw on his life-giving presence, which will manifest his glory and strength, and causes you to rise above the situation that tries to take your peace, steal your joy, and make you a victim of your circumstances.

Read Scripture:

2 Corinthians 4:8

Prayer:

Father God, I come before you today, asking you to forgive me for allowing myself to be a victim of my circumstance and allowing it to take control over my life. I thank you for forgiving me as I receive your forgiveness now. Holy Spirit, I need you. I ask you to help me and teach me how to draw on the Greater One who lives on the

---

* *Afflicted*—to distress with mental or bodily pain; trouble greatly or grievously.

inside of me; and how to draw upon him and his life-giving strength, his peace, and his joy; and how to stand victoriously over every situation as I put my hope in God. In Jesus' name, I pray. Amen.

Notes:

_____

_____

_____

_____

_____

_____

_____

_____

Friday, Day 6

(6) At one time or another, we have heard this saying, "That's the way the cookie crumbles." What that saying means is there is nothing we can do about the way things have unfolded, especially bad ones, so there is no reason to be upset about it. When you have embraced that saying, then you leave no expectation for God to move on your behalf or in your life. Therefore, do not *embrace* it, but look to God and *embrace what his Word says about your situation and wait expectantly for him to show up.

Read Scripture:

Psalm 62:5

Prayer:

Heavenly Father, I come to you, asking you to forgive me in embracing the things in my life that have come to hinder my expectation of you moving in my life. I thank you for your forgiveness as I receive it now. Holy Spirit, I need you. I am asking that you would help me to put my hope in God, and stir up my faith and expectation that God will perform and accomplish his Word, which is his will

---

* *Embrace*—to adopt or support and accept willingly or eagerly.

21

for my life to the degree to which I believe. I believe and therefore I receive it now. In Jesus' name. Amen.

Notes:

_____

_____

_____

_____

_____

_____

_____

_____

Saturday, Day 7

(7) Do you fear death? When you have accepted Jesus as your Lord and Savior, death is not a terrible fate of doom. Look at Jesus who was handed a death sentence, but he resurrected and is seated at the right hand of God. There is an eternal *destination* for you in the Lord, and when you die, your body will return to the earth as dust; but the real you, which is your spirit, will be returned to your Creator who gave you life as he receives you back to himself. Death is simply leaving your body here and leaving from here to your eternal place. *Destination heaven.

Read Scripture:

Ecclesiastes 12:7

Prayer:

Heavenly Father, I thank you that I do not have to fear death because I have accepted Jesus as my Lord and Savior. I know that death is only a separation of my body returning to dust, but the real me, which is my spirit, is returned to you, my Creator, and that you receive me back to yourself to live with you forever. Thank you that

---

* *Destination*—the ultimate purpose for which something is created or intended.

destination heaven is the very purpose that you have intended for me, where there is no more suffering, pain, sickness, and no more tears. What a glorious day it will be when I see you face to face, and for this, I give you thanks. In Jesus' name. Amen.

Sunday, Day 1

(8) the troubling things that we face in life may seem like they are too difficult to make it through, but they are only for a moment and are **temporal.* * God gives us his abundant grace to walk through the *temporal things, and we faint not because our inner man is strengthened and renewed day by day. try not to look at the things that you see going on outwardly, but take a deep breath and know that the short-lived pains of this life are creating for us an eternal glory that cannot compare to the difficulties that we go through here on earth.

Read Scripture:

2 Corinthians 4:17

Prayer:

Father God, I come before you now, asking to give me your strength to walk through the difficult time that I am facing right now. Thank you for your abundant grace that you give to me to face each day. I know that what I am experiencing right now cannot compare to the eternal glory that is created for me. Holy Spirit, you are

---

* *Temporal*—lasting only for a time; not eternal; passing or short lived.

my help, and I need you. Help me to take my focus off the temporal things that I see and are not eternal but short-lived, and help me to focus on the things that are unseen by my natural eyes. Open my eyes to the supernatural to see those things which are eternal and last forever. In Jesus' name. I pray. Amen.

Notes:

_____

_____

_____

_____

_____

_____

_____

_____

_____

Monday, Day 2

(9) From the time that you awaken in the morning to the time you lay your sweet head down, and even in your sleeping hours, the hand of God's *protection** is over you, under you, and all around you. He is guarding you and watching over you to keep you and your family safe from calamity and harm in this evil world we live in. It is as if you are under surveillance twenty-four hours a day, seven days a week, by an invisible force that surrounds you with *protection and safety. God protects his sheep.

Read Scripture:

2 Thessalonians 3:3

Prayer:

Heavenly Father, I thank you that I feel safe and secure knowing that wherever I go and however I get there, I am not alone because you have assigned your angels over me to make sure that nothing bad happens and that no harm shall come to me or near me. I thank you that whether I am awake or asleep that you have guarded me and

---

* *Protection*—supervision or support of one that is smaller and weaker, safety, and safekeeping.

my family. I thank you, Father God, for your divine protection over myself and my family. I am protected, I am safe, and most of all, I am loved by you. And for this, I thank you. In Jesus' name. Amen.

Notes:

_____

_____

_____

_____

_____

_____

_____

_____

_____

_____

Tuesday, Day 3

(10) Words have such power, and when words touch our ears, we should try them and judge them, and only receive that which is beneficial to our life. When others speak evil of you with their words, *counteract* it immediately by refusing to believe it. Understand that it is only their opinion, and do not accept it as truth. Treat their words as a plate of bad food set before you. Refuse to accept and push it away from you, and then replace those words with God's Word. Do not accept anything said about you that does not line up with what God's Word says about you.

Read Scripture:

Job 34:3–4

Prayer:

Father God, I thank you that you give me the ability to test the words that are spoken by others concerning me. If their words do not sit well with my spirit or line up with what your Word says about me, then I can and will refuse to accept it into my hearing or into my heart. With your strength, Holy Spirit, I will act against it

---

* *Counteract*—to act against, restrain, or to make in effective.

by pushing that plate of evil words away and reject it's lies, rendering it null void and powerless over my life. For every lie that is spoken to me, about me, or to me, I will replace it with your Word and what you say about me. In Jesus' name. Amen.

Notes:

_____

_____

_____

_____

_____

_____

_____

_____

_____

Wednesday, Day 4

(11) Faith is not walking blindly. Walking by faith is believing God's Word to be true. If God said it, then that should settle it. Once we have **resolved** that in our hearts, then we should delightfully walk it out. Faith is having full assurance that what God said in his Word is not just truth, but it is my truth and my reality. When you believe God's Word in your heart wholeheartedly, then you should stand expecting from God because he is the God of truth, and his Word is forever settled and established.

Read Scripture:

Hebrews 11:1

Prayer:

Father God, I ask you to forgive me for doubting you in any way and for not fully accepting what you said in your Word as solid truth and my reality. Holy Spirit, I ask you to help me as I have decided that I will not walk as one who is blind, but as one who believes that God's Word is real. It is not fraudulent or artificial, and it has already been settled and is immovable. I desire to apply it to every and all sit-

---

* *Resolved*—to reach a firm decision about.

uations that I face. Help me, Holy Spirit, to delightfully walk it out by faith and trust you. All of this I ask in Jesus' name. Amen.

Notes:

_____

_____

_____

_____

_____

_____

_____

_____

_____

Thursday, Day 5

(12) God has made both the day and the night. The nighttime that he has given you is a time for you to unwind, settle down, lie your body down, and close your eyes and rest. The promise of sweet sleep without fear is a blessing from God. There is an appointed time created by God for you to rest and **reboot** for the next new day, allowing you to start afresh. You are God's beloved, and God gives to you his beloved sweet sleep.

Read Scripture:

    Proverbs 3:24

Prayer:

    Father God, thank you for helping me to understand that rest for my body and mind is vital for me. I thank you that when I lay down at night, that I am not worried or anxious about anything because you are with me even during the nighttime. I thank you that my mind is at peace, that I am not afraid, and that you always give me the sweetest sleep that refreshes my entire being. I give you thanks

---

* *Reboot*—to start anew: to make a fresh start.

and praise for the night-time to reboot, and for awakening me afresh again to see and enjoy another day in you. In Jesus' name. Amen.

Notes:

_____

_____

_____

_____

_____

_____

_____

_____

Friday, Day 6

(13) Laundry day. Do you have a specific day set aside to do laundry? Laundry is a chore that many do not like to do. But have you ever considered that the day you accepted Jesus as your Lord and Savior is the day that the blood of Jesus, which is the real stain remover, forgave you, washed you, saved you, delivered you, and made you a new creation? Never view laundry day the same again; but make it a time to remember that Jesus cleansed you from the stain of sin, washed you free from all *impurities,* and made you brand new in him.

Read Scripture:

> Ephesians 1:7

Prayer:

> Father God, I thank you that even in my daily chores, such as doing the laundry, I can find traces of you in everything that I do. Today, I thank you for the blood of Jesus that was shed for me and the cleansing power to remove the stain of my sin, forgiving me and removing all the dirt of the world off me, washing me clean and pure.

---

* *Impurities*—lack of consistency or adulteration or a state of immorality; sin.

I thank you that the old me is dead, and I am a new person because of Jesus. For this, I will ever be grateful. In Jesus' name. Amen.

Notes:

_____

_____

_____

_____

_____

_____

_____

_____

_____

Saturday, Day 7

(14) God loves you as much as he loves Jesus! Let that sink in. Because of the sin of Adam and Eve, all of creation ended up *separated* from God. But God, in his love, did not want you to remain *separated from him, so he gave you Jesus, his precious Son, so that you would no longer be separated from him. He so desires to be close to you, and Jesus bridged the gap between us and God, bringing us near to him without any separation.

Read Scripture:

John 3:16

Prayer:

Heavenly Father, how I thank you for loving me beyond any love that I have ever experienced upon this earth and for sending your son Jesus so that I would no longer be far away from you. I thank you, Jesus, for the love that you had for the father to fulfill his will. Because of your obedience, Jesus, I have been reconciled back to my Father and will never be separated from him again. For this, I give you thanks and praise. In Jesus' name. Amen.

---

* *Separated*—to keep apart.

Notes:

_____

_____

_____

_____

_____

_____

_____

_____

Sunday, Day 1

(15) Hospitals and rehabilitation centers have physical therapy, occupational therapy, and speech therapy; and all are vital for someone's recovery. But the one valuable therapy that they are void of is Word of God therapy. Take one hour of Word therapy, which is spending *uninterrupted* time with God in his Word. This kind of therapy goes to the broken places of your heart and brings healing. When healing comes, it builds a better, healthier you from the inside out.

Read Scripture:

Jeremiah 17:14

Prayer:

Heavenly Father, I come to you, asking you to forgive me for not taking the time like I should to spend time daily with you in your Word. Holy Spirit, I need your help. When I get busy doing other things or when I am being hindered, please draw me by your presence to make time to sit in God's presence to read and study his Word because in doing so, it is like therapy. When I make time for Word therapy, it brings about healing to my innermost being and to

---

* *Uninterrupted*—not broken, discontinued, or hindered.

my mind and body, and it is good for my entire being. For this, I give you thanks and praise. In Jesus' name. Amen.

Notes:

_____

_____

_____

_____

_____

_____

_____

_____

_____

Monday, Day 2

(16) Trash day. Every community has a specific day when they set out their trash for the trash company to come, pick it up, and discard it for you. As you set out the trash on trash day, ask God to show you those things that he wants you to get rid of inwardly. As he shows you those things, confess them to him and prophetically dump them in the trash bin; and as you haul the trash bin to the curb, receive his forgiveness. Then as you watch the trash truck pick up the trash and drive off, say, "Take it away," and then thank God for helping you to discard all the *toxic* thoughts, and ways from your life.

Read Scripture:

1 John 1:9

Prayer:

Father God, I ask you to show me the toxic thoughts and ways that are within me that are hindering the plans that you have set out for my life. As you reveal them to me, Lord, I confess them and repent for these unhealthy thoughts. Thank you for your forgiveness as I receive it now. Holy Spirit, I need you. With your help and as an

---

* *Toxic*—harmful, unhealthy, poisonous, and lethal.

act of my will and prophetic act, I choose to dump all toxic thoughts and ways in the trash. I haul it to the curb, and I leave it there and say, "Take it away," as it is removed far from me and is taken away. As an act of my will, I will renew my mind to the Word of God, willingly embrace the thoughts and plans that God has for me. In Jesus' name, I pray. Amen.

Notes:

_____

_____

_____

_____

_____

_____

_____

_____

_____

Tuesday, Day 3

(17) When Jesus said, "It is finished," it was him fully completing the will of the Father. Jesus obeyed God and did his part, and he defeated Satan for you! Now the question is, are you doing your part?

Your part is enforcing or invoking the name of Jesus, his blood, and the Word of God by resisting the devil. You stand in the place of victory, not because of anything that you have done, but because of everything that Jesus has done. *Enforce** the name of Jesus, his blood, and the Word of God over the attacks of the enemy with full obedience to God and his Word.

Read Scripture:

1 John 3:8

Prayer:

Father God, the scripture says that Jesus came to defeat the devil and that he made a public spectacle of him, triumphing over him by the cross. I accept the finished work of the cross and what Jesus did in defeating my enemy, and that because of him, I stand in the place of victory over Satan and all of his evil works. Holy Spirit, I ask you

---

* *Enforce*—to put or keep in force by obedience.

43

to help me to enforce through obedience to your Word my victory over Satan by reminding him of his defeat through Jesus Christ, my Lord, and to resist him by standing firm on what Jesus has already done. Jesus died, was resurrected, and now sits at the right hand of the Father. I am seated with him in heavenly places using the authority that he has given me. In Jesus' name. Amen.

Notes:

_____

_____

_____

_____

_____

_____

_____

_____

_____

Wednesday, Day 4

(18) Real change comes from within, and no matter what we do *cosmetically*[*] to enhance our outer appearance, it does not take away the fact that God looks at the heart. There is nothing wrong with the care that is given to our outward appearance, but we should not forget our inward man. There is no makeup or cosmetic changes that we can use that can cover what's in the heart, so why attempt it? It's time to examine our own heart and be real with ourselves. God already knows us very well, and he loves us regardless.

Read Scripture:

Psalm 51:10

Prayer:

Heavenly Father, I come to you, first of all, thanking you that you love me. I ask you now to forgive me for any attempts made to cover up what is in my heart. I repent for doing all those things outwardly to look good on the outside for man's sake while ignoring those things on the inside of me that are not pleasing to you. I know

---

[*] *Cosmetically*—serving to modify or improve the appearance of a bodily defect, feature, or irregularity.

that there is nothing that can be hidden from you, and I am asking you, Holy Spirit, to create in me a pure heart. God, I ask you to renew a right spirit within me. In Jesus' name, I pray. Amen.

Notes:

_____

_____

_____

_____

_____

_____

_____

_____

Thursday, Day 5

(19) As a believer in Christ Jesus, you may face many attacks from the enemy; and many times, you can start to feel sorry for yourself. No matter what comes your way, do not give in to your flesh and call other's to take part in your pity party. Remember Jesus and what he endured and suffered all the way to cross for you. He did not quit, and you must not quit. *Aggressive* faith is putting your trust in God and never quitting. Have *aggressive faith. Defeat is not an option.

Read Scripture:

Mark 11:22

Prayer:

Father God, I come to you, asking you to forgive me for allowing my flesh to have a pity party with myself and wanting others to join in with me. I am sorry for allowing the situation and my feelings to dictate to me defeat and tempting me to quit. Thank you for your forgiveness as I receive it now. Holy Spirit, you are my help, and I am determined now to have faith in God and to trust him with all of my heart. As an act of my faith, I serve notice to self-pity, and I declare,

---

* *Aggressive*—assertive, bold, energetic, and determined.

"I have no room here for you to stay and as an act of my will, I evict you from my life and forbid you to come back." I declare that I am strong in the Lord and in the power of his might. In Jesus' name, I pray. Amen.

Notes:

_____

_____

_____

_____

_____

_____

_____

_____

_____

Friday, Day 6

(20) Giving is a kingdom of God lifestyle, but there are also simple things that we can sow besides monetary gifts. We all want a better world to live in, but did it ever occur to you that you can change the atmosphere around you one smile and one hug at a time? Each step that is taken when you *sow* those smiles and hugs generously will result in a much better atmosphere and give you a generous crop in return. But if you *sow only a few, then your crop or return will be small, so choose to sow generously. *Sow smiles and hugs today without limitations.

Read Scripture:

2 Corinthians 9:6

Prayer:

Father God, I want to thank you for another day to sow smiles and hugs into those that I come in contact with today. I make a conscious choice to be a sower of smiles, hugs, and kind words wherever I go today, knowing that one small act of kindness can brighten up someone's day, making a difference and changing the atmosphere

---

* *Sow*—to scatter or plant seed for the purpose of growth.

49

one person at a time. As I sow generously into the lives of others, I thank you that I can expect a generous and bountiful crop in return. In Jesus' name. Amen.

Notes:

_____

_____

_____

_____

_____

_____

_____

_____

_____

Saturday, Day 7

(21) There is no lack of the accounts in the Bible of those who faced disheartening circumstances and how God always encouraged them and told them to be courageous. When trouble comes, God does not want you to be afraid, alarmed, or discouraged. Remember that where-ever you go and whatever you do, God is with you always. So get rid of the "dis" in "discourage," and you're left with "courage." You are brave and *courageous,* and you've got this!

Read Scripture:

Joshua 1:9

Prayer:

Heavenly Father, you have commanded me to be strong and courageous. I thank you for reminding me that whatever I do and wherever I go, you are with me and will never leave me. I declare as an act of my faith in you that I am not afraid, alarmed, or discouraged when trouble comes my way. Because you have commanded me to be strong and courageous, and because I know that you have me

---

* *Courageous*—bold and unafraid.

covered with your divine protection and power, I can be courageous. For this, I thank you. In Jesus' name. Amen.

Notes:

_____

_____

_____

_____

_____

_____

_____

_____

_____

Sunday, Day 1

(22) Have you ever depended on someone that you thought you could trust, and they let you down and did not come through for you like they promised, and you found out that they were not someone that you can rely on or depend on? I am here to tell you that our God is *able!** He is depend*able* and reli*able*! You can depend on him and rely on him to do what he said he would do. He can be trusted. God is *able,* and blessed is he who puts his trust in him.

Read Scripture:

Psalm 84:12

Prayer:

Father God, you said in your Word that blessed is the man who puts his trust in you. I come to you now, asking you to forgive me if I have placed unrealistic expectations on others, expecting more of them than they are able to do for me. I extend the same forgiveness to them as well, and I thank you that I can depend and rely on you to do what you said that you would do because you are able. Father, I

---

* *Able*—having sufficient power or resources to accomplish something.

take you at your Word and thank you that you watch over your Word
to perform it in my life. In Jesus' name. Amen.

Notes:

_____

_____

_____

_____

_____

_____

_____

_____

_____

Monday, Day 2

(23) The Bible is not a set of rules for us to live by. It is a covenant between us and our loving heavenly Father, who *instructs** us with his words of wisdom. It is the wisdom of God, not the wisdom of the world, that we need to make important decisions concerning our life and family. God is your wise Father who desires to lead you through the instruction of his Word. Follow his instructions today and every day.

Read Scripture:

Proverbs 4:1

Prayer:

Heavenly Father, I come before you now, asking you to forgive me for treating your Word as if it was just rules to be followed instead of words of wisdom from you. Thank you, heavenly Father, that your Word is truth, and it directs me in the way that I should walk and live. You are a wise Father, and the instructions you give me through your Word always brings about the best results in my life when I hear

---

* *Instruct*—to teach someone how to do something.

and obey them. I give you thanks and praise today for ordering my steps in your Word. In Jesus' name. Amen.

Notes:

_____

_____

_____

_____

_____

_____

_____

_____

_____

Tuesday, Day 3

(24) We have all experienced a time when someone has made a promise to us and did not follow through on their end, leaving us *disappointed* and mistrusting in humanity. If we are not careful, we can also begin to see God the same way through the actions of those who did not make good on their promises to us. Our God is a faithful God, and he makes good on his promises that he has made to us through his Word. God is not a promise breaker, but a promise keeper.

Read Scripture:

Numbers 23:19

Prayer:

Father God, I come to you, asking you to forgive me for holding it against those who have made promises to me and have disappointed me. I release them now, and I forgive them as an act of my will. I thank you, God, that you are a good God and that everything that you have promised me in your Word for my life, you will do it because you are not a man that you could lie. I thank you that you

---

* *Disappointed*—saddened by the failure of an expectation or to be let down.

are a promise keeper and that I can put my trust in you to do what you said according to what is written in your Word. For this, I thank you and praise you. In Jesus' name. Amen.

Notes:

_____

_____

_____

_____

_____

_____

_____

_____

_____

Wednesday, Day 4

(25) Many women and even men spend untold amounts of money on anti-aging creams in hopes that it will make them look younger than they really are. There is nothing wrong with caring for your outward man; however, we should also give time to care for our spirit. Think of it this way, when you read, hear, and study God's Word daily and then you apply it to your life, it is likened to applying an anti-aging cream. Your youth will be *renewed* like the eagles. You will be rejuvenated, refreshed, lively, and ready to soar above any circumstance that tries to bring you down.

Read Scripture:

Psalm 103:5

Prayer:

Father God, today, I make a conscious decision to spend time reading, hearing, and studying your Word because it is beneficial to my very life. Thank you, Father, that your Word revealed to me can then be applied by me to my own life, and it renews me and strengthens me so that I am not caught off guard by any obstacles that may

---

* *Renew*—to make new. Restore.

try to get in my way today. Holy Spirit, you are my Teacher, and I am asking you to give me more revelation to know God through his Word and teach me how to apply his Word to my life, which causes me to rise and soar above any and all obstacles that stand before me. In Jesus' name, I pray. Amen.

Notes:

_____

_____

_____

_____

_____

_____

_____

_____

_____

Thursday, Day 5

(26) God has put a "no fishing" sign at the pond of your bad past, so drop your fishing pole! Going back to your past is like a dead fish that stinks. You cannot change the past, so do not allow the past to occupy your thoughts or mind. Speak to the memories of your bad past and render them null, void, and powerless in your life. Do not continue to *relive* your past. God never does, so neither should you.

Read Scripture:

Isaiah 43:18–19

Prayer:

Father God, I come before you, thanking you for the reminder that you have redeemed me from the past. Every mistake, has been forgiven and all regret washed away, and I do not have to relive my past anymore. As an act of my will, I lay down the fishing pole at the pond of my past, and I lift my hands in praise to you, thanking you for giving me a new life as I look forward to all the good things that you have in store for me. In Jesus' name. Amen.

---

* *Relive*—to undergo or experience again, especially in the imagination.

Notes:

Friday, Day 6

(27) As you look at your event calendar today, remember that you have a divine appointment to meet with the wonderful *Counselor,* so don't miss it. He is the Prince of Peace, and he is waiting for you and is looking forward to his time with you. Of all the appointments and tasks that you have to do today, this is of the utmost importance. If you have to cancel another appointment to pencil it in on your planner, then do so. It will be the best part of your day and will set the tone for the rest of your day.

Read Scripture:

Isaiah 9:6

Prayer:

Heavenly Father, I come to you right now, asking you to forgive me for allowing my busy schedule to cause me to miss my divine appointments with you. I thank you for your forgiveness as I receive it now. Holy Spirit, I need you. I ask you now to give me the desire to want to spend quality time in God's presence to worship, to study the Word, to pray, and to take the time to sit quietly to hear those

---

* *Counselor*—one who advises, consults, and mentors.

things that you have to say to me by your Spirit. For I know that you are my wonderful Counselor, and you have my best interest at heart. I thank you. In Jesus' name. Amen.

Notes:

_____

_____

_____

_____

_____

_____

_____

_____

_____

Saturday, Day 7

(28) Have you ever said something that as soon as the words left your lips, you regretted saying it, and you wanted to take those words back? Make a conscious effort today to think before you speak. The words that we speak produce a harvest in the lives of others but also in your own life. Have no *regrets.*

Read Scripture:

Proverbs 15:28

Prayer:

Father God, I come to you repenting for speaking carelessly and for any words that I have spoken that was hurtful to others. Thank you for your forgiveness as I receive it now. I now know that my words have power and can either hurt or bless others, and it is my heart's desire to speak words that build others and not tear them down. Holy Spirit, I need you, and I come to you, asking you today for your help because I know that I cannot do it without you. Holy Spirit, you convict my heart of any words that are not pleasing to

---

* *Regret*—the feeling of sorrow, disappointment, distress, or remorse about something that one wishes could be different.

God, and I ask that you, Holy Spirit, redirect my speech to speak the truth in love. All of this I ask in the name of Jesus. Amen.

Notes:

_____

_____

_____

_____

_____

_____

_____

_____

_____

Sunday, Day 1

(29) We have all been wronged by someone, and throughout our life, we have experienced hurt and pain at the words or hands of others. Love does not keep records of those who have hurt us, and it is time, so to speak, to burn the files that you have kept stored away in your mind or heart. Take *inventory** of the files that are in your possession and that you have kept on those who have hurt you. Bring them to God and leave them there.

Read Scripture:

    1 Corinthians 13:4–10

Prayer:

    Father God, I come before you now, asking you to show me those hidden files and records that I have stored away in my mind or heart of those who have hurt me in times past. Holy Spirit, I give you permission to reveal those hidden hurts and places where I have not extended forgiveness to those who have harmed me in any way. Father God, love does not keep records or does not tally the wrongs

---

* *Inventory*—a detailed, itemized list, report, or record of things in one's possession.

done to me by others. And by faith, as the Holy Spirit reveals to me those that I need to forgive, I choose as an act of my will to forgive them for every word or action done to me that caused me pain. I release them now, and I ask for your love and healing power to heal that part of my life, making me whole again. In Jesus' precious and holy name. Amen.

Notes:

_____

_____

_____

_____

_____

_____

_____

_____

_____

Monday, Day 2

(30) Have you ever tried in the middle of the night to walk to the bathroom without turning the lights on, and along the way, you stubbed your toe or walked into the wall or even tripped on a shoe that you did not know was in your path? To say the least, it is not safe to walk in the dark. Before we accepted Jesus as our Savior, we were children of the darkness, but now we are called children of light and are called to walk in the light. If you have ever allowed yourself to be caught up in the negativity that surrounds you in this world, then you're walking in darkness. Be determined today to walk in the light, and be the light in this dark world. Be free from *negativism.*

Read Scripture:

Ephesians 5:8

Prayer:

Heavenly Father, I thank you that you have called me out of darkness into your marvelous light. I am a child of light, and I ask you to help me today to walk in the light of your love and the light

---

* *Negativism*—the practice or habit of being skeptical, critical toward the views or suggestions of others.

of your Word. As I allow you to lead me each step of the way, I thank you that those that are walking in darkness would desire the same life that you have given me through Jesus Christ, my Lord, which is freedom from darkness and the liberty of walking as a child of light. In Jesus' name, I pray. Amen.

Notes:

_____

_____

_____

_____

_____

_____

_____

_____

Tuesday, Day 3

(31) Faith speaks to the mountain and laughs at impossibilities. Are you facing a mountainous problem that seems so big that you cannot see yourself on the other side of it? Regardless of the feelings that you are experiencing right now, and the fact that you do not feel like it, stand tall and begin to laugh at that mountain. Stand and face the problems that are before you and laugh at it. Begin to speak to the problem about your God instead of speaking to God about your problem. It is an act of your will and an act of faith, to say the least. Laughing at the problem will help you to rise above the doubt and discouragement that you are feeling, and faith will arise on the inside of you. Do not *doubt.*

Read Scripture:

Mark 11:23

Prayer:

Heavenly Father, I come before you, thanking you for the strength that I have in you to stand and face my problems head on. I choose to speak your Word to the mountain that is before me, and I

---

* *Doubt*—the state of being uncertain about the truth or reliability of something.

declare that you are my God, the God who takes the impossible and makes it possible. I laugh at the mountain, "Ha, ha, ha, ha," because I know that the mountain is not bigger than my God and that every mountain or problem has been laid low in comparison to the God that I serve. I do not doubt in my heart, but I believe you, God. I thank you that you will bring your Word to pass in my life. In Jesus' name. Amen.

Notes:

_____

_____

_____

_____

_____

_____

_____

_____

_____

_____

Wednesday, Day 4

(32) Have you ever prayed for something and you got tired of waiting for an answer from God? First of all, we must understand that God's Word is his will for us, and our prayers should line up with his Word. If you have asked God for something that lines up with his Word, then you must know and understand that he has heard you and that he will answer you. Once you have acknowledged that your prayer lines up with God's Word, then wait patiently and **persevere.** Perseverance is a continued effort to do or achieve something despite difficulties, failure, or opposition. Have an attitude of "I will not be defeated and I will not quit!" Be steadfast and stay in an attitude of gratitude, thanking God that he has heard your prayers and is taking care of things for you.

Read Scripture:

1 Corinthians 15:58

---

* *Persevere*—to persist in or remain constant to a purpose in the face of obstacles or discouragement.

Prayer:

Heavenly Father, I come to you now, giving you thanks for your Word. Your Word is your will for my life, and I can be reassured that when I pray out according to your Word, that you not only hear me, but you desire to give me what I have prayed for. As an act of my will, I continue to exercise patience; and I do persevere, knowing that I need not be anxious but I can have full confidence that what you said in your Word will surely come to pass. I continue to stay in an attitude of gratitude and thanksgiving, assured that you will do exactly what you have promised me that you would do according to your Word. In Jesus' name. Amen.

Notes:

_____

_____

_____

_____

_____

_____

_____

_____

_____

Thursday, Day 5

(33) *Gossip.* I hear a snake in there! Whether or not it's with a friend or a spouse, at one time or another, we have gossiped about someone. It is the sinful nature at work in us, and it is a natural inclination to sin. Given the choice to do God's will or our own, we tend to naturally choose to do our own thing. It is interesting that a snake tempted Eve to sin. However, Jesus has provided all believers with victory over their sin nature. "He himself bore our sins' in his body on the cross, so that we might die to sins and live for righteousness."

Read Scripture:

Psalm 34:13

Prayer:

Heavenly Father, I come before you now, asking you to forgive me for gossiping about others. I repent for the part that I have played in, whether it was starting it or giving ear to it. I acknowledge the hurt it has caused to the individual and also the hearer, and most of all, how it grieves the Holy Spirit. I thank you for your forgiveness as I receive it now. Holy Spirit, I need you. I am asking you for

---

* *Gossip*—a person who habitually spreads intimate or private rumors or facts.

your help in steering clear from conversations of gossip. Give me the power to walk away or to speak up against gossip, and doing it in love. Thank you for being such a loving and forgiving God. In Jesus' name. Amen.

Notes:

_____

_____

_____

_____

_____

_____

_____

_____

_____

Friday, Day 6

(34) When you were a child, did you have a favorite teacher that impacted your life in a way that you will never forget? One who took the time to answer your questions or made the extra effort to help you in an area that you were having difficulties? As a believer, God gave us the precious Holy Spirit to **teach** us the whole truth and nothing but the truth. There is no going wrong when we have a relationship with the Holy Spirit, allowing him to *teach us and remind us of the things that Jesus spoke while he walked upon the earth. The Holy Spirit is our Helper and a great Teacher.

Read Scripture:

John 14:26

Prayer:

Heavenly Father, I want to thank you that when Jesus went to sit at your right hand, he did not leave me or abandon me. Instead, he left a part of himself by sending the precious Holy Spirit to dwell on the inside of me. Thank you, Holy Spirit, that you are my Comforter, my Helper, my Counselor, my Teacher. You never speak

---

* *Teach*—to impart knowledge or skill to or to provide instruction.

on your own but you represent, act, and only speak to remind us of every word that Jesus spoke to us while he was here on the earth. Holy Spirit, I want to know you personally, and as an act of my will, I take your hand and allow you to instruct me in God's ways, because I need you every day. Thank you, Father God, for the Holy Spirit. In Jesus' name. Amen.

Notes:

_____

_____

_____

_____

_____

_____

_____

_____

_____

Saturday, Day 7

(35) Worry, is quite the heavy load to carry. To worry means to torment one-self with or suffer from disturbing thoughts, to fret. There are times in life when circumstances that are out of our control can cause us to worry even though we know that God tells us in his Word not to worry. God wants us to know that he tenderly cares for us. He wants us to take all those worries, lay them at his feet, and leave them there. Practice is what it takes. Start today by laying every circumstance that is stressing you out and causing you to worry at the feet of God, and let him take care of you. Give it to God. **Cast* or roll those cares on him.

Read Scripture:

1 Peter 5:7

Prayer:

Heavenly Father, you already know about my stressful circumstances that are causing me to worry. I come before you now, bringing every single care that I have, and I choose not to carry this heavy load anymore. As an act of my will, I willingly roll those cares to you,

---

* *Cast*—to roll or drop or to throw off.

and I lay it down at your feet. By faith, I walk away from these things that I have laid down before you, and I refuse to take them back up again. I have made the decision to trust you to take care of me, and I lay hold of the peace that comes in knowing that you tenderly and lovingly care for me. For this, I give you thanks and praise. In Jesus' name. Amen.

Notes:

_____

_____

_____

_____

_____

_____

_____

_____

_____

_____

Sunday, Day 1

(36) If you have ever been to a live play or musical, you will know that at the end of the program, they acknowledge the cast of characters and all the people who worked behind the scenes; and then the individual who plays the star role comes out and is acknowledged by applause and receives accolades. Life is much like a stage, and whether or not you have a platform, so to speak, everything you do should reflect your love for God and for others. Whether it is leading or serving, we should acknowledge God in everything that we do, and he will *direct* our steps.

Read Scripture:

Proverbs 3:6

Prayer:

Father God, I will never again look at life as just another day. I thank you that every day is a gift from you and an opportunity to live for you in all that I do. I thank you that I will never again look at my role as an employer or employee as just another job but an opportunity to lead and serve, and to reflect your love and joy in everything

---

* *Direct*—to cause to move in a certain direction. To give commands.

that I do. Thank you for directing my steps even on difficult days. I ask you to help me to keep my heart right before you, knowing that I represent you in the big stage of life, and I want others to see and know you through my actions. I ask this in Jesus' name. Amen.

Notes:

_____

_____

_____

_____

_____

_____

_____

_____

_____

Monday, Day 2

(37) When someone pays you a compliment, there is no denying that it feels wonderful. But when someone criticizes you, whether it is constructive or not, it hurts. If you had only bread to eat and nothing else, it would not **sustain** you in life. Likewise, you should not live your life on others' compliments or criticisms but instead, you should look to God's Word and find out what he has to say about you, for every word that proceeds from God will *sustain you.

Read Scripture:

Matthew 4:4

Prayer:

Father God, I come before you reflecting on how many times I have cherished others' compliments and harbored hurt from others' criticisms about me. As an act of my will, I forgive those who have knowingly or unknowingly hurt me by their words or actions, and I release them now. Father, I also ask you to forgive me for depending upon others' compliments of me and not spending time in your Word to find out what you say about me. Your Word is your

---

* *Sustain*—to support the spirits, vitality, or resolution of; encourage.

thoughts toward me, and through it, my whole being is nourished and strengthened. Your Word is encouraging to my heart and gives me hope to face each and every day, and shows me the love that you have for me and sustains me. Help me, Holy Spirit, and give me the desire and hunger for the Word of God so that I would grow in my relationship with God in a greater way. In Jesus' name, I pray. Amen.

Notes:

_____

_____

_____

_____

_____

_____

_____

_____

_____

Tuesday, Day 3

(38) Did you know that you are a beneficiary of all the *benefits* promised to you in God's Word? There is a will that was set in place by God, and you are designated as the recipient under that will; and when Jesus died, everything that belonged to him was passed down to you. Find out what *benefits are yours in the Word of God and take possession of those daily *benefits.

Read Scripture:

Psalm 103:2

Prayer:

Father God, I come before you, thanking you that your will for my life is found entirely in your will and testament. Give me a heart that desire to study your Word, which is your will for me, so that I will discover the benefits that you have for me. Holy Spirit, I ask you to teach me and give me understanding of God's Word and the wisdom to receive and steward all the good things that God has given to me. Thank you, Father God, for the full-coverage benefit

---

* *Benefits*—something that produces good or helpful results or effects or that promotes well-being.

package that covers me and my family for generations to come. In Jesus' name. Amen.

Notes:

_____

_____

_____

_____

_____

_____

_____

_____

_____

Wednesday, Day 4

(39) In the day and age we now live in, social media and technology take up so much of our time. It would almost be true to say that our phones, tablets, etc. have become idols; and time spent with God is becoming less and almost obsolete. We should always remember that a personal relationship with God is the most important aspect of a believer's life. God will not forget us, and we should not forget him. FaceTime with God, before you face the world. *Obeisance** to God is reverencing him.

Read Scripture:

    2 Samuel 14:4

Prayer:

    Father God, I come before you in absolute sorrow and repentance. I have allowed the trends of this world to take first place over time spent with you, and for this, I am truly sorry. I return to you, and I ask you sincerely to once again give me the love and desire to put you first in my life. There is nothing more important than my

---

*   *Obeisance*—an act of showing respect or submitting and surrendering to another.

FaceTime with you. Give me a heart fully devoted to you. As an act of my will, I submit and surrender to you. Holy Spirit, I am asking you to help me set aside the distractions that would try to draw me away from my Father God, so that I can enjoy my intimate, relational time in his presence. All of this I ask in Jesus' name. Amen.

Notes:

_____

_____

_____

_____

_____

_____

_____

_____

_____

Thursday, Day 5

(40) *Anger** keeps you from moving forward into the future that God has for you and keeps you in a place of constant stagnation like a fresh pool of water that has stopped flowing freely. Holding onto this *anger is like a foul flesh-eating disease that eats you up from the inside. It robs you of your peace, leaving you void of joy, and it also keeps you in a condition of mistrusting others who have not hurt you. It is time to let go of *anger.

Read Scripture:

Ephesians 4:26

Prayer:

Father God, I confess before you this anger that I have been holding onto, and I ask you to forgive me as it has kept me from walking in love and from moving forward in the things that you have for me. As an act of my will, I renounce, denounce, and break all agreement with this anger and command it to leave my heart and mind. I release those who I am angry at, and by faith, I forgive them

---

* *Anger*—a strong feeling of displeasure and belligerence aroused by a real or supposed wrong.

for hurting me. I thank you, Father God, for delivering me from anger, and I now receive your peace. Thank you for restoring my joy. In Jesus' name. Amen.

Notes:

_____

_____

_____

_____

_____

_____

_____

_____

Friday, Day 6

(41) Many would agree that we never would think of leaving our home half-dressed or naked. Did you know that as believers, we are to put on Christ daily? Putting Christ on means that we are to immerse ourselves in him to the degree that we will not **gratify** or yield to our sinful desires. It is making no provision for the flesh. As you prepare for your day, remember to put on Christ. He looks good on you.

Read Scripture:

> Romans 13:14

Prayer:

> Heavenly Father, today, as I prepare to dress for the day, I first take the time to worship you in your presence. As I read your Word, I take the time to meditate on it and allow you to minister to me as I minister to you. Before I dress my outer man, I take the time first to dress my inner man. I put on Christ who enables me to live this day with the ability and strength to stand clothed in the Spirit so that I

---

* *Gratify*—to give pleasure to (a person) by satisfying desires or humoring inclinations or feelings.

will not give in to my fleshy desires. Thank you that I am clothed in Christ Jesus, and there is no provision for the lust of the flesh today. In Jesus' name. Amen.

Notes:

_____

_____

_____

_____

_____

_____

_____

_____

_____

Saturday, Day 7

(42) Be thankful each and every day that God is not just a Sunday God! Saturday, Sunday, Monday, Tuesday, Wednesday, Thursday, and Friday, he is with you always. As a matter of fact, God is not even limited by our calendar because he is with you unto the end of the world. He is always teaching you his ways. How wonderful to know that although he is the invisible God and you can't see him with the natural eye, he is still right there with you, *Always.*

Read Scripture:

   Matthew 28:20

Prayer:

   Father, I want to thank you that although I cannot see you with my natural eye, I know that you are right here with me. Every day, every hour, and every minute, you are with me teaching me about your ways and revealing yourself to me. It is comforting to know that you will never leave me, and I thank you that I can depend on you to be near me, not just seven days a week, but unto the end of the world. For this, I am grateful. In Jesus' name. Amen.

---

* *Always*—forever at any time; in any event for all time.

Notes:

_____

_____

_____

_____

_____

_____

_____

_____

_____

Sunday, Day 1

(43) Prayer is an incredible force that *transcends* time and space. Even after you have left this earthly realm and entered into your eternal home, your prayers are still working. Your family's future is dependent upon the prayers that you pray today. Even though you may not be around to see the answer manifest, just know that God has heard and answered your prayer the second that you prayed. Pray for your today, and for your children and grandchildren's tomorrows.

Read Scripture:

Psalm 6:9

Prayer:

Heavenly Father, I come before you now, lifting up my children and grandchildren, and their children and their children's children for generations to come. I pray that the God of our Lord Jesus Christ, the Father of glory, may give unto them the spirit of wisdom and revelation in the knowledge of him. That the eyes of their under-standing be enlightened, and that they may know the hope of their calling, and the riches of the glory of their inheritance in the saints.

---

* *Transcend*—to go above and beyond a limit or expectation.

Thank you for hearing my prayer and that it is fulfilled this day that I have prayed and believed. In Jesus' name. Amen.

Notes:

_____

_____

_____

_____

_____

_____

_____

_____

_____

Monday, Day 2

(44) There is no doubt in saying that if we fail to feed our body the food that is necessary for our body's nutrition and that sustains us for life over a very long period of time, we will starve that body to death. The same goes for our spirit man. The strength of your spirit is dependent upon the nutrition of spiritual things such as time in God's presence, worship unto the Lord, and studying the Word of God. We should take as much time, if not more, to nourish our spirit as we would our natural body. Take time consistently to worship the Lord, and feed on God's Word to sustain your spirit. In doing so, you are feeding your faith, starving your doubts, and you will be able to believe for the *impossible.*

Read Scripture:

Mark 9:23

Prayer:

Father God, I come before you now, acknowledging that the condition of my spirit is not where it should be. I take full responsibility for this, and I ask you to forgive me for neglecting the most

---

* *Impossible*—an impossible situation that is difficult beyond reason or propriety.

important part of my being, which is my spirit man. I understand the importance of feeding my spirit by spending time with you in your presence, worshipping you, and spending time in your Word and prayer. Holy Spirit, you are my help, and I am asking you that you would help me in this area of my life as I know and understand that I cannot do it on my own. Father, I thank you for your love and forgiveness, and for bringing this to my attention so that I can get my priorities in order. In doing this, I will feed my faith and starve my doubts, making my spirit man strong in you, making it possible to believe that you will do the impossible. All this I pray in Jesus' name. Amen.

Notes:

_____

_____

_____

_____

_____

_____

_____

_____

_____

Tuesday, Day 3

(45) We have all experienced a time when someone has spoken words to us or over us that were hurtful and left us standing there, feeling unworthy. It's as if we were left there standing in a thick slime that paralyzes us and keeps us from moving forward. By the same token, we may have been the one who has regretfully spoken hurtful words to someone or over someone that left us feeling terribly ashamed. Words are powerful and can be used as a weapon to tear others down, or they can be used as a tool to build others up. Today, make a conscious effort to use your words to build others up. *Watch* your words.

Read Scripture:

Psalm 141:3

Prayer:

Heavenly Father, I come before you now in a time of reflection and examination of my own heart. I humbly acknowledge that I have been both one who was hurt by words spoken to me or over me, and have done the same in saying hurtful words to someone or over

---

* *Watch*—to act or proceed with care and caution.

someone. Father God, I confess my sin before you now, asking you to forgive me and asking you to cleanse me. I am sorry for the hurtful words that have come forth out of my mouth toward others, and thank you for forgiving me now. Father, as an act of my will, I stand before you now, forgiving those who have spoken hurtful words to me or over me. I do not hold any ill-will against them, and I forgive them and release them now. Holy Spirit, I need you. Please help me and keep watch over the door of my lips from speaking evil of anyone and to build and edify others. All of this I ask in Jesus' name. Amen.

Notes:

_____

_____

_____

_____

_____

_____

_____

_____

_____

Wednesday, Day 4

(46) Have you ever turned on the radio to listen to a specific program, but as it was playing, your mind was not in it and you wandered into a place where you tuned out of the program? Have you ever sat in church, and as the pastor was preaching, your thoughts went into thinking of what you were having for lunch after service and you did not hear what the pastor was saying? How many times have you set time aside to pray and study the Word, and you went through the motions, but your heart and mind were distracted with everything that you had to do that day? When you spend time with God and tune in to God's Word daily, it is important to tune your spirit in to the frequency of hearing God's Spirit disciplining our flesh to make it be still and setting our spirit in tune to hear what God has to say. *Attend* to God's Word.

Read Scripture:

Proverbs 4:20

---

* *Attend*—to look after; guard and to hear, listen and follow.

Prayer:

Heavenly Father, as I come before you acknowledging that there are distractions all around me. I repent and ask for forgiveness for allowing my mind to wander and my thoughts being on other things when I should be focused on hearing by the spirit what you desire to say to me. Holy Spirit, I need you, and I ask for your help. Teach me to discipline myself so that my flesh does not have control over me that my spirit will grow in the Lord, and that I would be disciplined in the Lord to tune in to the spirit's frequency to hear what the Spirit of God wants to say to me. All of this I ask in Jesus' name. Amen.

Notes:

_____

_____

_____

_____

_____

_____

_____

_____

_____

Thursday, Day 5

(47) The Sabbath Day is not just a day of rest for your body, but it has meaning that goes beyond your natural rest. The Sabbath is a rest from your own works and trusting in the finished work of Jesus Christ. It is when you get to the place where you realize that there is an absolute trust in God, where you take him at his Word and, meditate on that Word until it gets in your spirit. And instead of you trying to make it happen, you rest from the work of your own hands and trust that God said it, and it is settled as he brings about the manifestation of his Word, not based on what you have done, but on what Jesus has already accomplished for you through his death and resurrection. *Cease* from your own works and enter his rest.

Read Scripture:

Hebrews 4:10

Prayer:

Father God, I come to you now, admitting to myself and to you that I have tried to make things happen in my own strength without depending on you and trusting that what you said in your Word you

---

* *Cease*—to stop performing an activity or action; desist or refrain.

would do, that you would do it for me. I ask you to forgive me for getting in your way and taking control, and for trying to make things happen on my own without you instead of resting from my own works and giving you full control, trusting that your Word is true and that you will do what you said you would do. Today, I choose to lay down all my striving to make things happen, and I stay focused on your Word and trust you to bring your Word to pass in my life. I thank you for doing it for me because you love and care for me. In Jesus' name. Amen.

Notes:

_____

_____

_____

_____

_____

_____

_____

_____

_____

Friday, Day 6

(48) Have you ever been at a gathering and a specific individual walks in the room with a bubbly personality and the atmosphere of the room changes? It's as if the people in the room were infected by that person's personality, and the people loosen up and begin to have fun. As a believer in Jesus Christ, we should be a contagious carrier of his presence, power, joy, and peace; and when we walk in a room, the temperature and atmosphere of the room should change. Our faith in God should be so evident that we pass it on to others, and it increases their faith in God. Our faith in God should increase even the more and not decrease. Be a **contagious** believer so that when others hang around you awhile, they will catch it!

Read Scripture:

Matthew 5:16

Prayer:

Father God, I thank you that as I spend time in your presence today, you are imparting into me a part of yourself that becomes so much like you that whenever I walk into a room, your presence in me

---

* *Contagious*—spreading or tending to spread from one to another; infectious.

draws attention, not to me but to you. Use me today to be the express image of your love, power, joy, and peace in the midst of all whom I meet. Stir in them the desire to want to know this contagious presence that I carry with me. I thank you, Father, for giving me the opportunity to share with others with boldness and grace your love for them. In Jesus' name, I pray. Amen.

Notes:

_____

_____

_____

_____

_____

_____

_____

_____

Saturday, Day 7

(49) As we grow in our walk with God, we begin to understand that we are not our own and that apart from him, we can do nothing. This is when we will then be able to honor God in everything that we do. Walking in humility is refusing our flesh the right to brag about our accomplishments and resist *self-praise,* which is inappropriate. To God belongs all of the glory, all of the honor, and all of the praise. It belongs to him and him alone.

Read Scripture:

   Proverbs 27:2

Prayer:

   Father God, I come before you now, asking you to forgive me, first of all, for taking the credit for the things that I have done without acknowledging that it is only by your grace, by your strength, and with your help that I have been able to accomplish anything. Apart from you, I can do nothing, and I am sorry for praising myself for my accomplishments. Thank you for your love and forgiveness as I receive it now. I now ask you, Holy Spirit, to help me to always

---

* *Self-praise*—bragging on one's self.

remember that all of the glory, honor, and praise belong to God alone. When pride comes in, I give you the permission to convict me, Holy Spirit, with godly sorrow. I ask all of this in the name of Jesus Christ. Amen.

Notes:

_____

_____

_____

_____

_____

_____

_____

_____

_____

Sunday, Day 1

(50) For anyone who has traveled to another country, you would know that there is a currency exchange that must take place if you want to make purchases in that country. We experienced that when we went to India. Our American dollars had to be exchanged for the currency of India, which was Indian rupee. Because we are *citizens* of the kingdom of heaven, there is a heavenly currency for the believer. To obtain heavenly benefits, we must use the correct currency. Faith is the currency of heaven, and there are no spending limits. Whatever you need today, use your faith in God, and the reward of your faith will manifest in your life. You are a *citizen of the kingdom of God.

Read Scripture:

Hebrews 11:6

Prayer:

Heavenly Father, I thank you that you have given to me a measure of faith. Without it, I cannot please you; but with it, all things are possible. Whatever I need, I can ask you, believing that you will

---

* *Citizen*—an inhabitant of a city or town, especially one entitled to its privileges.

give it to me. Thank you that as a citizen of the kingdom of God, I can have access to all that you have provided for me by using my faith, which is the currency of heaven. Thank you because today, by exercising my faith in you, I have everything that I need and that there is no lack in my household, but abundance of provision has been made for me through Jesus Christ. I receive it all by faith right now. In Jesus' name. Amen.

Notes:

_____

_____

_____

_____

_____

_____

_____

_____

Monday, Day 2

(51) There is no doubt that we live in a very troubled world, and if we are not careful, we will allow despair to set in and open the door to fear. God wants us to know that in the latter days, we do not have to walk in fear. But we must know that he will instruct us; he will speak to us and give us his wisdom to live in these dire times. He is our Counselor, and he will help you to make good and godly decisions. Take time to sit at his feet today and bring all your concerns to him. Stay in the Word of God and allow him to counsel you and *guide* you through his Word.

Read Scripture:

Proverbs 19:20

Prayer:

Father God, I come before you now, thanking you that you are my wonderful Counselor who guides me by the instruction of your Word. You are my God who gives me wisdom in all matters. I do not fear even as the last days are upon us because you have not given me a spirit of fear, but of love, power, and a sound mind. I receive godly

---

* *Guide*—one who shows the way by leading, directing, or advising.

wisdom right now in all decision making concerning me and my family, and I give you thanks and praise for it now. In Jesus' name. Amen.

Notes:

_____

_____

_____

_____

_____

_____

_____

_____

_____

Tuesday, Day 3

(52) We have all experienced a time in our life when someone gave us their word from their lips, but they did not follow through with actions, leaving us in a place where we no longer trusted them. How many know that God is worthy of our whole heart, and we must draw close to him with our whole being and not just lip service. Let us not just *honor* him with the words of our lips, but let our life and actions be that of one who glorifies him through obedience.

Read Scripture:

Matthew 15:8

Prayer:

Father God, I come before you now, repenting and asking your forgiveness for the many times that I have come to you with the words of my lips that sounded so good and right, but in fact, my heart was not in it. My heart was so far from you. Thank you for your loving-kindness and forgiveness toward me, as I receive it now. Holy Spirit, you are my help, and I ask you to help me in this area of my life so that my heart and actions line up with you to bring glory

---

* *Honor*—to regard with great respect.

to my Father through complete obedience. In Jesus' name, I pray. Amen.

Notes:

_____

_____

_____

_____

_____

_____

_____

_____

_____

Wednesday, Day 4

(53) How many times have you reached into your refrigerator for that carton of milk, pouring yourself a tall glass; and as you took that drink and expected a refreshing drink, you discovered the milk was spoiled? Sour face and all, you look at the expiration date on the carton, telling you that milk will only be good until that date which has passed, so you then toss the entire carton of milk down the drain. The one thing that you can be sure of with God is that the Word of God has no *expiration* date. It remains good and is useful to you forever for all eternity.

Read Scripture:

Isaiah 40:8

Prayer:

Heavenly Father, I just want to thank you for your holy Word, which is your thoughts and your ways toward me. As I read your Word, I will remember that there is no expiration date to your Word for me and that it is useful for every aspect of my life. It is the one thing that I know you have given to me that I can hold onto and

---

* *Expiration*—coming to an end or no longer being valid after a period of time.

trust in forever until the end of time. I thank you that your Word sustains me, and it is the one thing that I can give to my children and grandchildren for generations to come. It will never lose its power, but it will continue to bless the hearer and the doer of your Word. The grass withers and dies, but your Word, God, stands forever. For this, I give you thanks and praise. In Jesus' name. Amen.

Notes:

_____

_____

_____

_____

_____

_____

_____

_____

Thursday, Day 5

(54) Do you find yourself in an impossible situation right at this moment? In this life, we face many trials; and at times, it will overwhelm us if we allow it to. Your impossible situation may be too hard for you to figure out, but it is not too hard for God. God specializes in the impossible and is waiting for you to turn that impossible situation that you are in over to him. Give it to him now. Lay it all down at his feet, for in doing so, you will receive rest from this *overwhelming** situation and partake of his peace for your soul.

Read Scripture:

Luke 1:37

Prayer:

Father God, I come to you right now, asking for your forgiveness. I have carried this impossible situation until it has weighed me down and overwhelmed me with doubt and unbelief. I am sorry for trying to do this on my own. As an act of my will, I lay down this situation at your feet, and I confess that you are the God of the impossible that makes all things possible to those who believe. I believe that

---

* *Overwhelm*—strong, powerful, and devastating.

you are God who cares for me, loves me, and will turn this impossible situation around and work it out for my good. I thank you for your rest and peace for my soul as I put my trust in you. In Jesus' name, I pray. Amen.

Notes:

_____

_____

_____

_____

_____

_____

_____

_____

Friday, Day 6

(55) We have all heard this saying, "Talk is cheap." Talk, without supporting it with action, means nothing, and those words have absolutely no value. Our words have no real value to them unless we support it with corresponding action. Talk is cheap, like faith without works is dead. "Faith" is an action word, and it moves us. God has already done everything he will ever do by sending his Son, Jesus Christ. We should take God's Word at face value in every area of our lives. Whether it is relationally, spiritually, financially, health, or any other area, we should *apply** God's Word to the situation by corresponding action and walk it out step by step.

Read Scripture:

James 2:26

Prayer:

Father God, I repent for taking your Word for granted and for not realizing that you gave me your most precious gift, your one and only Son, Jesus Christ. Faith in Jesus Christ means so much more to me now than ever. Everything that I need has been provided by you

---

* *Apply*—to put it into action.

through Jesus Christ. I thank you that I can take your scripture and apply it to my life with corresponding action. Meaning that when I hear your word, I confess it with my mouth, I believe it in my heart, and I receive it and walk it out by faith, knowing that it will manifest in my life because you are a faithful God. For this, I give you thanks and praise. In Jesus' name. Amen.

Notes:

_____

_____

_____

_____

_____

_____

_____

_____

_____

_____

Saturday, Day 7

(56) How much fun it was as children playing tug of war? The laughter, the screaming, and the strong determination as you worked with your team to pull your hardest with all of your strength to get that little red flag to your side; and in doing so, you win and walk in victory. There is an undeniable strength in God that you can rely on in times of life when you feel like giving up. Instead of believing that you are at the end of your rope, just know that God is at the end of your rope, and he is pulling for you. His power and might is gaining you the victory, and all you have to do is not give up! Pull on God's *undeniable* strength.

Read Scripture:

Ephesians 6:10

Prayer:

Father God, I come before you now, thanking you that I am not alone, but that you are with me. It is through your power and might that I can depend on you to get me through anything that I face today. I thank you that I can depend on your undisputed Word. I

---

* *Undeniable*—incapable of being denied or disputed; incontestable.

thank you that you are on my side, and you are pulling for me today. As an act of my will, I choose to depend on your mighty power and strength, and none of my own. What an absolute joy to know that you are on my team and that I can expect victory in my life today as I am strengthened and encouraged in you as I pull on your strength as you pull for me. All of this I pray in Jesus' name. Amen.

Notes:

_____

_____

_____

_____

_____

_____

_____

_____

_____

Sunday, Day 1

(57) As a child growing up, we can all remember a time when we asked our mother or father to please leave the light on when we went to bed because we were afraid of the dark. There is no doubt that the times we live in are dark. Be *reassured* that the Lord is your light in these dark times, and he is your salvation. You need not fear. He is the strength of your life, and you should fear no one or nothing.

Read Scripture:

    Psalm 27:1

Prayer:

    Father God, I acknowledge that you are my light in a dark world, and you are my salvation. There is nothing for me to fear or be afraid of. As an act of my will, I declare that you are my strength in whom I trust, knowing that no matter what is going on around me, you are there for me and with me. You will never leave me to face things alone. In you, I have life and strength. For this, I thank you and I praise you. In Jesus' name. Amen.

---

* *Reassured*—having confidence restored; being freed from anxiety.

Notes:

Monday, Day 2

(58) There are many things in this world that are trying to take you off course or change the direction of your life as a believer in Christ Jesus. This is called a distraction. Distractions can be people, places, or things to prevent you from obtaining your purpose and the plan that God has for you. When we allow the distractions in the world to sidetrack us and get us off our course for God, the scriptures say that the love of the Father is not in you. Our love for the Father should not be *sidelined* by these distractions.

Read Scripture:

1 John 2:15

Prayer:

Heavenly Father, I come to you, asking you to forgive me for allowing the distractions of the world to take me off the course that you have laid out for me. My love for you and what you have for me to do have become second place, and I realize now that my priorities have been wrong. I have been caught off guard with everything from family, job, sports, entertainment, and the busyness of living my life.

---

* *Sidelined*—to put out of action.

I repent and ask for you to forgive me. Thank you for your forgiveness as I receive it now. Holy Spirit, you are my help. I acknowledge that I need you every day to remind me and convict me when the people, places, or things have taken over my affections, and demands my attention above God. All of this I ask in Jesus' name. Amen.

Notes:

_____

_____

_____

_____

_____

_____

_____

_____

_____

Tuesday, Day 3

(59) Have you ever experienced waking up with a bad attitude for no reason at all? There is no doubt that this is an attack on your mind. However, you can refuse to carry it through this day. You can simply *counteract* this attack by choosing at that exact time to shout for joy and rejoice in the Lord. That bad attitude will fall off you by the act of your will to do the opposite of what you are feeling at that moment. You are righteous and upright in your heart, so be glad and shout the praises of God and watch this bad attitude leave you.

Read Scripture:

Psalm 32:11

Prayer:

Holy Father, as an act of my will, I choose today to shout for joy and rejoice in the Lord! I declare today that my feelings will not dictate to me the outcome of this day and as I praise your magnificent name! I oppose and refuse to carry the bad attitude that tried to attack me, and I command it now to go from me. I thank you that

---

* *Counteract*—to undo or prevent the effect of or to oppose and mitigate the effects of by contrary action.

I have so much to be thankful for today. I shout unto God with the voice of triumph and declare that his joy is my strength today. In Jesus' name. Amen.

Notes:

_____

_____

_____

_____

_____

_____

_____

_____

Wednesday, Day 4

(60) Without a consistent relationship with God, it is inevitable that this world, and all that is this world, will drain you. However, when you have a consistent relationship with him, spending quality, uninterrupted time with him in his presence, worshipping him, studying his Word, and serving him, you can trade in the stress, the striving, and the struggle for rest and restoration. It is much like hitting the *reset* button. It also allows him to lead you on the right path his way.

Read Scripture:

Psalm 23:3

Prayer:

Heavenly Father, I come before you now, asking you to forgive me for allowing myself to fall into the trap of the striving and struggling to make it in this world without acknowledging that you alone are the one who leads and guides me in paths of righteousness for your name's sake. Holy Spirit, I ask you to help me to give me the desire to consistently develop my personal relationship with God by spending quality time with him in worship and the Word. Instead

---

* *Reset*—to readjust and set anew.

of striving and struggling to make it in this world, my focus is my relationship with God that brings rest and restoration for my soul. In Jesus' name. Amen.

Notes:

_____

_____

_____

_____

_____

_____

_____

_____

_____

Thursday, Day 5

(61) In many public places, there are signs that tell you where you can find shelter in the event of a natural disaster such as a tornado. There are times in life where things all around us seem like a whirlwind of sorts. It is a time when we just need to be loved, and cared for. A place where we can find absolute rest. God's love for you is so extravagant that you can take *shelter* from the violent storms of life. You can come to him as a covering and know that you are safe under the wings of his love, care, and protection. Take some time right now to take cover in him. Receive sweet rest for your soul. Take shelter in him.

Read Scripture:

Psalm 36:7

Prayer:

Heavenly Father, I come before you now in need of rest for my soul. As an act of my will, I come to you and take cover under your wings. With you, I feel safe and secure from the chaos that is all around me. Under your umbrella and shelter, I receive your peace

---

* *Shelter*—the state of being covered or protected.

and your strength that revives me and allows me to gain your insight for what lies ahead of me. It gives me the absolute assurance to know that I can come to you at any time and take comfort in your complete care of me. Thank you for loving me so. In Jesus' name. Amen.

Notes:

_____

_____

_____

_____

_____

_____

_____

_____

_____

_____

Friday, Day 6

(62) Have you ever done something that made you feel as if you were an absolute failure and you could not shake it off no matter how hard you tried? This is called *brooding.* It's when you continually dwell on it and meditate on it to the point of leaving you in a pit of depression. You are not alone. We have all made mistakes and done things that were total failures. However, in Jesus Christ, you are not defined by your past failures. You are a new person, and God desire that you do not despair over the past, but live your life in the fullness of joy that he has given to you now. No more *brooding.

Read Scripture:

1 John 2:8

Prayer:

Heavenly Father, I come to you now, thanking you that I am not defined by my past failures. Forgive me for giving in to the despair of my past decisions and failures that have kept me from living in your fullness of joy. As an act of my will, I choose to stop brooding and dwelling on the past, and I make the decision now to look forward

---

* *Brooding*—to focus the attention on a subject persistently and moodily; worries.

to the newness of life that you have given me through Jesus Christ, our Lord. I will enjoy this life that you have given me. In Jesus' name. Amen.

Notes:

_____

_____

_____

_____

_____

_____

_____

_____

_____

Saturday, Day 7

(63) *You* plus *time with God* equals *less of you and more of him.* T-I-M-E is the equation for increased spiritual development and growth. Time can never be **recovered** once it has passed. Time with God, in his presence—worshipping him, talking to him, studying his Word, and walking in—is vital for growth. Make time for worship, prayer, and the Word. You are the bride, and Jesus is the bridegroom. When we take time to know him and be with him, then we take our place as his bride, stepping to his side as he takes the center stage.

Read Scripture:

John 3:30

Prayer:

Father God, I come to you asking to forgive me for neglecting my relationship with you and for not giving you the time of day that you so desire. I ask you to give me an unquenchable hunger to know you. Help me, Holy Spirit, to manage my time wisely and to keep my time of worship, prayer, and the Word a priority so that I would become transformed, becoming less, so that Jesus would increase

---

* *Recovered*—to get back something lost or taken away

even the more. I acknowledge that Jesus is the bridegroom and that I am the bride who steps to his side and allows him to take center stage in my life. In Jesus' name, I pray. Amen.

Notes:

_____

_____

_____

_____

_____

_____

_____

_____

_____

Sunday, Day 1

(64) There is a vast difference between reading the Word of God and studying the Word of God. If you can admit that you do not know how to *study* God's Word, ask him to show you how or to bring those people in your life who are willing to take the time to sit with you and share their study resources with you. When we study the Word of God, we should study with the intent, the purpose, and the resolve to act it out by living it out throughout our day.

Read Scripture:

2 Timothy 2:15

Prayer:

Father God, I come to you, asking you to give me the desire to go beyond just reading your Word. I desire to study your Word so that I can know you in a more intimate way. I desire to know you through your Word, and I ask you to give me the revelation to understand what you are saying to me through the Scripture. I ask you, Holy Spirit, to help me to study the Word of God with the intent,

---

* *Study*—the application of the mind to the acquisition of knowledge, as by reading, investigation, or reflection.

purpose, and resolve to walk it out and to act it out in my own life. In Jesus' name. Amen.

Notes:

_____

_____

_____

_____

_____

_____

_____

_____

_____

Monday, Day 2

(65) Growing up as a child, many of us can recall the song, Down in the valley, valley so low. Hang your head over; hear the wind blow. Hear the wind blow, dear; hear the wind blow. If you sang this long enough, you would surely find yourself dragging your body so low that you could not look up. We all have what is known as the *valley* experiences, but we also have a God who is able to comfort us as we walk through those times, and a God who is able to strengthen us and give us a view of the light at the end of the *valley, being assured that he will bring us through. You are not alone in the valley, and you don't have to hang your head down, but look upward to him who is able to keep you during this time.

Read Scripture:

    Psalm 23:4

Prayer:

    Heavenly Father, I come to you now as I walk through the valleys of life. I give you thanks that I do not walk alone for you are with me, and I have nothing to fear. I thank you for the Holy Spirit

---

* *Valley*—a low point or interval in any process, representation, or situation.

who is my Helper and who guides me through every low valley. As an act of my will, I choose to look to you instead of the valley. I know that even in the valleys, your plan and purpose for my life have not changed. I refuse to give up, and I continue to receive comfort and strength from you every step of the way. I declare that this valley is not the end, but part of the journey to discovering you as my never-ending companion. All of this I pray in Jesus' name. Amen.

Notes:

_____

_____

_____

_____

_____

_____

_____

_____

_____

WEEK 10

Tuesday, Day 3

(66) Your words have the power and ability to bring healing to others; or you can also slice, dice, and destroy with your words. It is a decision that we most often don't even think about. Today, be aware of the decision you make on how your words affect others. Be careful not to sling your tongue all over the place with *careless* words that slime others, leaving them feeling bad about life. Instead, choose words that will encourage and bless others. Your words can bring healing in such a hurtful world.

Read Scripture:

Proverbs 12:18

Prayer:

Heavenly Father, as I am about to face this day, I take just a few moments to come before your presence to worship you and thank you that you have given me the God-given ability to speak words that bring healing to others. I ask for your forgiveness for any words that I have spoken to others that bring destruction, and I thank you for forgiving me. I ask you, Holy Spirit, to help me to take inventory

---

* *Careless*—done with or acting with insufficient attention: negligent.

of my words today, and help me to think before I speak so that the words that I speak unto others will bring healing to them in this hurtful world. All of this I pray in Jesus' name. Amen.

Notes:

_____

_____

_____

_____

_____

_____

_____

_____

Wednesday, Day 4

(67) We live in a world where there are many distractions that try to take our precious time away from our relationship with God. In our busyness, if we allow things to become more important to us, it will draw us further away from God and *intimacy* with him will be lost. We cannot afford to lose that precious intimacy with our Creator. In this world, we need him more today than ever. The definition of "distraction" is: "dis" means to separate, and "traction" means the state of being drawn. Take just a few minutes today and ask yourself these questions, who or what is drawing me away from him? Who or what is trying to separate me from *intimacy with my God? Who or what is distracting me?

Read Scripture:

Deuteronomy 30:16–17

Prayer:

Heavenly Father, I come before you now, asking you to forgive me for all of the distractions in this world that I have allowed to separate me and pull me away from you. Please forgive me for my

---

* *Intimacy*—close or warm friendship or understanding; personal relationship.

busyness and letting those things pull on my heart to the degree that I have not made time for your presence, worship, and your Word; and my intimacy with you has been affected. Thank you that I am forgiven. Right now, I say, Holy Spirit, I need you! I am asking you, Holy Spirit, to help me daily to discipline myself to never begin a day without first spending time with my Father. Show me, Holy Spirit, when the distractions of this world are trying to separate me from the one who means the most to me. All of this I pray in Jesus' name. Amen.

Notes:

_____

_____

_____

_____

_____

_____

_____

_____

_____

Thursday, Day 5

(68) Have you ever considered how much power lies in your thoughts? A thought that is allowed to remain *unchecked,* so to speak, will eventually produce feelings, whether good or bad. And the more that you meditate on that thought, it will eventually lead to an action. Today, make a conscious effort to arrest those thoughts that do not line up with what God says about you and others in his Word. You have the power within you to allow a thought to remain, or you can cast that thought far away from you. Fasten your thoughts to God's Word and stay heavenly minded, keeping your thoughts out of the gutter.

Read Scripture:

Philippians 4:8

Prayer:

Gracious Father, I come before you now, and as an act of my will, I ask for your forgiveness for every single thought that I have allowed in me to produce feelings and actions that are contrary to your Word. Forgive me for not casting those thoughts down and for

---

* *Unchecked*—not restrained or controlled.

allowing them to run rampant in my life. I thank you as I receive your forgiveness now. Holy Spirit, I ask you to help me to train and discipline myself to think thoughts that are pure, holy, merciful, and kind. Holy Spirit, I ask for you to help me to filter and confront every thought that is contrary to the Word of God and help me to cast them away from me. Help me to fasten my thoughts firmly to God's Word and to keep my mind on heavenly thoughts today. I pray in Jesus' name. Amen.

Notes:

_____

_____

_____

_____

_____

_____

_____

_____

_____

Friday, Day 6

(69) There are times in our life where the things going on all around us will attempt to *wear down** on you and wear you out, and if you are not careful, you will want to throw in the towel, so to speak. Today, take a moment to sit in God's presence and thank him for preserving you in difficult times. "Preserve" means "to keep safe from harm or injury; to protect or spare." If God was able to preserve the Israelites' clothes and shoes for forty years, he is able to keep you from wearing down to.

Read Scripture:

Deuteronomy 29:5

Prayer:

Father God, I come to you today, acknowledging my weaknesses and asking you to forgive me for depending on my own strength to get me through difficult times. I thank you for your forgiveness toward me and for your hand upon my life to preserve me, and that you are always watching out for me to keep me safe and in your care at all times. Thank you that it is in my weakness that you are made

---

* *Wear down*—to break down or exhaust by relentless pressure or resistance.

strong and that I can depend on you to strengthen me in my inner being to continue my walk with you by faith. I declare that I will not be defeated, and I will not quit, or throw in the towel. I will not wear down as I depend on you this day and every day. I pray in Jesus' name. Amen.

Notes:

_____

_____

_____

_____

_____

_____

_____

_____

Saturday, Day 7

(70) We all like to experience new places when we go on vacations. At times, we will set up a tour with a tour guide who has the knowledge and the history of the place that we are touring. The insights of the tour guide are fascinating and helpful to us as we view every sight along the way. God has given to every believer the precious Holy Spirit as a personal guide in this life, who always leads us and guides us into all truth. He never speaks of himself but always speaks and does what the Father does. The Holy Spirit never fails, and you will never go wrong when you make the decision to follow him *wholeheartedly.*

Read Scripture:

　　1 Thessalonians 4:8

Prayer:

　　Gracious heavenly Father, I come before you, giving you thanks and praise for giving to me the precious Holy Spirit. As an act of my will, I choose to follow the leading of the Holy Spirit as he always leads and guides me into all truth. Today, I will yield myself to the

----

* *Wholeheartedly*—free from all reserve or hesitation or uncertainty.

Holy Spirit as he leads me on paths of righteousness, and shows me and reveals to me the wonderful mysteries of the kingdom of God that have been given unto me as an heir of salvation. All of this I pray in Jesus' name. Amen.

Notes:

_____

_____

_____

_____

_____

_____

_____

_____

_____

Sunday, Day 1

(71) Fear. We have all experienced it at one time or another. If you were to stand on a railroad track and a train was coming toward you, it would indeed produce fear of danger. You would surely jump off those railroad tracks before the train would hit you. That train was a real threat and not imagined. There is a fear that goes beyond fear of impending danger which God's Word tells us is a spirit of fear that God did not give you. When this spirit of fear has come upon you, there is the absence of faith and a presence of timidity. Fear and faith cannot dwell in you at the same time. When fear comes, then we must hear the Word of God, as faith only comes by hearing the Word. Then, and only then, can faith come, overthrow, and *evict* the fear that has tried to occupy your life.

Read Scripture:

2 Timothy 1:7

Prayer:

Father God, I come before this day, thanking you that you have not given me a spirit of fear or timidity, but of power, love, and a

---

* *Evict*—to forcefully put out or to expel or drive out.

sound mind. I understand that fear and faith cannot dwell within me at the same time, and I thank you that as I hear your Word, faith comes and overthrows the fear that has tried to come and occupy my life. Faith comes only by hearing your Word, so as an act of my will, I choose to hear and read your Word for myself, taking a stand against the spirit of fear and walking in victory over it. In Jesus' name, I pray. Amen.

Notes:

_____

_____

_____

_____

_____

_____

_____

_____

_____

Monday, Day 2

(72) When we become a born-again believer, we become a new creature in Christ Jesus. Old things are passed away, and all things become new. It is still our responsibility to renew our minds to the Word of God, which produces more than a behavior modification. It works in us a great *transformation,* first of the mind, in our thoughts; and we begin to take on God's character. The change is beyond anything that we can do on our own. Take some time in his presence today to find out what God says in his Word about you. Read it for yourself and meditate on it until you see yourself as God sees you.

Read Scripture:

Romans 12:2

Prayer:

Heavenly Father, I come before you now, asking you to forgive me for neglecting your Word which has the power to renew my thoughts and transform my life to be what you have created me to be. I receive your forgiveness now. Holy Spirit, you are my help. I ask you to help me with the desire to read God's Word, which leads to

---

* *Transformation*—change in form, appearance, nature, or character.

the renewing of my mind, and transforms and changes me to have the characteristics of God and makes me more like him. All of this I pray in Jesus' name. Amen.

Notes:

_____

_____

_____

_____

_____

_____

_____

_____

_____

Tuesday, Day 3

(73) Have you ever just stood under a nice hot shower without a care in the world, enjoying the refreshing touch of the water flowing over every part of your being and not wanting it to end? We should have great *expectation* for the showers of blessings that God has for us to flow over our lives in such a way that we experience a great refreshing in our lives that we can't keep it to ourselves, but we want to pass it on to others to enjoy as well. Today, have faith *expectation for those showers of blessings to overflow in your day.

Read Scripture:

Ezekiel 34:26

Prayer:

Heavenly Father, I come before you, giving you thanks for the many blessings that you have for me today. Holy Spirit, I ask for your help today. Help me to see and recognize those blessings before me, and help me to have faith expectations to take hold of every blessing that comes to me so that I do not miss out on what God has for me. No matter how big or how small these blessings are, I receive every

* *Expectation*—belief about the future.

one of them to enjoy and to share these blessings with others. In Jesus' name. Amen.

Notes:

_____

_____

_____

_____

_____

_____

_____

_____

_____

Wednesday, Day 4

(74) Before we accepted Jesus Christ as our Lord and Savior, sin had a hold on us, and we were like prisoners in bondage and chains. Jesus shed his blood, and his body was broken for us when he went to the cross. Jesus has broken the chains of sin and bondage in our life, and he resurrected victoriously to sit at the right hand of the Father. We can now stand firm in our freedom. Today, you can walk as a free man or woman, and you do not have to be *entangled* with yokes of bondage anymore because you have been liberated and set free.

Read Scripture:

Galatians 5:1

Prayer:

Father God, I come before you today with a heart of thanksgiving. I have received your greatest gift to me, which is your Son, Jesus Christ, who has removed the yoke of bondage and has liberated me. Today, I walk in this freedom and stand firm against sin; and as an act of my will, I refuse to be entangled with the yoke of bondage to

---

* *Entangle*—to involve in a complicated situation or in circumstances from which it is difficult to disengage.

sin from which Jesus Christ has paid the price with his broken body and his blood. The chains that once held me as prisoner have been broken off my life. In Jesus' name. Amen.

Notes:

_____

_____

_____

_____

_____

_____

_____

_____

_____

Thursday, Day 5

(75) We have all seen in the movies where a ship cannot withstand a forceful storm that causes the ship to take on water and begin to sink, and the people on board are seen jumping overboard and hanging on for dear life to anything that will keep them above water. If you are facing a difficult circumstance that you find is tempting you to *shipwreck* your faith in God, cling to your faith in Christ, and keep your conscience clear. Faith in God's Word will keep you afloat and above the circumstance, and you will reach your destination victoriously.

Read Scripture:

1 Timothy 1:19

Prayer:

Father God, I come to you today because you are my anchor in the storms of life. As an act of my will, I reach out to the life ring of faith in Christ which keeps me afloat and above the circumstance so that I am not overwhelmed and drowned by it. I hold fast to the Word of God in this circumstance and declare that I will not be

---

* *Shipwreck*—a complete failure or ruin.

overcome by this wave of circumstances. My faith in you will not be shipwrecked, but I will overcome by faith. In Jesus' name. Amen.

Notes:

_____

_____

_____

_____

_____

_____

_____

_____

_____

Friday, Day 6

(76) Have you ever experienced a time when you heard someone who carelessly wagged their tongue with constant *nagging* and you had to leave the room? Words of the tongue are so powerful, and it affects everyone within ears' reach. God's Word has such wisdom and breeds life to those who hear it. You can choose to speak words of righteousness and can choose to hear these words of wisdom instead of the wag and nag of the tongue. Today, make an effort to speak and only give ear to words of righteousness.

Read Scripture:

Psalm 119:172

Prayer:

Heavenly Father, I come before you now, asking you to forgive me for either wagging or nagging my tongue around others or if I have given ear to this from others as well. Thank you for your forgiveness as I receive it now. Holy Spirit, I need you. Help me today, Holy Spirit, to resist the temptation to wag or nag my tongue but

---

* *Nagging*—to annoy by persistent faultfinding, complaints, or demands.

instead, to choose words of righteousness that will bless God and build those up around me who hear it. In Jesus' name, I pray. Amen.

Notes:

_____

_____

_____

_____

_____

_____

_____

_____

_____

Saturday, Day 7

(77) Can you imagine God's mercy being so plenteous that it never runs out? He is a good God and a forgiving God. Just as there is plenty of God's mercy to go around, should we also extend mercy toward an offender who has wounded us? No matter how many times in a day we are hurt, we should extend mercy, forgiveness, and *pardon* to the offender just as we would hope that others would do for us.

Read Scripture:

Psalm 86:5

Prayer:

Heavenly Father, I come before you today, asking you to forgive me for holding unforgiveness toward anyone who has hurt me. I release them now, and I thank you for your forgiveness toward me as I receive it now. Holy Spirit, I cannot and will not do this without you. Help me to walk in forgiveness and to extend God's mercy to others as it has been extended to me time and time again. All of this I ask in Jesus' name. Amen.

---

* *Pardon*—to release (a person) from punishment or disfavor for wrongdoing or a fault.

Notes:

_____

_____

_____

_____

_____

_____

_____

_____

_____

Sunday, Day 1

(78) What an amazing sight to see a total eclipse, where the sun disappears when the moon comes between it and the earth, or of the moon, when the earth's shadow falls across it. God's love for us did not just eclipse our mistakes and failures, but all of mankind's *sin.* He loved us enough to send us Jesus to completely come between us and death, and when his blood fell to the earth, it covered all of us. What love for former present and future generations. Next time you step out and see an eclipse, remember how his love covers you, your children, and your children's children for generations to come.

Read Scripture:

Romans 5:8

Prayer:

Father God, I come before you today, in awe of your love for me; but more than that, your love for former, present, and future generations to come. While we were yet sinners, you commanded your love toward us. Jesus came between us, death, hell, and the

---

* *Sin*—a condition of estrangement from God resulting from such disobedience.

grave and has redeemed us. Thank you that we are covered by your precious eclipse of love today and every day. In Jesus' name. Amen.

Notes:

_____

_____

_____

_____

_____

_____

_____

_____

Monday, Day 2

(79) When you spend time with God in his presence, worshipping him and studying his Word, it is more than you becoming *acquainted* with him. It is getting to know him personally for yourself. You can then perceive his thoughts, and understand his ways. Knowing him is liberating and brings a life of freedom in him. He is the truth, and knowing him makes you free to be who he has created you to be in him. Go beyond being *acquainted with God and enter into a place of intimacy.

Read Scripture:

John 8:32

Prayer:

Heavenly Father, I come before you now, asking you to forgive me for neglecting my time with you in your presence worshipping you, and the study of your Word. Thank you for forgiving me as I receive your forgiveness now. Holy Spirit, I need you. Help me, Holy Spirit, to prioritize my day to include the most important part of my life, which is knowing God through his Word, as his Word are his

---

* *Acquainted*—familiarity but not intimacy.

thoughts and his ways. Give me the desire to spend time personally getting to know him as the truth that sets me free. In Jesus' name, I pray. Amen.

Notes:

_____

_____

_____

_____

_____

_____

_____

_____

_____

Tuesday, Day 3

(80) Did you know that you are more *valuable** to God than many sparrows? If God takes care of these small creatures, don't you think he will take care of you? If every single hair on your head is numbered by God, then guaranteed he knows what you need. You are God's most treasured possession, and you have no need to worry or be afraid. He will take care of you. Ask your Father for those things that you have need of today. He's waiting.

Read Scripture:

Luke 12:7

Prayer:

Father God, I come to you now, asking you to forgive me worrying about those things that you said you would take care of. I thank you for your forgiveness as I receive it now. Holy Spirit, I need you, and I am asking you to help me bring to God every need and lay it down with full assurance, knowing that he will take care of me and

---

* *Valuable*—having desirable or esteemed characteristics or qualities or of great use of service.

my family because we are his most treasured possession. All of this I pray in Jesus' name. Amen.

Notes:

_____

_____

_____

_____

_____

_____

_____

_____

_____

Wednesday, Day 4

(81) Whenever you are called upon to do anything and positioned to do so, remember that God has put you there. Use your gifts, talents, and opportunities for him; and do not draw the attention to yourself as if you did this on your own. When God gives you a *platform,* use it for his glory and shine for him.

Read Scripture:

1 Peter 4:11

Prayer:

Heavenly Father, I come to you now, asking you to forgive me for the times where I have been flattered by the applause of man, and the acknowledgments and praises that I have received from others without giving you the credit you so deserve. I thank you for your forgiveness as I receive it now. Holy Spirit, I need you. Help me, Holy Spirit, to remember that I have not nor can I do anything without your help. Help me to walk in humility and to always shine for

---

* *Platform*—if someone has a platform, they have an opportunity to tell people what they think or want.

Jesus, giving him all the glory and honor for any accomplishments that are done through me. All of this I pray in Jesus' name. Amen.

Notes:

_____

_____

_____

_____

_____

_____

_____

_____

Thursday, Day 5

(82) Have you ever seen a small child try to put on their dad or mom's shoes and *walk** in them? The child could not tell by looking at the shoes that they would not fit; but without reservation, they put them on, stood up, and began to *walk even though they would fall due to the shoes being too big for them. Regardless, what a delightful picture to see. There is a *walk of faith that Jesus walked while on this earth, and we can wear those same shoes of faith. Yes, by faith, we can *walk in our Daddy's shoes.

Read Scripture:

2 Corinthians 5:7

Prayer:

Father God, I come to you now, thanking you that you have given me eyes of faith. This faith goes beyond seeing with the natural eyes into pursuing you and believing that what you have said in your Word is the truth, and it teaches me how to conduct my own life. I declare that each step that I take by faith pleases you and brings forth

---

* *Walk*—to pursue a course of action or way of life: conduct oneself.

your will and your plan for my life upon this earth just as it is in heaven. For this, I give you thanks and praise. In Jesus' name. Amen.

Notes:

_____

_____

_____

_____

_____

_____

_____

_____

_____

Friday, Day 6

(83) A *limitation* is a restriction that keeps us from succeeding in life. It is our own limitations that keep us from achieving our God-given dreams, desires, and goals. Take time to examine your life and the *limitations that you have placed on yourself, and be loosed from those *limitations. God created you to succeed, and he put those dreams on the inside of you. By all means, don't limit God or tempt God by saying you can't do it.

Read Scripture:

Psalm 78:41

Prayer:

Heavenly Father, I come to you now, asking you to forgive me for placing limitations on myself concerning the dreams, desires, and goals that you have placed in my heart. For in doing this, I have limited you in my life as well. Thank you for your forgiveness as I receive it now. Holy Spirit, I need you. You are the greater one living on the inside of me, and I ask you to help me with the strength and ability to let go of the limitations that hinder me from accomplishing my

---

*   *Limitations*—the state of being bound or restricted.

God-given assignments. As an act of my will, I release all limitations that have restricted me from making forward progress in the things that God has for me. Thank you that I am released into starting and completing every God-given dream, desire, and goal. In Jesus' name. Amen.

Notes:

_____

_____

_____

_____

_____

_____

_____

_____

_____

Saturday, Day 7

(84) Have you ever experienced riding in a car with shocks so worn down that you could feel every bump in the road, and instead of it being a smooth ride, it was such a bumpy and uncomfortable ride? Faith in God and his Word is like a shock absorber over the bumpy roads of life. When your spirit man is *built up* in the Word and you have faith in God, it can handle the weight of your problem and the wounds that come with it. It sustains you through it.

Read Scripture:

> Proverbs 18:14

Prayer:

Father God, I come to you now, thanking you that through every road of life—potholes, bumps, and all that—my spirit can sustain me through it when I build myself up in your presence, in worship, in the Word, and in prayer. Holy Spirit, when life gets challenging, draw me to you to spend quality time building myself up in my most holy faith so that my spirit man rules and moves me, and not the situation at hand. In Jesus' name, I pray. Amen.

---

* *Built up*—to strengthen gradually.

Notes:

_____

_____

_____

_____

_____

_____

_____

_____

_____

Sunday, Day 1

(85) Today, you woke up to see another day. Give thanks to God for every breath that you take. As a matter of fact, take a minute to inhale and exhale, and *appreciate* the air that surrounds you. You are blessed, and this very day was made for you to enjoy. The Bible tells us that we should rejoice in the day the Lord has made, so praise him this morning!

Read Scripture:

Psalm 118:24

Prayer:

Father God, how I thank you today for giving me this day to enjoy. I rejoice in you and give you praise, glory, and honor for blessing me with every breath that I take. Today is such a gift, and I will treat it as such. I ask you for nothing, but instead, I just want to thank you for your gift of life to see another day and to spend this day right here now in your presence and with my family, friends, and co-workers throughout the day. Thank you, my precious Father. In Jesus' name. Amen.

---

* *Appreciate*—to be thankful or show gratitude for.

179

Notes:

_____

_____

_____

_____

_____

_____

_____

_____

_____

Monday, Day 2

(86) We have all experienced a time in our life when someone has come against us and treated us as if we were their enemy. Then somewhere along that road, you heard that something happened to that person that either made you feel bad for them or perhaps you showed some gratification that they got what they deserved. The Bible tells us that when those who come against you experience **calamity,** we shouldn't be happy about it. We can even go a step further into kindness and pray for them as we would want someone to pray for us.

Read Scripture:

Proverbs 24:17

Prayer:

Heavenly Father, I come to you now, asking you to show me and bring to my remembrance any bad situations that have occurred to someone who has hurt me and my heart was glad about it. As you reveal it to me, I ask that you would forgive me for my thoughts and actions that were not pleasing to you. I thank you for your forgive-

---

* *Calamity*—an event that brings terrible loss, lasting distress, or severe affliction; a disaster.

ness as I receive it now. Holy Spirit, I need you to lead and guide me in all areas of my life, especially in relationships. When calamity strikes someone that considers me to be their enemy, please give me a heart of compassion and mercy to pray for them as I would want others to pray on my behalf. All of this I ask in Jesus' name. Amen.

Notes:

_____

_____

_____

_____

_____

_____

_____

_____

_____

Tuesday, Day 3

(87) Reliving your past is like having weights on your feet that hold you back from your future and the good things that await you. Don't let the weight of failure, mistakes, and regret hinder your walk and keep you from reaching ahead into the future that God has for you. *Forget* about those things that are in the past and step freely without restraint into your best life yet.

Read Scripture:

Philippians 3:13

Prayer:

Father God, in the name of Jesus I declare that every past failure, mistake, and regret of the things that I have done cannot and will not restrain me or weigh me down from walking in the wonderful future that you have set forth for me. As an act of my will, I choose to forget those things that are behind me, and I take hold of those things that lay ahead for me. I thank you for it. In Jesus' name. Amen.

---

* *Forget*—to fail to think of; take no note of.

Notes:

_____

_____

_____

_____

_____

_____

_____

_____

_____

Wednesday, Day 4

(88) It is true that we are drawn to certain people whether or not it is by the Spirit or just because you like their personality or the kindness that you feel when you're around them. It may be that you find you have a lot in common with them, but in all honesty, God commands us to love everyone so we don't get to *choose* who. Today, take a minute to look around you and reach out to someone who needs to experience God's love through you. You can make a big difference in this world.

Read Scripture:

Deuteronomy 10:19

Prayer:

Father God, in the name of Jesus, I come before you now, offering myself up to you to be your vessel of love to those around me today. Holy Spirit, lead me today to those who are in need of God's love, not by my choosing, but by God's choosing. Give me the words to say to them or show me a kind gesture to do for them that will

---

* *Choose*—to determine or decide.

minister your love in a way that they can receive it. In Jesus' name, I pray. Amen.

Notes:

_____

_____

_____

_____

_____

_____

_____

_____

_____

Thursday, Day 5

(89) Sometimes, we have great expectations that we place on God to move mightily and powerfully. It is all right to have such great faith in such a big God, except we should never **discredit** the small things, as God works in the small things to. Take note of the small things that you see God do in the midst of you today.

Read Scripture:

   1 Kings 19:12

Prayer:

   Heavenly Father, I come before you now, asking you to forgive me for having preconceived ideas that you only move in certain ways and placing expectations upon you to do things according to my understanding. You alone are God and can move in many ways, whether it's an earthquake, fire, or a still, small voice. Thank you for showing me that you work through the small things as well as the great things. In Jesus' name. Amen.

---

* *Discredit*—lack of belief or confidence, or to refuse to accept as true or accurate.

Notes:

Friday, Day 6

(90) Cease and seize. God's Word contains many promises to you, and his promises never cease, come to an end, discontinue, or stop. So seize, grab, grasp, and take *possession* of them! Yes, I agree. And amen, it is *so*!

Read Scripture:

2 Corinthians 1:20

Prayer:

Father God, I thank you that your Word is your promise to me as your child and that my *yes* means I agree, and *amen* means it is so. So, right now, I take hold of your promises for my life and family by faith, and I trust you to bring it to pass this day. In Jesus' name. Amen.

---

* *Possession*—ownership or legal rights to take.

Notes:

_____

_____

_____

_____

_____

_____

_____

_____

_____

Saturday, Day 7

(91) Are you one of the few who finds yourself always encouraging others around you? Are you drawn to those who look like they can use a kind word? You can take heart in knowing that God said in his Word that those who encourage others will himself be encouraged! Because of your generosity to refresh others, you yourself will also be *refreshed.*

Read Scripture:

Proverbs 11:25

Prayer:

Heavenly Father, I come to you now, giving you thanks and praise for allowing me the privilege and honor to encourage others when they are down and in need of encouragement. I thank you that in doing this, I myself am also refreshed, filled up again, and encouraged according to your Word as is written in Proverbs 11:25. In Jesus' name. Amen.

---

* *Refreshed*—to fill up again; replenish.

Notes:

_____

_____

_____

_____

_____

_____

_____

_____

_____

Sunday, Day 1

(92) Have you ever made a call and experienced hearing this recording? "All customer service representatives are currently assisting other callers. Your call is *important* to us. Please hold for the next available agent. All calls will be answered in the order that they are received." We should be so thankful that with God, we can expect this instead: "This is God. Your prayers are *important to me. Please expect your answer as all available angels are currently assisting you. I am God, and I hear and answer you when you call on me."

Read Scripture:

Psalm 4:3

Prayer:

Father God, I come to you in the name of Jesus, thanking you that you are omnipresent and that you are never too busy to hear me, your child, when I cry out to you. Thank you that all of my prayers reach your ears, that you answer my prayers as they come before you as sweet smelling incense, and that I can expect what I pray according

---

* *Important*—something that is important is very significant, valuable, or necessary.

193

to your will, which is your Word, to come to pass in my life. In Jesus'
name. Amen.

Notes:

_____

_____

_____

_____

_____

_____

_____

_____

_____

Monday, Day 2

(93) When we submit ourselves to God and his Word, we can begin to see things the way that he sees them. So instead of seeing it as you're the sick trying to get healed, you see it through his eyes as you're the healed resisting sickness. Submit, yield, or surrender to God and his Word; and *resist* all sickness and disease.

Read Scripture:

James 4:7

Prayer:

Father God, I come to you in the name of Jesus, asking you to forgive me for not submitting to you and your Word, which is your will for my life. I thank you for your forgiveness as I receive it now. I humbly submit to you, and I resist the devil and every lie that he has spoken to me that is opposed to your Word, which is the truth. I take a stand for truth, declaring that I am not the sick trying to get healed, but I am the healed resisting all sickness and disease. In Jesus' mighty name. Amen.

---

* *Resist*—to oppose an influence or idea.

Notes:

_____

_____

_____

_____

_____

_____

_____

_____

_____

_____

Tuesday, Day 3

(94) Have you ever made a purchase online for what you thought was an authentic designer item and you found out that it was not an *original?* Instead, you ended up with what they call a knockoff item, which looks like an *original but is in fact a replica or copy of the *original? In life, there is only one of you, and the Bible says that you are fearfully and wonderfully made. Today, the Father celebrates you because you are an original.

Read Scripture:

Psalm 139:14

Prayer:

Heavenly Father, I come to you today, giving you thanks and praise for reminding me that I am fearfully and wonderfully made. There is only one of me, and in your eyes, I am valuable to you. I receive your love knowing that there is only one of me, and today, I celebrate everything that you made me to be. I thank you that I do not have to pretend to be someone else but that I can fully accept

---

* *Original*—not derived or copied or translated from something else but a master copy original. Not an imitation.

that you made me who I am and that I am precious in your sight.
Thank you for loving me. In Jesus' name. Amen.

Notes:

_____

_____

_____

_____

_____

_____

_____

_____

_____

_____

Wednesday, Day 4

(95) Are you sick in your body? No one likes to be sick. We all want to be well. Are you in need of a touch from God? We all *desire* healing in our body when we are not feeling well, but you cannot have faith for healing without faith in the healer. You cannot have faith in the healer if you think he has put the sickness on you. Do not receive that lie as he will never put sickness and disease on you because he is a loving Father, and he is the Healer.

Read Scripture:

Exodus 15:26

Prayer:

Heavenly Father, I come to you now, asking you to forgive me for believing the lie that you put sickness on me to teach me something. I break agreement with that lie; and I render it null, void, and powerless in my life. I give you thanks that you are a loving Father who does not put sickness and disease on your children. Instead, you are the God that heals, and I receive your healing touch upon my

---

* *Desire*—to long or hope for.

body right now. I thank you for being my Healer. In Jesus' name. Amen.

Notes:

_____

_____

_____

_____

_____

_____

_____

_____

_____

Thursday, Day 5

(96) Have you ever had a day where you just needed some encouragement? We have all experienced a time where we needed encouragement, but there was no one around to encourage us. The Bible says that David, in his time of *distress,* encouraged himself. Sometimes, you just have to encourage yourself instead of waiting on someone else.

Read Scripture:

1 Samuel 30:6

Prayer:

Father God, I thank you for your Word which shows me a great example through David when he encouraged himself in the Lord. I thank you that I do not have to wait around for others to encourage me when I am in distress but that I can encourage myself in the Lord as David did. As an act of my will, I boldly speak into my own ears that "I am strong in the Lord and in the power of his might." I thank you, Father, that as I lift my hands in praise to you now, all distress

---

* *Distress*—anxiety or mental suffering.

leaves me, and my heart is encouraged in you. For this, I thank you. In Jesus' name. Amen.

Notes:

_____

_____

_____

_____

_____

_____

_____

_____

_____

Friday, Day 6

(97) Have you ever done something that left you feeling so disappointed in yourself, and instead of moving on from it, you got stuck in park? So you blew it. There is not a single person who has never made a mistake or sinned. Repent and ask God to forgive you. Forgive yourself and move on. God's *mercy* is new toward us every day, and you don't have to stay stuck in park. It is time to put yourself in drive, move ahead, and start afresh.

Read Scripture:

Lamentations 3:22–23

Prayer:

Heavenly Father, I come to now, asking you to forgive me for being so hard on myself when your mercies are new for me daily. I thank you for your forgiveness as I receive it now. Holy Spirit, I need you. I ask you to help me to shift out of park and into drive, and move forward from my shortcomings and rely on God's mercy that is new toward me daily. As an act of my will, I choose to start

---

* *Mercy*—an act of kindness, compassion, or favor.

afresh today. I thank you and praise you, Father God. In Jesus' name. Amen.

Notes:

_____

_____

_____

_____

_____

_____

_____

_____

_____

Saturday, Day 7

(98) Special agents are *assigned* to protect some of the most important leaders of our nation. They stay close to these individuals, ready to lay down their life for these leaders. Are you aware that God has *assigned to you, your own secret service protection? That's right. There are angels on special assignment who follow you and go with you, and they have been given special orders to protect you wherever you go, defending you from all harm.

Read Scripture:

Psalm 91:11

Prayer:

Father God, I come to you today, giving you thanks for your love for me. I thank you that I do not have to be afraid for I know that you have assigned heavenly angels to go with me wherever I go and that no harm will come to me or my family today. Thank you that in this chaotic world that I live in, I have your divine protection over my life and the life of my entire family today. In Jesus' name. Amen.

---

* *Assigned*—to appoint as a duty or task.

Notes:

_____

_____

_____

_____

_____

_____

_____

_____

_____

Sunday, Day 1

(99) We have never lived in a day like the current day, where there are so many swindlers that prey on *vulnerable* individuals who buy into the sweet talking con artist on the other end of the phone line. Many have lost precious savings on scams that sounded too good to be true. As a believer, we have an adversary who comes to steal, kill, and destroy. How can you know that it is a lie? A lie is always contrary to what God's Word says. If it does not agree and line up with the Bible, then it is more than likely a lie. Don't be scammed by the devil's lies.

Read Scripture:

John 10:10

Prayer:

Heavenly Father, I come before you today, thanking you that I do not have to fall prey to the devil's lies which are totally opposite of what you say in your Word. Holy Spirit, you are my help, and I need you to help me to discern the lies of my enemy and to resist those lies by replacing the lie with the Word of God over my life. As an act of

---

* *Vulnerable*—someone who is vulnerable is weak and without protection, with the result that they are easily hurt physically or emotionally.

my will, I submit myself to the truth of God's Word and walk in the victory over my own thoughts and the enemy's suggestive thoughts. I declare that I will not be a vulnerable victim but a victor. In Jesus' name. Amen.

Notes:

_____

_____

_____

_____

_____

_____

_____

_____

_____

Monday, Day 2

(100) Have you ever asked yourself the question, "I wonder what the future holds?" God doesn't only direct your steps, but he will direct your life according to his purpose. You do not have to try to figure it out on your own. Ask him to teach you how to tune in to his voice to hear what he wants to *reveal* to you by his Spirit.

Read Scripture:

Jeremiah 33:3

Prayer:

Heavenly Father, I come to you today, in awe of who you are and how you desire to reveal to me your plans for my future. As I take time to study your Word, I ask you to reveal and show me by the Spirit and confirm it with your Word your plans for me. Holy Spirit, I need you, and I ask you to show me how to pray out all of God's plans and his purpose for my life. In Jesus' name, I pray. Amen.

---

* *Reveal* to make known through divine inspiration and lay open in order to view or see.

Notes:

_____

_____

_____

_____

_____

_____

_____

_____

_____

Tuesday, Day 3

(101) A trespass is a sin or an offense that someone has committed against another person, showing no regard for them and wounding their feelings. To forgive means to pardon or *release* them from the offense that they have committed. Forgiveness is not an option but a commandment. When you forgive someone, it doesn't mean they're right, it just keeps you free.

Read Scripture:

Matthew 6:15

Prayer:

Father God, I come to you in the name of Jesus, asking you to show me if I have any unforgiveness toward anyone. As an act of my will, I choose by faith to forgive. I pardon them for all offense and wrongs committed against me, and I do not hold it against them. I thank you, Father God, that in doing so, I am obeying your commandment because forgiveness is not an option but a direct command from you. So I choose to obey and walk it out by faith in you,

---

* *Release*—to release a hostage and to set someone free.

and continue to live in the freedom that you have so graciously given to me. In Jesus' name. Amen.

Notes:

_____

_____

_____

_____

_____

_____

_____

_____

_____

Wednesday, Day 4

(102) God's Word fuels our strength to *stand* in times when opposition comes, and when our faith in God is tested and we are under attack by the adversary. We are not made strong to fight; we are made strong to *stand. Put on the full armor of God and *stand against the wiles of the devil.

Read Scripture:

Ephesians 6:11

Prayer:

Heavenly Father, I come before you now, thanking you that my loins are girded about with the truth of your Word. And having on the breastplate of righteousness, my feet shod with the preparation of the gospel of peace; and above all, taking the shield of faith, wherewith I shall be able to quench all the fiery darts of the wicked. I take the helmet of salvation, and the sword of the Spirit, which is the Word of God, and I stand against the wiles of the devil. I maintain

---

* *Stand*—to resist successfully; withstand: to maintain one's position against an attack.

my position of victory that was accomplished for me by Jesus Christ, my Lord. Amen.

Notes:

_____

_____

_____

_____

_____

_____

_____

_____

_____

Thursday, Day 5

(103) Everyone has emotions, and emotions are not bad unless you let them take over and move you out of faith. Our thoughts lead to emotions, and emotions are strong feelings that can cause psychological changes, such as an increased heart-beat, and can also bring a manifestation of crying or shaking. You don't have to ride that roller coaster of your emotions, but you can take every thought captive and make it subject to the obedience of Christ. You have the power to *harness* your emotions and submit them to God's will.

Read Scripture:

   2 Corinthians 10:5

Prayer:

   Heavenly Father, I come to you in the name of Jesus, asking you to forgive me for allowing my emotions to get the best of me. I thank you for your forgiveness and receive it now. Holy Spirit, I need you. Help me and teach me how to take captive those thoughts that would try to take me out of faith in God and his Word, and to make them subject to the obedience of Christ. As an act of my will,

---

* *Harness*—to bring under control and direct the force of.

I submit my thoughts and emotions daily to God's will, which is his Word. Holy Spirit, help me to use God's Word to redirect the force of my emotions under the control of the spirit of God on the inside of me. In Jesus' name, I pray. Amen.

Notes:

_____

_____

_____

_____

_____

_____

_____

_____

_____

Friday, Day 6

(104) Have you ever just wanted to do right by God in every area of your life but wondered if it was even possible? Did you know that God gave you the Holy Spirit to **lead** you into all truth? There is no going wrong when you follow the Holy Spirit because he is truth-centered, Christ-centered, and Christ glorifying; and he never does anything on his own or apart from God's Word.

Read Scripture:

John 16:13

Prayer:

Heavenly Father, I come to you now in the name of Jesus, thanking you that you have given the Holy Spirit to indwell on the inside of me. Right now, as an act of my will, I submit my life to you, Holy Spirit, today. I ask you to lead me and guide me, direct me and keep me on the path of righteousness in everything that I do today so that my life would bring glory and honor to God alone. In Jesus' name. Amen.

---

* *Lead*—to guide or direct in a course.

Notes:

_____

_____

_____

_____

_____

_____

_____

_____

_____

_____

Saturday, Day 7

(105) Have you ever listened to someone who constantly talks about their past and you think it just happened yesterday, but what they are talking about happened over twenty-five years ago? God gave your eyes the ability to look at what is ahead of you. Why do you keep turning around and looking back at the past? Can you picture this? If God wanted you to *continually** look behind at your past, don't you think that he would have given you eyes at the back of your head?

Read Scripture:

Proverbs 4:25

Prayer:

Heavenly Father, I come before you now, asking you to forgive me for always looking back to my past and for not looking straight ahead, and fixing my eyes on what lies before me. Thank you for your forgiveness as I receive it now. Holy Spirit, I need you. As an act of my will, I submit my life to your leading as I follow you. Help me to set my focus on what good things God has ahead for me instead

---

* *Continually*—in a constantly repeated manner over and over again.

of looking back at my past decisions, disappointments, failures, and regrets. In Jesus' name, I pray. Amen.

Notes:

_____

_____

_____

_____

_____

_____

_____

_____

Sunday, Day 1

(106) I cannot imagine living without seasons. God has appointed the moon and the sun for seasons. A season is each of the four divisions of the year-spring, summer, autumn, and winter. There are also different seasons in our life as well, and it is good to know that the seasons in our life are *subject to change* for the better.

Read Scripture:

Psalm 104:19

Prayer:

Heavenly Father, I come to you now, giving you thanks and praise that just as the seasons are meant to bring about change, so are the seasons of my life. I thank you that seasons are also not meant to stay that way forever, and for each season that I go through, it is subject to change for the better. As an act of my will, I submit to you through every season, knowing that you are able to bring me through this season and the next, and the results will develop spiritual growth and maturity in my life. In Jesus' name. Amen.

---

* *Subject to change*—the conditions set are prone to or likely to be affected by change.

Notes:

_____

_____

_____

_____

_____

_____

_____

_____

_____

Monday, Day 2

(107) Our God is such a loving God, and the only thing he takes away is the sin of the world. God is not a God of lack or loss, but he is a God of increase and multiplication. Anytime God says, " *Surely,* I will bless you," we should have a firm belief that what he is saying is true and that there is no doubt that he will bless us. He will add to us with increase and multiplication.

Read Scripture:

Hebrews 6:14

Prayer:

Father God, I come before you in the name of Jesus, asking you to forgive me for doubting in my heart that you would bless me to the degree of adding and increasing those things in my life that you have promised to me. I thank you for your forgiveness and receive it now. Holy Spirit, I need you. Help me to renew my mind to the truth of God's Word to know that God is not a God of lack who wants me to be in need or without; but he is a loving and caring God

---

* *Surely*—with confidence and without fail or without doubt.

who gives, adds, increases, and multiplies his precious promises to me. In Jesus' name. Amen.

Notes:

_____

_____

_____

_____

_____

_____

_____

_____

_____

Tuesday, Day 3

(108) Words that are spoken can be as smooth as butter coming forth from the lips, but in the heart, there can be a drawn sword of war ready to destroy. God always looks at the heart, and we should examine our heart daily and rid ourselves of any intentions to hurt those who have hurt us. Speaking smooth words and having war in our heart at the same time is a *destructive* force that wounds us from the inside and wounds others.

Read Scripture:

Psalm 55:21

Prayer:

Heavenly Father, in the name of Jesus, I come before you, asking you to examine my heart and show me if there is any offense that I have taken up that will cause me to operate with a drawn sword, ready to hurt others. I ask you to forgive me, and I thank you for your forgiveness as I receive it now. Holy Spirit, I need you. I ask you to help me to always have a renewed heart daily so that there will never be war in my heart and smooth as butter words that come forth

---

* *Destructive*—causing great damage, harm, or injury.

from my lips that damage, harm, or injure others; and that my heart is kept pure. In Jesus' name. Amen.

Notes:

_____

_____

_____

_____

_____

_____

_____

_____

_____

Wednesday, Day 4

(109) Many times, there are distractions in this world that pull us away from precious, intimate time with the Lord in his presence, worship, and the Word. In all honesty, there can be people who can distract us as well. We all know of Martha who distracted Mary who had the greatest desire to sit at the feet of Jesus. Take note of the people in your life that can be a distraction and set a healthy *boundary.* Always make time to sit at his feet.

Read Scripture:

Luke 10:38–42

Prayer:

Father God, I come to you in the name of Jesus, asking you to forgive me for being distracted not only by the things in the world but also by those people closest to me. Thank you for your forgiveness as I receive it now. Holy Spirit, I need you. I ask you to help me to be balanced with my time with the Lord and my social life. Show me how to prioritize my time, and when I am out of balance

---

* *Boundary*—a limit you can set on what you will accept of another person's words or actions. Boundaries can be material, physical, mental, or emotional.

and spending so much time with friends, family, and other social gatherings that may pull me away from you. I ask you, Holy Spirit, to teach me how to set healthy boundaries. All of this I pray in Jesus' name. Amen.

Notes:

_____

_____

_____

_____

_____

_____

_____

_____

_____

Thursday, Day 5

(110) Have you ever watched a child playing pirates looking for **treasure** and you could not help but get involved in their playtime, going beyond your imagination to a place where you physically created the outfits, the eye patch, plastic swords, and even a treasure chest filled with loot? In obeying God's Word, there is such great reward, and we should value and honor the Word of God as our greatest **treasure. It is more valuable than gold.

Read Scripture:

Psalm 19:7–11

Prayer:

Father God, I come before you, asking you to forgive me for neglecting to see your Word as my greatest treasure that you have given me. I thank you for your forgiveness and receive it now. Holy Spirit, I need you. I ask you now to help me to see God's Word as holy, and as valuable and beneficial to my life. Teach me, Holy Spirit, how to seek out the depths of God's wisdom found in the scriptures

---

* *Treasure*—something of great worth or value.

and how I can apply it to my life. All of this I ask in Jesus' name. Amen.

Notes:

_____

_____

_____

_____

_____

_____

_____

_____

_____

Friday, Day 6

(111) Did you have a parent or parents who would not allow you as their son or daughter to continue to be around someone that they knew was a bad **influence** on you, and they were concerned that their attitudes and behaviors could rub off on you? Even as adults, we should choose wisely the company we keep and those that we associate our self with.

Read Scripture:

1 Corinthians 15:33

Prayer:

Father God, I come to you, thanking you for giving me your guidance in choosing those who I am to keep continual company with. If bad company corrupts good morals, then I want to always be in the company of those who are of like faith and are influencers of good and not evil. Holy Spirit, I ask you to always direct me into right relationships and friendships that are godly and beneficial to my life. All of this I pray in Jesus' name. Amen.

---

* *Influence*—the capacity to have an effect on the character, development, or behavior of someone or something, or the effect itself.

Notes:

_____

_____

_____

_____

_____

_____

_____

_____

_____

Saturday, Day 7

(112) How many times have we been in a situation where we needed advice and good counsel, and how many times have we turned to people first instead of coming to God first and looking to his Word for direction and guidance? Whatever *difficulty* comes your way, take a minute and turn to God's Word first to hear what he has to say about it. Then if you need someone to stand with you in agreement with God's Word concerning the situation, you have a scripture that you can stand in agreement with.

Read Scripture:

Ezekiel 18:1

Prayer:

Heavenly Father, I come before you now, asking you first to forgive me for the times that I have gone to others first and looked to them solely for answers when I should have come to you and sought direction and guidance from your Word. I thank you for your forgiveness as I receive it now. Holy Spirit, I need you. I ask you to help

---

* *Difficulty*—a problem or condition or state of affairs almost beyond one's ability to deal with and requiring great effort to overcome.

me and to teach me how to depend on God to the degree that I seek him first in every difficult situation and to get his thoughts on the matter at hand. All of this I pray in Jesus' name. Amen.

Notes:

_____

_____

_____

_____

_____

_____

_____

_____

_____

_____

Sunday, Day 1

(113) Almost everyone has the desire to *please* God, and we know that Scripture tells us that we can't *please God without faith. The opposite of faith is unbelief. It is like watching someone who is visibly drunk, and you knew they were because of the way they staggered around. God does not want us to stagger around in unbelief but encourages us to be strong in faith.

Read Scripture:

Romans 4:20

Prayer:

Heavenly Father, I come before you now, asking you to forgive me for every single time in my life where I have staggered around in unbelief instead of walking by faith in your Word. I thank you for your forgiveness as I receive it now. Holy Spirit, I need you. I ask you now to give me the desire to hear God's Word as faith comes by hearing and hearing by his Word. As an act of my will, I submit myself to the Word of God and build myself up to be strong in faith which

---

* *Please*—to give pleasure or satisfaction; to be agreeable.

pleases God, leaving no opportunity to stagger around in unbelief. All of this I pray in Jesus' name. Amen.

Notes:

_____

_____

_____

_____

_____

_____

_____

_____

_____

Monday, Day 2

(114) We live in a world where there is sin all around us, but if God can save the world from sin, he can keep you from sinning in this world. Before Jesus went to sit at the right hand of the Father, he prayed for God the Father not to take us out of this world but to keep us from evil. Jesus knew what it was like to live in a world of evil all around him, yet he sinned not. You have the **power** of the Holy Spirit to live free from sin just as Jesus did.

Read Scripture:

John 17:15

Prayer:

Heavenly Father, I come to you, giving you thanks for Jesus who was and is my example to follow. Jesus was all man, yet he never sinned because of his love for you, God, and his desire to be one with you. He was also led by the Spirit of God. When Jesus left this world, he prayed that you would not remove us from the world but to keep us from the evil one. Thank you, Father, that you are able to keep me from all evil in this world that I live in, and for this, I am thankful.

---

* *Power*—the ability or official capacity to exercise control; authority.

Holy Spirit, I ask you to teach me to exercise the God-given authority that I have over evil in this world. In Jesus' name, I pray. Amen.

Notes:

_____

_____

_____

_____

_____

_____

_____

_____

Tuesday, Day 3

(115) No one can deny the fact that the days that we live in are evil. Even in these evil times, we have a heavenly Father, who will care and *provide* for us in ways that we can never fully comprehend. He is a God of more than enough, and you will have enough for yourself and your family, and enough to be a blessing to others too Trust him to meet not only your needs but also to have enough to share with others around you. Believe and you will have plenty and be satisfied.

Read Scripture:

Psalm 37:19

Prayer:

Heavenly Father, I come before you in the name of Jesus, knowing full well that the days that we live in are evil. However, I also know that you are a good God who provides for his children everything that we need on a daily basis. I give you thanks and praise, Father, and I trust you to meet my needs beyond more than enough until I am satisfied. I also thank you for the overflow of plenty that I

---

* *Provide*—to give something wanted or needed to someone or to make something available to someone.

can share with others. All of this I pray in the powerful name of Jesus Christ. Amen.

Notes:

_____

_____

_____

_____

_____

_____

_____

_____

_____

Wednesday, Day 4

(116) When you accepted Jesus as your Lord and Savior, you first heard the good news, you received it as good news, and you believed it in your heart. Therefore, you began to speak it out of your mouth and *confess* it by your words that Jesus is your Lord. You have that same spirit of faith on the inside of you that moved you from a life of sin and death into life in Christ Jesus. Whenever you hear the good news of the gospel on any subject, believe it to be true, receive it in your heart, and confess it with your mouth by that same spirit of faith.

Read Scripture:

2 Corinthians 4:13

Prayer:

Heavenly Father, I come before you now, giving you thanks and praise for my salvation which came by faith. As an act of my will, I submit myself to the same spirit of faith to live by daily. Holy Spirit, I need you, and I ask for your help to lead me into truth. By your power living on the inside of me, help me to continue to hear the

---

* *Confess*—to declare in faith or a formal profession of belief and acceptance of.

good news, believe it, receive it, and speak it into my life as the spirit of faith on the inside of me works to obtain all the fullness of God in my life. In Jesus' name, I pray. Amen.

Notes:

_____

_____

_____

_____

_____

_____

_____

_____

_____

Thursday, Day 5

(117) The Bible tells us that we are to love our enemies. The problem is how can we do that if we can't even love those around us who are not our enemy? God is love, and we are commanded to walk in love and to be good to our enemies. It is good to *evaluate* our love walk. When we find it difficult to obey God's command of love, then we should take the time to evaluate our heart. Could it be that we have strayed away from the one who is love?

Read Scripture:

> Luke 6:27

Prayer:

> Father God, as I examine my life and judge my own self, I have come to realize that I have not loved those around me, much less my enemies. For this, I repent and say, "I am sorry." This love you have even for my enemies is something that I cannot do apart from you or without your help, so as an act of my will, I submit my will over to the Holy Spirit who is my help. According to God's Word, his love has been shed abroad in my heart by the Holy Ghost, which

---

* *Evaluate*—to look, assess, or judge one's own self.

is given unto me. So by faith, I receive the unconditional and pure love of God into my heart; and I choose to love others, including my enemies, the way that you love them. I thank you for it now. In Jesus' name. Amen.

Notes:

_____

_____

_____

_____

_____

_____

_____

_____

Friday, Day 6

(118) Have you wondered why some Christians seem to have it all together financially and you thought to yourself that God just loves them more than you? The truth is that God is *not a respecter of persons,* but he is a respecter of faith in him. Those who live by faith will never lack, or go without their needs being met.

Read Scripture:

Philippians 4:19

Prayer:

Heavenly Father, I come to you in the name of Jesus, asking you to forgive me for the lack of faith on my part. I thank you for your forgiveness as I receive it now. You are a God who provides everything that I need according to your riches in glory by Christ Jesus, and according to my faith, I position myself to receive your provision in my life. Thank you that not one of my needs is forgotten, but you supply me with all that I need. For this, I give you thanks and praise. In Jesus' name. Amen.

---

* *Not a respecter of persons*—a person whose attitude and behavior is uninfluenced by consideration of another's rank, power, wealth, etc.

Notes:

_____

_____

_____

_____

_____

_____

_____

_____

_____

Saturday, Day 7

(119) Do you look around you and see chaos and *confusion,*[*] and you think to yourself, "What is this world coming to?" We can and should pray daily about the things that surround us, but we also must always look to Jesus and know that even in this chaotic world that we live in, that we can also receive what we need from God to live in this world. He is the God of peace, and he is the God that blesses his people with his peace.

Read Scripture:

Psalm 29:11

Prayer:

Father God, I come to you now, thanking you that even in a chaotic world, there is a peace that comes from you that will keep me from entering into a place of unrest. As an act of my will, I draw upon this peace from you. I will not be afraid of the things that the world is afraid of, for you have blessed me with your perfect peace which makes me secure in you and gives me strength to face the day. I

---

[*] *Confusion*—the state of being bewildered or unclear in one's mind about something.

am not bewildered or puzzled, and I thank you that you are my God, the God of Peace that keeps me grounded. I thank you for blessing me with your perfect peace today. In Jesus' name. Amen.

Notes:

_____

_____

_____

_____

_____

_____

_____

_____

_____

Sunday, Day 1

(120) The devil is a liar and the father of lies, and he operates through the power of suggestion and deception. But you are the one who has the choice to authorize, endorse, or *empower* the lie in your life. The only way to know if it's a lie is to apply the Word of God, and if it does not line up with the Word, then it is a lie.

Read Scripture:

John 8:42–45

Prayer:

Father God, I come to you in the name of Jesus, asking you to forgive me for receiving the lies of the enemy that are contrary to your Word. Thank you for your forgiveness as I receive it now. Holy Spirit, I need you. I am asking you to help me to be disciplined to apply God's Word to every thought or suggestion that comes to me to discern whether or not it lines up with God's Word. When it does not, then I know how to resist and reject the lie because I am empowered to endorse God's Word in my life. In Jesus' name, I pray. Amen.

---

* *Empower*—to give ability to or enable or permit.

Notes:

_____

_____

_____

_____

_____

_____

_____

_____

_____

_____

Monday, Day 2

(121) When you say, "I can't," have you ever considered that you are in God's way and have taken your eyes off him? That "I can't" phrase is a blind spot in your vision that needs to be corrected. If you are in that state right now, it is time to make the *adjustment* by taking that one step to get out of the way of the "can't" that is in front of you. Place your focus back on him and what he says about you in his Word. Then, your vision will become clearer, and you can see it his way. When he says to you that you can do all things through Christ who is your strength and you receive it, there is nothing that you cannot do without him!

Read Scripture:

Philippians 4:13

Prayer:

Father God, I realize now that my vision was impaired. I come to you, asking you to forgive me for standing in the way and saying, "I can't," when you have told me that I can do all things through Christ who strengthens me. I thank you for your forgiveness as I

---

* *Adjustment*—making a suitable alteration or a change for the better.

receive it now. Holy Spirit, you are my help, and I need you. I know that I can do all things through Christ when I depend on you to give me strength to do everything that God has called me to do. I am convinced and know that "I can do all things through Christ who gives me strength." Thank you, Father, for hearing my prayer. In Jesus' precious name. Amen.

Notes:

_____

_____

_____

_____

_____

_____

_____

_____

Tuesday, Day 3

(122) Growing up, has anyone ever told you, "Don't *complain.* Somewhere in the world, there is someone worse off than you." We have all heard this saying at one time or another in our lifetime. Many times, we focus on what is going wrong and never really look at when things are going right in our life. Today, count your blessings because the sum or grand total of them is more than your problems.

Read Scripture:

Psalm 118:1

Prayer:

Heavenly Father, I come before you now, asking you to forgive me for any complaints that have proceeded from my mouth instead of thanking you for the many blessings that are so evident in my life. Thank you for opening my eyes to see every blessing in this day that I often overlook or take for granted so that I may give you thanks. You are good, and your love endures or remains forever. For this. I thank you. In Jesus' name, I pray. Amen.

---

* *Complain*—to express feelings of pain, dissatisfaction, or resentment.

Notes:

_____

_____

_____

_____

_____

_____

_____

_____

_____

Wednesday, Day 4

(123) Growing up, you may have heard a parent telling a child, "Stop crying, or I will give you something to cry about." In other words, they are saying, "Don't cry for nothing." I thank God that our God is a Holy God, but he tells us to cry out to him with our voice and he will hear us. Whatever it is you are going through right at this moment, just know that God wants you to call out to him. He hears you, and he will surely *respond* to you. He will not disappoint you.

Read Scripture:

Psalm 3:4

Prayer:

Father God, I come before you now with everything that is in me, and I call out to you without holding anything back. I lift my voice to you, and I know that you hear me. My cry does not fall on deaf ears, and for this, I am thankful. As an act of my will, I release everything to you this day, and I give it to you. As I cry out to you, I do declare that you are my help, and you are the Glory and the One who lifts my head. It is you who causes me to rise up, and it is your

---
* *Respond*—to react favorably.

255

strength which gets me through this day. For this, I say thank you. In Jesus' name. Amen.

Notes:

_____

_____

_____

_____

_____

_____

_____

_____

Thursday, Day 5

(124) Growing up, we all had a hero that we looked up to. Whether it was imagined or a real war hero, we had one that we admired for courage, outstanding achievements, or noble qualities. The scriptures in the book of Hebrews give us a great example of the heroes of faith. It speaks of them being established in faith, rooted in faith, living by faith, and going through by faith. What they endured, they did with their faith in God. *Determine* in your heart that you will face your day with faith in God. Faith, don't leave home without it.

Read Scripture:

Colossians 2:7

Prayer:

Heavenly Father, I come to you now, giving you thanks and praise for the great heroes of faith who have gone on to glory but have left such a tremendous testimony of how their faith in you helped them to endure any and all hardship. As an act of my will, I yield to the greater one on the inside of me, and I keep the switch of faith on through every situation that comes my way to try me. In

---

* *Determine*—decide upon or fix definitely.

faith, by faith, and through faith, I boldly and confidently face this day knowing that my faith in God is fixed; and his Word, which is his will for my life, can and will get me through any trying circumstance. In Jesus' name. Amen.

Notes:

_____

_____

_____

_____

_____

_____

_____

_____

Friday, Day 6

(125) We all remember a time as parent's when we had plans to go on an outing with children in tow, giving them firm instructions to take our hand and do not let go for any reason lest they get separated from us and that child gets lost in the crowd. Our Father desires that we take the hand of the Holy Spirit, allowing him to lead and **guide** us down the right path. You are God's child, so take the hand of the Holy Spirit and let him lead you today.

Read Scripture:

Psalm 5:8

Prayer:

Heavenly Father, what a comfort it is to know that you have given me the Holy Spirit to lead me and guide me into all truth. As an act of my will, I place my hand in the hand of the Holy Spirit and yield myself to his leading, knowing that he will help me to make right choices for my life. Every decision made by me with his help will keep me in line with your Word and keep me on the right path

---

* *Guide*—one who shows the way by leading, directing, or advising.

for your name's sake. For this, I give you thanks and praise. In Jesus'
name. Amen.

Notes:

_____

_____

_____

_____

_____

_____

_____

_____

_____

Saturday, Day 7

(126) As a child, when the circus came to town, there was always such excitement and anticipation of such a great sight to see. Often, there were three rings to the circus; and in each ring, there was something different going on. It was hard to see everything all at one time. Even though there were three acts going on at once, they all followed the ring-master's lead. Jesus, not mammon, is our master; and when we devote ourselves to him, our life is not a three-ring circus but Christ-focused. He takes full center stage, and we will *serve* him.

Read Scripture:

Luke 16:13

Prayer:

Heavenly Father, I thank you that you are the God that blesses us with wealth for your kingdom purpose. I thank you, Jesus, that you are my Master and the Lord who governs my life. I declare that the spirit of mammon, which is wealth and regarded as an evil influence or false object of one's worship and devotion, does not have a hold on me. As an act of my will, I yield to the greater one on the

---

* *Serve*—to give homage, honor, and respect, and obedience to.

inside of me. I ask you, *Holy Spirit, to help me to obey the Word of God so that my life does not ever resemble a three-ring circus*, but that my focus and attention would always be to honor God and his Word in everything that I do to steward the wealth that he has provided me for his kingdom work. In Jesus' name. Amen.

Notes:

_____

_____

_____

_____

_____

_____

_____

_____

_____

Sunday, Day 1

(127) We may see words as just a way to communicate with others, but our words have tremendous power. Our words have the power to *create* and the power to bring about change. In the beginning, God said, "Let there be light," and it was so. Did you ever consider that the words that you speak today *create your tomorrow? Your words have the power to bring health to every bone in your body and healing to your soul. Today, speak God's Word, which is his will for your life, because it may very well manifest in your tomorrow.

Read Scripture:

Proverbs 16:24

Prayer:

Heavenly Father, I thank you that your Word is your perfect will for my life. My words have the power to form my tomorrow, and I desire to speak life-giving words that are in agreement with your Word. So as I take time to hear, study, meditate, and give life to your Word through speaking it forth into my life and the life of my children and my children's children, I thank you for the manifes-

---

* *Create*—to cause to exist; bring into being.

tation of your will being done here in my life and in the lives of my children and their children for generations to come. In Jesus' name, I pray. Amen.

Notes:

_____

_____

_____

_____

_____

_____

_____

_____

_____

Monday, Day 2

(128) When you make the choice to hear and obey God's Word, you are not only *pressing** into the blessings of God for your life, but you are pressing to know him in a more intimate and personal way. When you know him, then you can embrace his blessings, knowing that you have first sought to know the one who blesses.

Read Scripture:

Deuteronomy 28:2

Prayer:

Father God, I thank you for your Word, which is getting to know your thoughts and your ways as I spend time in your presence. I want to know you in an intimate and personal way. Holy Spirit, you are my help. I am asking you to help me to press into the discipline of spending time in God's presence, hearing, studying, meditating on God's Word, and receiving his life-giving instruction. Help me to submit my will to his will in full obedience to walk out his Word in my life in spite of the difficulties, which will undoubtedly produce God's will for my life. In Jesus' name. Amen.

---

* *Press*—to continue a course of action, especially in spite of difficulties.

Notes:

Tuesday, Day 3

(129) When we draw close to God to get to know him *personally,* then it is out of that personal relationship with him that his love begins to move us toward ministering to others. Get to know him and minister to the Lord, first and foremost, and he will then minister to others through you.

Read Scripture:

Solomon 2:13

Prayer:

Heavenly Father, I come before you now, asking you to forgive me for the times where I have sensed you drawing me to yourself and I have failed to answer the call. I thank you for your forgiveness as I receive it now. Holy Spirit, I need you. I am asking you now to help me recognize when you are tugging on my heart or prompting me to a quiet place and setting that time aside with the Father to know him personally. Help me to minister to him first, above all else, and

---

* *Personally*—doing something oneself, not having or letting someone else do it on one's behalf.

to allow him to impart into me his love which enables me to then minister to others. In Jesus' name, I pray. Amen.

Notes:

_____

_____

_____

_____

_____

_____

_____

_____

_____

Wednesday, Day 4

(130) We have all been there when someone comes to us and says something about another person, and without hearing the other person's side of it, we have the tendency to want to take that person's side. But once we hear the other person's account of the story, we hear a whole different side to the matter. We should never take offense against someone on the part of another. Remember that there are two parties to the story, or two sides to a coin. Remain *neutral* and pray for both parties to prevent you from getting tangled in the middle of it, then pray for God's wisdom on how to handle the matter.

Read Scripture:

Deuteronomy 19:15–21

Prayer:

Heavenly Father, I come before you now, asking you to forgive me for being quick to take sides on behalf of one person without hearing both parties' stories. I thank you for your forgiveness as I receive it now. Holy Spirit, I need you. I am asking you to help me

---

*   *Neutral*—belonging to neither side in a controversy.

to always think before I speak on a matter and remain neutral, and stand in the position of prayer for both parties and receive instruction from you on how to handle the matter so that I am your vessel who stands for what is right and true, bringing about results that are pleasing to you always. In Jesus' name, I pray. Amen.

Notes:

_____

_____

_____

_____

_____

_____

_____

_____

_____

Thursday, Day 5

(131) We live in a society where people feel, think, and act based upon **impulse;** and there is an instability that it brings. As a believer, we have to present ourselves to God daily and renew our minds to the Word of God to bring about change in the way that we think, feel, and act in order to be transformed and brought in line with God's perfect will so that we do not act impulsively. Take time to think about your decisions and ask God for his wisdom.

Read Scripture:

> Romans 12:1

Prayer:

> Father God, I come before you in the name of Jesus, asking you to forgive me for failing to present myself to you daily in worship, the Word, and fellowship with you. I thank you for your forgiveness as I receive it now. Holy Spirit, I need you. I am asking that you would help me to understand how important it is to present myself to God daily and to renew my mind so that my thoughts line up with God's

---

* *Impulse*—doing things on a whim without thinking about it first.

Word and that I am led in my decisions by the Spirit and not by impulsive thoughts. All of this I pray in Jesus' name. Amen.

Notes:

_____

_____

_____

_____

_____

_____

_____

_____

_____

Friday, Day 6

(132) Exceedingly abundantly means to go beyond with awe-inspiring things, *immeasurable** things, and plentifully. It is God who is able to go beyond. Although he is the One, he works it all in you and through you because he is a much more God! Receive his power that works from within to manifest his *immeasurable greatness in you and through you.

Read Scripture:

Ephesians 3:20

Prayer:

Father God, I come before you now, thanking you that you are the God who does exceeding, awe-inspiring things, immeasurable things, and plentiful things according to your mighty power which works in me and through me. It surpasses anything and everything that I could ever do on my own, and it manifests your immeasurable greatness on the inside of me and also outwardly and expressively to those around me so that you are glorified in and upon this earth. In Jesus' name. Amen.

---

* *Immeasurable*—impossible to measure; limitless.

Notes:

Saturday, Day 7

(133) Every time you spend time fellowshipping with the Father in his presence, worshipping him, studying his Word, he is *pouring* into you. God pours into you so that you can pour into others to bring healing, raise the dead, and cast out devils. "Pour" means flowing forth, especially a downpour of rain. It is God who heals, raises the dead, and casts out devils; but you release the power of God pouring through you. As you have received from him, now give it out to others who come across your path today.

Read Scripture:

Matthew 10:8

Prayer:

Heavenly Father, I give you thanks and praise. When I spend time with you in your presence, worshipping you and studying your Word, you are pouring into me more of your heart, your presence, your power, and your compassion, love, and mercy. Use me as your vessel to pour out the contents of what you have poured into me out

---

* *Pouring*—to send forth, produce, express, or utter copiously or abundantly as if in a stream or flood.

upon a hurting world. Freely, you have given unto me; and freely, I give to those who come across my path today as I am led by your Spirit. In Jesus' name. Amen.

Notes:

_____

_____

_____

_____

_____

_____

_____

_____

_____

_____

Sunday, Day 1

(134) To every problem that we face upon this earth, there is a heavenly *solution.* God is looking for intercessors, or individuals, who will intervene, pray, or mediate on behalf of others. It is time for intercessors to arise and answer the call on the behalf of others to pray out these heavenly *solutions in the lives of our families, our government, and for all men. Pray for someone who comes to your mind today. God hears and answers prayers.

Read Scripture:

   Ezekiel 22:30

Prayer:

   Father God, I come before you in the name of Jesus, asking you to forgive me for my selfishness in praying for my needs only and not considering that others are in need of prayers too. I thank you for forgiving me as I receive your forgiveness now. Holy Spirit, I need you, and I am asking for your guidance and your help to show me who I can pray for today. I ask you, Holy Spirit, to help me to pray out the desires of God's heart and lead me to the scriptures to pray

---

*   *Solution*—the answer or result.

for the individuals or entities that I am praying for. Help me, Holy Spirit, to always pray according to God's will, plan, and purpose. In Jesus' name. Amen.

Notes:

_____

_____

_____

_____

_____

_____

_____

_____

_____

Monday, Day 2

(135) The old saying, "Before, you were a twinkle in your father's eyes," is a term that we may have heard at some time in our life. Scripture says that before you saw the light of day, God recorded in his book the number of days that he has planned for you. Our parents were the vehicle to get us here, but we are God's. We have often heard that God does not make mistakes. That is in fact true, and before you were you, God knew you. He planned your life. One translation says, "You saw me growing, changing in my mother's womb. Every detail of my life was already written in your book. You *established* the length of my life before I ever tasted the sweetness of it."

Read Scripture:

  Psalm 139:16

Prayer:

  Abba Father, I come to you today in awe of you! Your Word has brought encouragement to me, and the words that you speak to me are life giving and refreshing to my soul. I renounce, reject, and no longer adhere to the lies that have been spoken about me that I was

---

* *Established*—settled securely and unconditionally.

unwanted, unplanned, and a mistake. I boldly confess God's love for me and toward me, and I choose to fulfill and live out in God, every established and recorded day of my planned life. I am not rejected, but I am accepted by my heavenly Father, who loves me and created me in his perfect image. For this, I am eternally grateful. In Jesus' name. Amen.

Notes:

_____

_____

_____

_____

_____

_____

_____

_____

_____

Tuesday, Day 3

(136) As the days grow, more evil and *darkness* seem to be all around. Remember that God is everywhere and he brings light into the night. It is impossible for God to leave you. He has been with you since you were in your mother's womb. Even if *darkness lurks all around us, his very essence is light, and his presence emanates in the darkest of times and shines the light of his glory, leading us on the path of righteousness and keeping us from stumbling.

Read Scripture:

Psalm 139:11

Prayer:

Heavenly Father, I thank you today that even in the darkest of times, it is impossible for you to leave me as you have been with me since I was in my mother's womb. I declare that when darkness is all around, you are my light and my salvation. Your presence goes before me and lights up the path that is right ad true, and as an act of my will, I choose to walk that path of righteousness that is laid before

---

* *Darkness*—the absence of moral or spiritual values and the absence of light.

me. As you illuminate it before me, I will walk it and follow after you as I trust you. In Jesus' name. Amen.

Notes:

_____

_____

_____

_____

_____

_____

_____

_____

_____

Wednesday, Day 4

(137) Have you ever sat down to the table and the food that was set before you looked absolutely delicious, yet when you took that first bite, it was bland and not flavored with any seasoning, but tasteless? The Bible says to us that our speech should be seasoned with grace. If we are talking like the world and we are not disciplined in our speech, then we are not speaking according to his grace given unto us. We are to be like salt, and if we become bland, how can our "salt-iness" be restored? *Flavorless* salt is good for nothing and will be thrown out and trampled on by others. "You are the salt of the earth and your lives light up the world."

Read Scripture:

> Colossians 4:6

Prayer:

> Heavenly Father, I come before you in the name of Jesus, asking you to forgive me for speaking as the world speaks, instead of my speech being seasoned with grace. I thank you for your forgiveness as I receive it now. Holy Spirit, I need you. I ask you now as I yield

---

* *Flavorlessness*—a lack of excitement, liveliness, interest, or being dull.

my tongue and speech to God's will to convict me of tasteless speech before it comes forth. Give me the strength and power to be the salt of the earth that is full of life and vitality, speaking forth God's Word which has the power and ability to set the captives free, bless the hearer, and bring glory to God. In Jesus' name, I pray. Amen.

Notes:

_____

_____

_____

_____

_____

_____

_____

_____

Thursday, Day 5

(138) We have all heard it too many times to count. "I'm just a sinner saved by grace." You are not a sinner or just a sinner saved by grace. Anytime we make that statement, we are speaking *contrary* to what his Word says. As far as God is concerned and according to what God says about you in his Word, you are a new creature in Christ Jesus.

Read Scripture:

2 Corinthians 5:17

Prayer:

Father God, in the name of Jesus I come before you, asking you to forgive me for speaking words that are not the truth about who you say I am. I thank you for your forgiveness as I receive it now. Holy Spirit, I need you. You always speak truth. The old me has passed away, and I am now a new creature in Christ Jesus. Holy Spirit, as I study God's Word, please reveal to me and show me who I am in Christ so that my perception of who I really am will be known and understood by me. In Jesus' name, I pray. Amen.

---

*   *Contrary*—the opposite of what is true.

Notes:

_____

_____

_____

_____

_____

_____

_____

_____

_____

Friday, Day 6

(139) The Bible warns us that in the last days, there shall be some that will *depart* from the faith because they gave heed to seducing spirits and doctrines of devils. The Word of God is the truth, and we can discern when the truth is not preached. We can reject and not give ear to false doctrines. We do not have to board the train of unbelief and *depart from our faith in God.

Read Scripture:

1 Timothy 4:1

Prayer:

Father God, in the name of Jesus, you said that faith comes by hearing and hearing by the Word of God. Therefore, as an act of my will, I yield myself over to your Word, which is your will for my life. I thank you for giving me a discerning heart to know when anything other than your Word is preached so that I will not be led astray by seducing spirits or doctrines of devils, and I never depart from my faith in God and his Word. In Jesus' name, I pray. Amen.

---

* *Depart*—to move away or go in another direction.

Notes:

Saturday, Day 7

(140) During the **trials** you face, at times it seems as if you are going under and can't take it another day. It seems like a whirlwind or a flood, but you are not going to go under. With the strength of God, you have stamina, and you are going to go through to the other side. Rejoice in the Lord as you go through, as it will not last forever, but it will come to an end.

Read Scripture:

Psalm 66:6

Prayer:

Heavenly Father, I come to you now, asking you to forgive me for looking at the whirlwind of the trial that I am facing instead of looking to you. I thank you for your forgiveness as I receive it now. I look to you and receive your strength. I rejoice in you, knowing that I am not alone in this and that this too shall pass. I will make it to the other side of this difficult time without going under, as you will bring me through it. In Jesus' name, I pray. Amen.

---

* *Trials*—the act or process of testing, trying, or putting to the proof of one's faith.

Notes:

Sunday, Day 1

(141) All of God's promises are for us, but not everyone receives them. Faith in God is required to acquire everything that God has for us. Jesus obtained for us every promise of God for us. Faith is simply receiving everything that Jesus Christ has *accomplished* for us through the cross and his resurrection. It is positioning us to simply receive it by faith. Take it because it is yours.

Read Scripture:

Romans 5:1

Prayer:

Father God, I come to you in the name of Jesus, thanking you that I stand as the righteousness of God in Christ Jesus. I thank that you have given to me everything that I need that pertains to life and godliness. I have acquired every promise that you have given to me because of what Jesus Christ has accomplished for me, and because I am the righteousness of Christ Jesus, I am now positioned to receive it by faith. In Jesus' name. Amen.

---

* *Accomplished*—successfully completed and achieved.

Notes:

_____

_____

_____

_____

_____

_____

_____

_____

_____

Monday, Day 2

(142) Have you ever considered that a big tree is started by a little seed? As you look up toward the top of the biggest trees, you never imagined that the tall tree was first a little seed before it grew to be a big tree. Scripture says that you are like a tree that is *planted* by the streams that never run dry and that the fruit that you produce ripens in its season. Your leaf never dries or fades and that no matter what you do prospers. This is good news, so draw your nourishment from God in his presence in worship, in the Word, and prayer. Let your roots grow in God even more. Remember that it does not happen overnight but that it is a process.

Read Scripture:

Psalm 1:3

Prayer:

Heavenly Father, I come to you now, asking you to forgive me for neglecting my time in your presence worshipping you, studying the Word, and in prayer. I thank you for your forgiveness, and I receive it now. Holy Spirit, I need you, and I ask you now to help

---

* *Planted*—deeply seeded, deeply rooted; firmly fixed or held.

me and remind me when other things begin to draw me away from my time in God's presence. For I know that I derive my nourishment and strength from him alone, and I know that I must remain in him deeply rooted and fixed in order for my life to produce fruit after the God kind. All of this I pray in Jesus' name. Amen.

Notes:

_____

_____

_____

_____

_____

_____

_____

_____

Tuesday, Day 3

(143) We can all recall as a child hearing another shouting, "Liar, liar, pants on fire, hanging from a telephone wire," and anyone caught lying was in big trouble. It would be foolish to say that we have never lied even as adults. Bending the truth just a little is as much a *lie* as telling a blatant *lie. We all know that lies come from the pit of hell, and lying is essentially aligning ourselves with the father of lies, the devil. Lies are deceptive and are certainly not the truth. God help us to cling to the truth.

Read Scripture:

John 8:44

Prayer:

Father God, I come to you now in Jesus' name, asking you to search my heart and to show me the times where I have bent the truth or unashamedly told a lie. I thank you, Holy Spirit, for revealing this to me now. Father, I am sorry for every lie that has come forth out of my mouth, and I ask you to forgive me now. I thank you

---

* *Lie*—a false statement deliberately presented as being true; a falsehood or something meant to deceive or mistakenly accepted as true.

for your forgiveness as I receive it now. Holy Spirit, I need you. I am asking you to help me and show me immediately when I am about to think, speak, or act out on a lie. As an act of my will, I yield my mind to the spirit of truth, and I yield my tongue to only speak what is truth. I align myself with the truth of God's Word today. In Jesus' name, I pray. Amen.

Notes:

_____

_____

_____

_____

_____

_____

_____

_____

_____

_____

Wednesday, Day 4

(144) It has been said of some that he or she has followed in his or her mother or father's footsteps. Depending on whether our parents followed the Lord or not, that can be a good thing or it can be a bad thing. Regardless of the *examples* we had to follow growing up, we do not have to settle for what they did. Instead, we can pursue God to the degree where we firmly follow him every step of the way, being firmly established in him; and God, our Father, will take great delight in us as we walk in his footsteps. Jesus is our godly *example.

Read Scripture:

Psalm 37:23

Prayer:

Heavenly Father, I come before your presence now with a heart of thanksgiving. I thank you that you are my Father who delights in me when I follow in your footsteps. As an act of my will, I yield myself to you today; and I am asking you to lead, guide, and order my steps. Holy Spirit, I thank you that you are my help and that you assist me in all things. I yield the members of my whole being to you

---

* *Example*—one that is worthy of imitation or duplication.

today and will follow where you lead me, knowing that you always lead me in truth and in the complete will of my Father every step of the way. In Jesus' name, I pray. Amen.

Notes:

_____

_____

_____

_____

_____

_____

_____

_____

_____

Thursday, Day 5

(145) It would be fair to say that no one likes the seasons in life where we are in distress due to a difficult circumstance that we are facing. These difficult times are tribulations or great times of anguish and suffering. "Tribulation" means an experience that tests one's *endurance,* patience, or faith. Believe it or not, these times of tribulation serve their purpose and that purpose is to work the fruit of patience in us. Every believer has the fruit of patience on the inside of them, as it is one of the traits of our Father God. We must learn to draw on his strength to exercise this patience, which undoubtedly produces *endurance in hardship. Sounds like Jesus to me, and he is our example to follow.

Read Scripture:

Romans 5:3

Prayer:

Heavenly Father, I come before you in the name of Jesus, asking you to forgive me for complaining about my circumstances, and letting the distress and care of it to overwhelm me. I thank you for

---

* *Endurance*—the act, quality, or power of withstanding hardship or stress.

your forgiveness as I receive it now. Holy Spirit, I need you, and I am asking for your strength to uphold me in this time to empower me to withstand this hardship by exercising the fruit of patience which produces endurance in me. In Jesus' name, I pray. Amen.

Notes:

_____

_____

_____

_____

_____

_____

_____

_____

_____

Friday, Day 6

(146) When Adam and Eve fell into sin, the entire world was in the same state. But when Jesus Christ came and paid the debt for our sin, then we came alive in Christ. Life is so much more than just surviving. We should be thriving, very lively, profitable, and flourishing in all things. The life of God in you through Jesus Christ has made you alive to succeed. Spend time in his presence and receive his power to *thrive.*

Read Scripture:

1 Corinthians 15:22

Prayer:

Heavenly Father, I come before you now, asking you to forgive me for accepting the norm to survive and not walking in all that you have for me. I thank you for your forgiveness as I receive it now. Holy Spirit, I need you today. As I spend time in God's presence, I am asking you to give me revelation of the power that has been given to me to thrive and succeed in life, as the life of Jesus Christ in me empowers me to move in new things that I have never had the con-

---

*   *Thrive*—to grow strong and vigorously.

fidence to do. I thank you, Jesus, that you always cause me to grow, flourish, and bloom into that person that you have designed me to be. In Jesus' name, I pray. Amen.

Notes:

_____

_____

_____

_____

_____

_____

_____

_____

_____

Saturday, Day 7

(147) Growing up, Doris Day was a very popular actress and singer. There was one familiar song that she sang called, "Que Sera, Sera." It was about a little girl who asked her mother if she would be rich and pretty, and her mother replied, "Que sera, sera. Whatever will be, will be." As a believer, God does not want you to be a "que sera, sera "Christian and have the attitude in your life that whatever will be, will be. God tells us in his Word that he knows the plans that he has for your *future* and that these plans are not to harm you nor are they plans of evil. His plans are to give you a hope and a *future. Look forward to all that God has for you and resist being a "que sera, sera" Christian.

Read Scripture:

Jeremiah 29:11

Prayer:

Father God, I come before you now, asking you to forgive me for acting like a "que sera, sera" Christian and believing in hopelessly unchangeable situations, embracing the un-changeability of it

---

* *Future*—the time yet to come or what lies ahead.

all. Thank you for your forgiveness as I receive it now. Holy Spirit, I need you, and I am asking you to help me to fully embrace God's plan that he has for me. I thank you that I can expect my future with hope, just knowing that God's plan for me is good, and I can fully trust him to help me to walk in the fullness of what he has planned for me as I receive it now. In Jesus' name. Amen.

Notes:

_____

_____

_____

_____

_____

_____

_____

_____

_____

Sunday, Day 1

(148) We all have memories of our childhood school days and the teachers that we had. We may have a fond memory of that one teacher that we took a special liking to because he or she took extra time to explain something to us that we did not understand the first time. Little did they know that they affected our future with that one small act of kindness that changed the course of our life for the better. As believers in Jesus Christ, we have the precious Holy Spirit who is our *Teacher,* who leads and guides us in righteousness and always keeps us aligned with the will of God. Trust the Holy Spirit as your Teacher; he will always lead you into God's truth.

Read Scripture:

Psalm 143:10

Prayer:

Heavenly Father, I come before you, giving you thanks and praise for the precious Holy Spirit that you have given to me and who always leads and guides me into all truth. As an act of my will, I surrender and yield to the Holy Spirit today with a teachable heart,

---

* *Teacher*—a coach, instructor, tutor, or guide.

with the full assurance that he will lead me on paths of righteousness and will teach and reveal to me your ways so that I can walk in obedience to your will. I declare that I am empowered to live in the fullness of Gods' Word. In Jesus' name, I pray. Amen.

Notes:

_____

_____

_____

_____

_____

_____

_____

_____

_____

Monday, Day 2

(149) The next time you are enjoying the great outdoors and have the opportunity to walk in the fields of grass, think about the goodness of God. Have faith in God to meet your needs, and remember that after all, you are much more valuable to God than the fields of grass that he has clothed. How much more will he clothe you and meet your needs. God is a **good** God, and you can put your trust in him.

Read Scripture:

Luke 12:28

Prayer:

Heavenly Father, I come before you in the name of Jesus, giving you thanks for meeting every one of my needs. Just as you have clothed the grass, I know that you will clothe me and will provide for me and my household. God, you are a good Father, and by faith, I trust you to do it. I give you thanks and praise for loving and caring for me the way that you do. In Jesus' name. Amen.

---

* *Good*—of moral excellence; upright and reliable; real, true and sure.

Notes:

_____

_____

_____

_____

_____

_____

_____

_____

_____

_____

Tuesday, Day 3

(150) As a believer in Christ Jesus, we have to be reminded that when you accept Jesus, he becomes your mighty Savior. He rejoices over you with such joy! He will never mention your past sins, and he will never even *recall* them to his mind. If he does not recall them to mind, neither should you. Know that he calms you with his love, and he sings over you with his songs. Sit in his presence for a moment and inhale his precious presence as he wraps his loving arms around you and sings his songs over you.

Read Scripture:

Zephaniah 3:17

Prayer:

Heavenly Father, I come before you now, thanking you that you never recall my past sins. I ask you to forgive me for replaying my past in my mind. I thank you for your forgiveness as I receive it now. Holy Spirit, I need you. I am asking you now to help me to understand that the tapes have been erased, so to speak, and there is nothing on record to recall back to my memory. As I sit in God's

---

* *Recall*—to bring back from memory; recollect; remember.

presence, he calms me with his love as he sings over me today. In Jesus' name. Amen.

Notes:

_____

_____

_____

_____

_____

_____

_____

_____

_____

Wednesday, Day 4

(151) Jesus has **infused** you with his power to conquer every difficulty, and if you think that you can overcome, then you will. Soak in his presence today until you are permeated with the fullness of his strength. Know that apart from him, you can do nothing; but through Christ Jesus, you can do all things.

Read Scripture:

Philippians 4:13

Prayer:

Father God, I come to you now, asking you to forgive me for taking for granted the fact that you have seen me through the difficult times in my life. I thank you for your forgiveness as I receive it now. Holy Spirit, I need you. I am asking you to remind me that through Jesus Christ, I can do all things. He has infused me, or poured into me, his ability to overcome every single difficult situation that I face; and because of that, I am an overcomer. For this, I give you thanks and praise. In Jesus' name. Amen.

---

* *Infused*—to fill or cause to be filled with something.

Notes:

_____

_____

_____

_____

_____

_____

_____

_____

_____

Thursday, Day 5

(152) Have you ever been around someone who has exhibited absolute hopelessness, and you could not be around them long because it started to affect you? Being *pessimistic* is the same as being hopeless. Eeyore on *Winnie the Pooh* was one such character. He would say things like, "I would look on the bright side, if I could find it." As a believer, we put our hope in the Lord and his strength. God gives us the courage to see the opportunities, or chances, for advancement on the other side of hopeless situations. In order to hope in God, you must first be willing to take that care and lay it before him. Lay it down, look up, and be of good courage today. Put your hope in God.

Read Scripture:

Psalm 31:24

Prayer:

Heavenly Father, I come before you today, asking you to forgive me for giving any place to pessimism instead of putting my hope in you. I thank you for your forgiveness as I receive it now. Holy Spirit, I need you. I am asking you to help me to see that difficult

---

* *Pessimistic*—expecting the worst possible outcome.

circumstances are opportunities to see God's mighty hand move on my behalf as I place it in his hands and put my hope in him. Thank you, Holy Spirit, for giving me the courage to believe and to trust God to breakthrough for me as I lift my head and look to him. In Jesus' name, I pray. Amen.

Notes:

_____

_____

_____

_____

_____

_____

_____

_____

_____

Friday, Day 6

(153) Was there ever a time in your life when you lost your patience with someone and they said, "Please bear with me"? What they are essentially saying is "Be patient with me." Forbearance is having patient restraint. And when we have a difficult time bearing with others, we should remember that God was gentle, patient, loving, and tolerant of us. He did not give us what we deserved, which was death, and he was forbearing as he sent Jesus Christ to take on the sin of the whole world. Surely, we can *bear with one another* in his love.

Read Scripture:

Ephesians 4:2

Prayer:

Father God, I come before you in the name of Jesus, asking you to forgive me for being impatient with others when you have extended to me such great grace and patience. I thank you for your forgiveness as I receive it now. Holy Spirit, I need you. I am asking

---

* *Bear with one another*—to hold up and support and to remain patient and attentive, especially during a lengthy or problematic situation that may cause one to want to quit or leave prematurely.

you to help me to exercise the fruit of patience toward others, and to always remember the forbearance of God the Father toward me and his ability and strength to do the same for others. In Jesus' name, I pray. Amen.

Notes:

_____

_____

_____

_____

_____

_____

_____

_____

_____

Saturday, Day 7

(154) Maya Angelou once said that we may encounter many defeats, but we must not be *defeated.* You must determine in your heart that defeat is not an option and that through every frustration, you will rise again stronger than before. When you are facing what looks like defeat, say to yourself, "I will not be defeated, and I will not quit." Do not separate yourself from God's presence during times of difficulty, but go after him even the more, and you will be strengthened to rise above defeat and not be *defeated. You are more than a conqueror.

Read Scripture:

Romans 8:35–37

Prayer:

Heavenly Father, I come before you now, asking you to forgive me for allowing the frustration of life's difficulties to bring me down. I thank you for your forgiveness as I receive it now. Holy Spirit, I need you, and I am asking you to help me to press into God's presence instead of separating myself from him during this time. As I worship the Lord, study his Word, and pray, I am arming myself with

---

* *Defeated*—beaten or overcome, not victorious.

God's power and strength that causes me to rise above the situation. I declare that I will not let the circumstances defeat me. I will not be defeated, and I will not quit. In you, Lord, I have conquered defeat, and I thank you. In Jesus' name. Amen

Notes:

_____

_____

_____

_____

_____

_____

_____

_____

Sunday, Day 1

(155) Before we came to Christ Jesus, we were all prisoners, or slaves, to sin. We were owned by the god of this world until God expressed his love for us by sending his one and only Son to buy us back and free us from our bondage. God brought us out with his mighty hand, *redeemed* us out of the house of the bondman, and set us free! Let the *redeemed of the Lord say so!

Read Scripture:

Deuteronomy 7:8

Prayer:

Heavenly Father, I come before you today, giving you thanks for loving me enough to send your only Son, Jesus, to pay the debt in full for my release from the prison of darkness, sin, shame, and eternal damnation. By your mighty hand, you have set me free from the wicked bondsman. You have redeemed me from sin and its consequences, and I declare that I am the redeemed of the Lord. I will praise you to the ends of the earth. In Jesus' name. Amen.

---

* *Redeemed*—to save, a person or soul, from a state of sinfulness and its consequences.

Notes:

_____

_____

_____

_____

_____

_____

_____

_____

_____

Monday, Day 2

(156) The skilled hand of Father God, is your Creator who made you in his image, and he has ordained you by virtue of his superior authority unto good works that you should walk in them. You are his treasured possession, and today, you have the power and ability to carry out and *fulfill* all those good things that he has for you to do.

Read Scripture:

Ephesians 2:10

Prayer:

Heavenly Father, I come to you today, thanking you that I am your workmanship created in Christ Jesus to do good works. As an act of my will, I submit my life, my hands, and my feet to you. Thank you that you have given me the power and ability through the Holy Spirit to carry out, fulfill, and complete all that you have prophesied over my life and every good work that you have for me to carry out for you today. In Jesus' name, I pray. Amen.

---

* *Fulfill*—to carry out or bring to realization, as a prophecy or promise.

Notes:

_____

_____

_____

_____

_____

_____

_____

_____

Tuesday, Day 3

(157) Have you ever experienced someone who is introducing their young child to you and this child is not at all interested in meeting you but instead clings, or *cleaves,* for dear life to the parent's leg or arm? The Bible says that we are to cleave unto God, meaning we are to adhere, or stick fast, to him and to be faithful to hear his voice, serve him, and obey him, walking after him. *Cleave to your Father God, with everything that is in you.

Read Scripture:

Deuteronomy 13:4

Prayer:

Heavenly Father, I come to you now, asking you to forgive me for the times where I have not been faithful when I have heard you speak and did not obey. I thank you for your forgiveness as I receive it now. Holy Spirit, I need you, and I am asking you to convict me when I am leaving and not cleaving to my heavenly Father, God. As an act of my will, I surrender my own will and desire unto the will and desire of my Father God, to hear, obey, serve, and cleave, resist-

---

* *Cleave*—to remain faithful to one's principles and to resist separation.

ing separation from him and remaining faithful to him. In Jesus'
name, I pray. Amen.

Notes:

_____

_____

_____

_____

_____

_____

_____

_____

_____

Wednesday, Day 4

(158) God's way is perfect, and his Word has been tried. Meaning, it has been thoroughly tested and proved to be good and *trustworthy.* Throughout the generations, man has tested and tried God's Word to disprove it, and they have found it proven to be good and trustworthy. We can put our trust in God, knowing that he is our Buckler, our Shield, and we can put our full trust in him and his Word.

Read Scripture:

2 Samuel 22:31

Prayer:

Father God, I come before you in the name of Jesus, asking you to forgive me for the times where I have not fully trusted in you or your Word. I thank you for your forgiveness as I receive it now. Holy Spirit, I need you. I am asking you to help me to hold fast to the truth of God's Word, and to know and understand that God is my Shield and my Buckler that protects me from the blows of life. For this, I am grateful. In Jesus' name. Amen.

---

* *Trustworthy*—worthy of being trusted, honest, reliable, or dependable.

Notes:

_____

_____

_____

_____

_____

_____

_____

_____

_____

_____

Thursday, Day 5

(159) Have you ever prayed concerning something and wondered why it seemed as if God did not hear you, and you questioned whether or not he would answer? And then someone close to you tells you it will happen in due time, and you wondered what that meant when they said it? "In due time" means eventually or at an appropriate time. Daniel, the prophet, said that all wisdom and power belong to God, and he sets the times and ages. When you pray according to the Word, which is God's will, know that God heard your prayer, and there is an *appointed time* when the answer will manifest. Continue to thank God for the due time he has promised.

Read Scripture:

Daniel 2:20–21

Prayer:

Heavenly Father, I come before you in the name of Jesus, asking you to forgive me for the times where I have wavered after bringing my petitions before you. Thank you for your forgiveness as I receive it now. Holy Spirit, I need you. I am asking you to help me to stand

---

* *Appointed time*—at a specific, designated time.

firm in my faith and trust in God because I know that he has heard my prayers as I have prayed according to his Word. I thank you, Father God, that there is an appointed time for the answer to manifest. In Jesus' name. Amen.

Notes:

_____

_____

_____

_____

_____

_____

_____

_____

Friday, Day 6

(160) The scriptures tell us that when Jesus was on earth traveling, there was a man who called him Good Teacher, and Jesus asked him why he was calling him good. Jesus told him that there is only one that is good, and that one is God and God alone. Jesus was right in saying so because God is the only one who is morally right—*righteous.* One Bible translation says, "No one is essentially good by nature except God alone." We do not hear this often enough, but the God we serve is indeed a righteous God.

Read Scripture:

Mark 10:18

Prayer:

Heavenly Father, I come to you today, not asking you for anything but to thank you for reminding me of your goodness. There is no one as good as you, and today, I lift my hands in worship to you, giving you the praise, the glory, and the honor that is due your magnificent name; and I declare that you are indeed a righteous and a good, good God. In Jesus' name. Amen.

---

* *Righteous*—morally upright; without guilt or sin.

Notes:

_____

_____

_____

_____

_____

_____

_____

_____

_____

Saturday, Day 7

(161) Scripture tells us that there should be no schism in the body of Christ. A schism is division, disharmony, discord. Being a part of the body of Christ means that we are members, and each of us should care for each other with mutual *concern.** When one member of the body suffers, we should suffer; and when one member rejoices, we should rejoice with them. As a believer, we should make it a practice to examine our own hearts so that there would be no schisms between us and any other member in the body of Christ.

Read Scripture:

1 Corinthians 12:25

Prayer:

Father God, I come before you in the name of Jesus, asking you to reveal to me any part that I have had in bringing disharmony, discord, or division in the body of Christ. I ask you to forgive me, and I thank you for your forgiveness as I receive it now. Holy Spirit, I need you. I am asking you to help me to continually examine my own heart and help me to treat my brothers and sisters in the body

---

* *Concern*—to relate to; be connected with.

of Christ with the same mutual concern. When one suffers, show me so that I can stand with them in their time of need. I will also rejoice with them when they rejoice. In Jesus' name, I pray. Amen.

Notes:

_____

_____

_____

_____

_____

_____

_____

_____

Sunday, Day 1

(162) Some of you have experienced *rejection* as a child, where a parent refused to give sufficient parental affection or care to you. Then as adults, some individuals have totally been disregarded by others and have been pushed aside as if you never existed. If you have been rejected by others and you have accepted Jesus as your Lord and Savior, you need to hear that he will never turn you away, but he fully embraces you because he never rejects or sends someone away who comes to him.

Read Scripture:

John 6:37

Prayer:

Heavenly Father, I come before you now in the name of Jesus. As an act of my will and by faith in Jesus Christ, right now, I choose to forgive those individuals who have rejected me in both my childhood and my adulthood. I release the root of rejection that it produced in my life. I declare that by the power of the Holy Spirit, the root of rejection is uprooted and rendered null, void, and powerless

---

* *Rejection*—to shun or turn away from or refuse to accept.

in my life and that I am set free! I thank you, Father God, that in your love, you fully embrace me as your own, and you will never turn away from me. In Jesus' name. Amen.

Notes:

_____

_____

_____

_____

_____

_____

_____

_____

_____

Monday, Day 2

(163) Can you recall a time when someone said something terrible to you and how it affected you? What about the very words that come out of your own mouth? Are you aware that those words affect you as well? Be aware of the things that you say today, and let your words line up with what God says about you. Speak life-giving, *wholesome* words released into your life and not toxic poison.

Read Scripture:

Proverbs 15:4

Prayer:

Father God, in Jesus' name, I come before you now, asking you to forgive me for the words that I have spoken into my life that were contrary to what you say about me. I thank you for your forgiveness as I receive it now. Holy Spirit, I need you. I am asking you to help me to guard my lips and tongue so that I do not release toxic words. Instead, as an act of my will, I surrender my tongue; and by the power of the Holy Spirit, I speak forth life-giving, life-changing,

---

* *Wholesome*—moral, decent, clean, pure, uplifting, respectable, ethical, healthy, good, and beneficial.

God-filled words that are beneficial to my life. In Jesus' name, I pray. Amen.

Notes:

_____

_____

_____

_____

_____

_____

_____

_____

_____

Tuesday, Day 3

(164) We all have feelings and emotions, but they should never control our actions and move us away from God. How many times have you allowed your feelings to *dictate* you and direct your life? Feelings can be fickle. It causes us to change our mind constantly and shows instability. We should never allow our feelings to direct our footsteps or take command of our life. Our relationship with God is what orders our steps.

Read Scripture:

Job 23:11

Prayer:

Heavenly Father, I come before you now, asking you to forgive me for the times that I have allowed my feelings to dictate, dominate, or rule over me, directing my steps away from you and your Word. I thank you for your forgiveness as I receive it now. Holy Spirit, I need you. I am asking you to help me to put my relationship with my Father God, first place as I make time to study his Word, and he orders my steps. In Jesus' name, I pray. Amen.

---

* *Dictate*—to give orders: to boss, dominate, or rule.

Notes:

_____

_____

_____

_____

_____

_____

_____

_____

_____

Wednesday, Day 4

(165) There are so many things in life that we *take for granted.* Breathing, for example, is one. How many times in the day or in life have we even considered breathing? Your very first breath of the day is a gift. Remember to give thanks to your Creator for allowing you to see another day, for it is he who has made you and has given life to you.

Read Scripture:

Job 33:4

Prayer:

Heavenly Father, in the name of Jesus, I come before you now, asking you to forgive me for the many things that I have taken for granted. I thank you for your forgiveness as I receive it now. Holy Spirit, I need you. I am asking you to help me to be sensitive to the many things that God has blessed me with and to never take it for granted, but to always appreciate and have a heart of thanksgiving for all things, big or small. In Jesus' name, I pray. Amen.

---

* *Take for granted*—to underestimate or undervalue someone or something or to not properly recognize or appreciate someone or something.

Notes:

Thursday, Day 5

(166) The scriptures give such wonderful insight about God's loving and caring heart for us. He tells us that when we are old, when our limbs grow tired, our eyes are weak, and our hair is silvery gray, that he will *carry** us as he always has. Such comfort knowing that from the beginning of our life to the end of it, God is there for us!

Read Scripture:

    Isaiah 46:4

Prayer:

    Heavenly Father, in the name of Jesus, I come before you now with overwhelming love and thanksgiving for you. I receive such comfort from your Word, which tells me that when I am old, tired, and my eyes are weak and my hair is gray that you will always carry me. Thank you, Father God, for always being there. From the very beginning of my life to the end of it, you are still there. For this, I give you thanks and praise. In Jesus' name. Amen.

---

*   *Carry*—to move while supporting.

Notes:

Friday, Day 6

(167) Criticism and gossip are church going demons that prey on wounded people. Scripture says that one who gossips are merely revealing the wounds of his own soul and that his or her slander penetrates the innermost being. Next time you are *tempted* to start gossiping or give ear to gossip, stop and ask yourself this question: where is my soul wounded, and where did the wound come from? When it has been revealed to you, then forgive those who have been the source of that wounding. Wounded people wound people.

Read Scripture:

Proverbs 18:8

Prayer:

Heavenly Father, I come before you now in the name of Jesus, asking you to examine my heart. Please show me when I have gossiped or have given ear to gossip. As you reveal it to me, I bring to you and I ask you to forgive me as I receive your forgiveness now. Holy Spirit, show me any deep wounds within me that have come from others who hurt me right now. As an act of my will, I release

---

* *Tempted*—incline, entice, or lure.

those individuals who have wounded me; I forgive them. Heavenly Father, I thank you for healing me now from those wounds so that I will not wound others. In Jesus' name. Amen.

Notes:

_____

_____

_____

_____

_____

_____

_____

_____

_____

Saturday, Day 7

(168) Sometimes in life, we get tired of waiting for God's answer to our prayers, and we **settle** for solutions instead of his promises. Abram and Sarai *settled for a solution when they decided to do it their way. Abram laid with Hagar, and their son Ismael was born. It was not for another ten years that the promised son Isaac was born. Don't *settle for a solution and do things your way. Instead, wait on God for your promise.

Read Scripture:

> Joshua 23:14

Prayer:

Father God, in the name of Jesus, I come to you with a repentant heart, asking you to forgive me for settling for the solution by doing things my way instead of waiting on your promises. I thank you for your forgiveness as I receive it now. Holy Spirit, I need you. I am asking you to help me and show me when I am about to settle for the solution, doing things my way instead of standing firm on God's promise no matter how long it takes, knowing that God will not fail

---

* *Settle*—accept despite lack of complete satisfaction.

me but he will accomplish all that he has said in his Word. In Jesus'
name, I pray. Amen.

Notes:

_____

_____

_____

_____

_____

_____

_____

_____

_____

Sunday, Day 1

(169) There is no doubt that we are living in a world where there is much *negativity.* All you have to do is watch the news for five minutes and you will see all the *negativity and the things that are going all around us. What we hear can rub off on us. Sometimes, we need to make a conscious effort to fast from all *negativity, and God will break that yoke. When fasting from all *negativity, be prepared, because it may mean separating yourself from certain people.

Read Scripture:

Isaiah 58:6

Prayer:

Heavenly Father, I come before you now in the name of Jesus, asking you to forgive me for allowing negativism to affect my life. I repent for being critical toward others' suggestions, and for allowing pessimism and the tendency to stress and have the gloomiest possible view of things. I thank you for your forgiveness as I receive it now. Holy Spirit, as an act of my will, I choose to fast from all negativity.

---

* *Negativity*—the practice or habit of being skeptical, critical, or pessimistic, especially toward the view or suggestions of others.

With your help, you will loosen the bands of wickedness, undo all heavy burdens, break every yoke, and set me free. In Jesus' name, I pray. Amen.

Notes:

_____

_____

_____

_____

_____

_____

_____

_____

_____

Monday, Day 2

(170) God's Word is an indispensable weapon. It is absolutely necessary and essential for us believers. We must spend time studying the Word, *meditating* on the Word, and confessing the Word so that when a situation arises in our life, we can successfully use the sword of the Spirit. So the question is: how sharp is your sword?

Read Scripture:

Ephesians 6:17

Prayer:

Heavenly Father, in the name of Jesus, I come to you now, asking you to forgive me for the lack of time that I have spent studying your Word. I thank you for your forgiveness as I receive it now. Holy Spirit, I need you, and I yield to you now, asking you to help me prioritize my life by putting the most important things above everything else. Holy Spirit, as I spend time studying God's Word, give me the revelation of the scriptures so that I can apply them to my life and effectively use the sword of the Spirit in every and all circumstances. In Jesus' name, I pray. Amen.

---

* *Meditating*—to think or reflect, especially in a calm and deliberate manner.

Notes:

_____

_____

_____

_____

_____

_____

_____

_____

_____

_____

Tuesday, Day 3

(171) Scripture tells us that it is easier to conquer a strong city than to win back a friend that we have *offended* because their walls go up, making it nearly impossible to win them back. We all have had friendships that we hold dear to our hearts. More than likely, at some time or another, we may have offended a friend. Sometimes, we should take the time to ask our friends if we have ever offended them and ask them for forgiveness. Remember that even though your intent was not to offend, sometimes others' perception of the situation may have brought about a rift between you; and you should be willing to talk it through.

Read Scripture:

  Proverbs 18:19

Prayer:

  Heavenly Father, I come before you in the name of Jesus as I examine my heart, asking you to show me if I have offended any of my friends. As you show me, I ask you to forgive me, and I thank you for your forgiveness as I receive it now. Holy Spirit, I need you. I

---

* *Offended*—to cause displeasure, anger, resentment, or wounded feelings.

am asking you to help me as I prepare myself to approach the friends that I have offended and ask them to forgive me. Holy Spirit, be in our midst and have your way. I trust you to bring about resolve and restoration between me and any of my friends that I have wounded. In Jesus' name, I pray. Amen.

Notes:

_____

_____

_____

_____

_____

_____

_____

_____

Wednesday, Day 4

(172) When Jesus went to sit at the right hand of the Father, he did not abandon us. Instead, he sent the precious Holy Spirit to dwell on the inside of us. He was given to us to help us, to teach us, to *comfort* us. The Holy Spirit always leads and guides us into all truth and points to the Father always. The Holy Spirit enables us to be all that we are called to be, and he empowers us to do all that he has called us to do. Yield to the Holy Spirit. He is the Genius on the inside of you.

Read Scripture:

John 14:16

Prayer:

Heavenly Father, I come to you in the name of Jesus, thanking you that you did not abandon me when Jesus went to sit at your right hand. Instead, you sent the precious Holy Spirit to dwell on the inside of me to be my Guide and to enable me to be all that you have called me to be. He has empowered me to do all that you have called me to do. As an act of my will, I surrender to the Holy Spirit

---

* *Comfort*—a feeling of freedom from worry or disappointment and to soothe in times of affliction or distress.

who causes me to overcome, and he is the Greater One who lives on the inside of me. For this, I give you thanks and praise. In Jesus' name. Amen.

Notes:

_____

_____

_____

_____

_____

_____

_____

_____

_____

Thursday, Day 5

(173) We have all heard the saying that the Bible is God's Basic Instructions Before Leaving Earth. The Bible is called the Word of God because it is God's thoughts and God's will for us. His Word *instructs* us, teaches us, and imparts unto us his thoughts and his righteous ways so that we may live according to them. We should take hold of his instruction by and through the Word of God, and never let it go. Let God's Word *instruct you, teach you, correct you, and lead you.

Read Scripture:

Proverbs 4:13

Prayer:

Heavenly Father, in the name of Jesus, I come before you as I examine my heart and life. I ask you to forgive me for not placing importance on your Word as your thoughts and your will for my life. Please forgive me for neglecting the study of your Word. I thank you for your forgiveness as I receive it now. Holy Spirit, I need you. I ask you now to help me to see when I am neglecting and straying

---

* *Instruct*—train, educate, prepare, and develop.

from time spent studying God's Word. Thank you, Father, that you instruct, teach, and correct me by and through your Word. In Jesus' name, I pray. Amen.

Notes:

_____

_____

_____

_____

_____

_____

_____

_____

_____

Friday, Day 6

(174) We are a three-part being-spirit, soul, and we live in a body. Our spirit is perfectly made in the image of God. Our soul is our mind, will, and emotions. Our mind is our thoughts. Our will is what we want or do not want to do, and our emotions are our feelings. Our body is the tent that houses our spirit and soul. Jesus told us in scriptures that we should love the Lord, our God, with all of our heart, soul, and mind. We are to love him with everything that is in us-our *entire* being-spirit, soul, and body. We do that by submitting our will to God's will, by renewing our mind to God's Word, and by taking thoughts that do not line up with his Word and making them subject to the Word. We present our body to him as the temple of the Holy Spirit and care for it accordingly.

Read Scripture:

Matthew 22:37

Prayer:

Heavenly Father, I come to you today. As an act of my will, I willingly submit my spirit, soul, and body to your will without res-

---

* *Entire*—with no reservations or limitations; complete.

ervations. I renew my mind with your Word, which is your will for my life. I take every though captive that would exalt itself above the knowledge of Jesus Christ and bring it into submission to the Word of God. I thank you for the Holy Spirit who helps me to live by faith in you, God, and not according to my feelings. I submit my body, which is the temple of the Holy Spirit, to care for it accordingly. Above all, God, I give you my heart, which is the center of all physical and spiritual life. In Jesus' name. Amen.

Notes:

_____

_____

_____

_____

_____

_____

_____

_____

_____

Saturday, Day 7

(175) Abraham is known as the *father* of faith because he believed God. When we read about Abraham, we should not just see historical events that took place, but we should see a real person who put his full trust in God. God called Abraham his friend, and he became the father of many nations. If you are in Christ Jesus, then you are Abraham's seed that lives upon the earth. Scripture tells us that a true child of Abraham will have the same faith as their father Abraham. One translation says that people who trust in God are the true sons and daughters of Abraham.

Read Scripture:

Galatians 3:7

Prayer:

Heavenly Father, I come before you now, thanking you for your Word that says that the true sons and daughters of Abraham are the ones who put their trust in you. As I examine my heart today, I confess to you that I have not always put my trust in you, and I am asking you to forgive me. I thank you for your forgiveness as I receive it

---

* *Father*—a person who founds a line or family; forefather.

now. Holy Spirit, I need you. God said in his Word that faith comes by hearing and hearing by the Word. So I am asking you to stir up within me a great desire to hear the Word by which faith comes, and to be a doer of the Word as Abraham was by believing it and receiving the promises of God as he did. In Jesus' name, I pray. Amen.

Notes:

_____

_____

_____

_____

_____

_____

_____

_____

_____

Sunday, Day 1

(176) The Bible instructs us not to wise in our own eyes. One translation tells us not to be impressed with our own wisdom, and instead, we are to fear the Lord and turn away from evil. There is wisdom from this world system that we can attain that leads to pride, and this wisdom of the world cannot compare to the wisdom of God. No philosopher or expert scholar can debate with God and win because the wisdom of this world is utter *foolishness* to God.

Read Scripture:

1 Corinthians 1:20

Prayer:

Father God, I come before you in the name of Jesus. As I examine my heart, I realize the times where I have been wise in my own eyes, which is pride. I come with a repentant heart, asking you to forgive me for the sin of pride. I thank you for your forgiveness as I receive it now. Holy Spirit, I need you, and I ask you to always convict my heart when I am operating out of the foolishness of the

---

* *Foolishness*—lack of good sense or judgment; stupidity.

wisdom of this world. Help me to fear the Lord and turn away from evil and worldly wisdom. All of this I ask in Jesus' name. Amen.

Notes:

_____

_____

_____

_____

_____

_____

_____

_____

_____

Monday, Day 2

(177) Have you ever wondered why it took the Israelites forty years to get to their Promised Land when according to Deuteronomy 1:2, it was only supposed to take them eleven days?

The Israelites acted like rebels, and their repeated *rebellion* against their leader Moses was evident by their complaining, murmuring, and coming against him. Yet God's repeated mercy and discipline was on his people. Are you facing a hardship that has become an obstacle where you have lost the view and sight of the promises that God has made to you? Do not let your heart be hardened by your circumstances, and do not reject the promises of God through his Word to you. Keep believing.

Read Scripture:

Numbers 14:11

Prayer:

Father God, I come to you in the name of Jesus. As I examine my heart, I ask you to forgive me for straying from your promises to me, and for murmuring and complaining about my circumstances.

---

* *Rebellion*—resistance or defiance to authority.

I thank you for your forgiveness as I receive it now. Holy Spirit, I need you. I ask you to help me to stand firm in the belief that God's promises to me shall be fulfilled in his time, his way, and that I will not grow weary in my faith in God nor will I allow my heart to be hardened in the waiting. As an act of my will, I will praise him continually and thank him for what he has promised me is on its way. In Jesus' name, I pray. Amen.

Notes:

_____

_____

_____

_____

_____

_____

_____

_____

_____

Tuesday, Day 3

(178) We do not worship angels, but as believers, we know that angels do exist. According to scripture, angels are heavenly *messengers.* Scripture tells us that angels listen and act on God's very Word. Angels stand ready to do his will. What is God's will? God's will is his Word for us, so when we speak the Word of God, we are speaking the will of the Father, and the angels hear his Word and are ready to move on our behalf.

Read Scripture:

Psalm 103:20

Prayer:

Heavenly Father, I come to you now, giving you thanks for this day and for showing me in Scripture that there are heavenly messengers standing ready to do your will. I thank you that your Word is your will for my life; and when I speak forth your Word according to what has been written in the Bible, I am speaking out your perfect will for my life, and the angels hearken and move on my behalf to fulfill your perfect will in my life. Holy Spirit, I need you and ask

---

* *Messenger*—one that carries messages or is a bearer of news.

you to help me to always attend to the Word of God to hear, believe, confess, and expect. In Jesus' name, I pray. Amen.

Notes:

_____

_____

_____

_____

_____

_____

_____

_____

_____

Wednesday, Day 4

(179) We have all seen a court case play out on television. When the verdict is read out loud and the judge says, "Not guilty," the defendant then sighs with great relief and will sometimes even show great emotion and break down and weep. In the courts of heaven, when you have accepted Jesus as your Lord and Savior, Father God, has declared you **not guilty.** You have been pardoned. "Pardoned" means to allow an offense or fault to pass without judgment. Jesus took our judgment upon him and paid the penalty for our sin, and because of it, we become the righteousness of God through him.

Read Scripture:

Romans 3:25

Prayer:

Heavenly Father, I come before you, giving you thanks and praise for Jesus Christ who paid the penalty in full for my sin. I have become the righteousness of God through him and have been pardoned because of his great love for me. I thank you, Jesus, for taking my place at the cross and for the remission of my sins, releasing me

---

* *Not guilty*—blameless or innocent.

from a debt that I could not pay from the penalty or punishment for my sin and for your forgiveness. In Jesus' name. Amen.

Notes:

_____

_____

_____

_____

_____

_____

_____

_____

_____

Thursday, Day 5

(180) The Bible says that the Israelites heard God's good news just as we have but that the preached Word did not do them any good because it was not combined with faith. How many times have we heard the Word of God being preached and say that it was a good word, but when we get home and go about the week, we forget that word or we do not apply it to our life? The preached word only profits you when you **mix** it with faith. So the next time you hear the word preached, add your faith to it, mix it, and you will profit or benefit from it.

Read Scripture:

Hebrews 4:2

Prayer:

Heavenly Father, I come to you now, asking you to forgive me for taking your Word for granted and for not combining my faith to the preached word. I thank you for your forgiveness as I receive it now. Holy Spirit, I need you, and I ask you to help me to remember that when I hear the preached word, I can combine my faith and

---

* *Mix*—to add, combine, or join.

join myself to the word that is preached. The Word of God will then produce fruit, and I will receive the benefits from it in my life. In Jesus' name. Amen.

Notes:

_____

_____

_____

_____

_____

_____

_____

_____

_____

Friday, Day 6

(181) In the Old Testament, we read about the exodus of God's people. The Israelites form the **oppression** and slavery of the Egyptians who were enemies of God and his people. They had a fearless leader in Moses, and many times, Moses would tell them not to fear. In scriptures, we read that Moses told the Israelites to stand their ground, to witness how the Lord would rescue them, and to take a good look at the Egyptians because they would never see them again. Time and time again, the Israelites had to be reminded that God was with them to deliver them. Today, be reminded to fear not, stand still, and see the Lord's salvation!

Read Scripture:

Exodus 14:13

Prayer:

Father God, in the name of Jesus I come before you now, asking you to forgive me for giving in to fear when you have spoken to us in your Word to fear not. I thank you for your forgiveness as I receive it now. Holy Spirit, I need you. I am asking you to help me to see and

---

* *Oppression*—a feeling of being weighed down in mind or body.

know that God's hand of deliverance is there when the enemy rises against me, and because my enemies are God's enemies, God is able to annihilate them just as he did when he delivered the Israelites from the fear of the Egyptians. I declare that I will not fear, but I will stand still and see God's hand of deliverance from all oppression in my life. In Jesus' name. Amen.

Notes:

_____

_____

_____

_____

_____

_____

_____

_____

_____

Saturday, Day 7

(182) When you first gave your life to the Lord and received him as Savior, did you ever have anyone tell you that you were being brain-washed? As a believer in Jesus Christ, there is a *sanctification* process where when we begin to read and study the Word of God, our minds are being washed with the water of the Word. Our thoughts are being renewed and our life being transformed. So the next time someone tells you that you are brain-washed, don't argue with them, but let them know that it is true. Your mind and thoughts are being cleansed, and the Word is changing you and that they too can be brainwashed.

Read Scripture:

Ephesians 5:26

Prayer:

Father God, in the name of Jesus, I thank you that I am set apart to you and for you. By the washing of the water of your Word, my thought life is being cleansed from old ways of thinking, old

---

Sanctification—the state of growing in divine grace as a result of Christian commitment.

habits, old attitudes, and old practices. I am being renewed, and it is bringing about a transformation and change in me into the ways of Jesus to live, forgive, and love as he did. For this, I am grateful. I give you the praise, glory, and honor. In Jesus' name. Amen.

Notes:

_____

_____

_____

_____

_____

_____

_____

_____

_____

Sunday, Day 1

(183) Scripture tells us that God's wisdom is a gift from him and that he is a generous God. Every single word that God speaks is full of revelation, and God reveals his own nature and his purpose for mankind. This is the revelation that God gives to those who train their heart to listen when he speaks and when we open up our spirit wide to expand discernment. God wants us to cry out for *comprehension* and intercede for insight, and to seek his wisdom as treasure. When we seek, we will surely discover the fear of the Lord and discover the true knowledge of God.

Read Scripture:

Proverbs 2:1–6

Prayer:

Heavenly Father, I come before you today, in awe of you and what precious treasure that we have in your Word, which is your will for my life. Through your Word, you disclose or uncover for us to see your nature and your purpose for us and for mankind. Holy Spirit, I need you. As an act of my will, I yield myself whole-heartedly to

---

* *Comprehension*—the capacity for understanding fully.

you to expand my discernment through you as I cry out to God for understanding and intercession for insight into the kingdom of God, to know him intimately in a deeper way, and to discover the true knowledge of who he is to me personally in my life. All of this I pray in Jesus' name. Amen.

Notes:

_____

_____

_____

_____

_____

_____

_____

_____

Monday, Day 2

(184) We have all seen the documentaries on television of the nature of animals and the dangers of other animals preying on them, lying in wait to kill them. Sometime in our walk as a believer in Jesus Christ, we will experience other's coming against us, and the first thing we do is tell someone else. That is our human nature at work. However, God does not want us to expose another's weakness or fault, and he certainly does not want them to become our prey or for us to attack, devour, or *victimize.* If we do this, then we are the one who is becoming prey for the devil. Scripture tells us that we are to love, bless, and pray for our enemies; and if we are honest with our self, we know that it is not something that comes easy for us. But we can ask God to help us, and he will.

Read Scripture:

Matthew 5:44

---

* *Victimize*—to punish someone or discriminate against selectively or deliberately treat unfairly.

Prayer:

Heavenly Father, I come to you, giving you thanks for your Word which constantly reminds me of how much I need you. Your Word tells me that I am supposed to love, bless, and even pray for my enemies. I come asking, first of all, admitting that I find this very hard to do, and I ask you to forgive me for not asking or looking to you for help to do this. Instead, I have handled my way, which is more than not the wrong way. I repent now, and thank you for your forgiveness as I receive it. Holy Spirit, I need you. As an act of my will, I yield to your leading; and I ask you to teach me how to forgive, love, bless, and pray for my enemies. In Jesus' name, I pray. Amen.

Notes:

_____

_____

_____

_____

_____

_____

_____

_____

_____

Tuesday, Day 3

(185) Throughout the day, we endure so many things that can and will steal your joy and peace if you let it. Peaceful, restful, quiet, still, calm, soothing, and *undisturbed* rest is what God wants you to have in the night hours when you lay your body down. But what about your mind and your thoughts? Be determined to take the events of the day and those thoughts that came from the day's events, and lay them at the feet of Jesus before you lay down to sleep at night. God always watches over you as you sleep. Why not enjoy his peace.

Read Scripture:

Numbers 6:26

Prayer:

Heavenly Father, I come to you now asking for forgiveness for carrying the events of the day and the thoughts that have robbed me of my joy and peace. I thank you for your forgiveness as I receive it now. Holy Spirit, I need you. I am asking you to help throughout the day to take the thoughts and events of the day that bring weariness to my soul and to cast them at the feet of Jesus; I willingly lay

---

* *Undisturbed*—quiet, still, calm, peaceful, serene, restful.

379

it all down. And in its place, I receive peaceful, restful, quiet, still, calm, soothing, and undisturbed rest for my mind and body. In Jesus' name, I pray. Amen.

Notes:

_____

_____

_____

_____

_____

_____

_____

_____

_____

Wednesday, Day 4

(186) Because God's Word is his will for us and we pray according to his will, which is his Word, then whatever we ask for in prayer, believing we shall receive. We do not have to *perform* for God to receive it because Jesus already achieved every precious promise for us so that all we have to do is position ourselves to receive, and we do that by faith in him. "Achieve" means "to bring to a successful conclusion; to accomplish; attain and receive means to get something; come into possession of." Jesus achieved so we could receive, so take it by faith.

Read Scripture:

Matthew 21:22

Prayer:

Father God, in the name of Jesus, I come before you now, thanking you that you are a good God. I thank you that I do not have to perform for you to receive your promises because Jesus has already obtained and achieved this for me when he went to the cross and was resurrected from the dead. Because of this, I am the righ-

---

* *Perform*—to carry out or do or to execute or do something.

teousness of God and positioned to receive all that you have given to me by faith in Jesus Christ. As I hear your Word, believe, and pray according to your Word, asking you, I shall receive as you have said. In Jesus' name. Amen.

Notes:

_____

_____

_____

_____

_____

_____

_____

_____

Thursday, Day 5

(187) Smokey the Bear said it so well when he said, "Only you can prevent forest fires." As a believer in Jesus Christ, we know and understand how small the tongue is and how grand speeches can be made with this small member of our body. We also know how damaging our words can be from this same member known as our tongue. Scripture tells us that a tiny spark from our tongue can set our whole world on fire, *corrupting* our entire body, and that our life is set on fire by hell itself. Therefore, we should guard our tongue lest we want to see the destruction of hell's fire.

Read Scripture:

James 3:3–6

Prayer:

Father God, I come before you now with a repentant heart, asking you to forgive me for the many times that I have spoken and uttered lies, factions, unwholesome talk, or anything that is contrary to your Word. I thank you for your forgiveness as I receive it now. Holy Spirit, I need you, and I am asking you to help me keep my

---

* *Corrupting*—to infect or taint, harmful to the mind or morals.

heart and tongue in check. Set a guard over my tongue, preventing me from speaking evil or wicked, which corrupts my whole body and allows hell to set my whole life on fire for destruction. Holy Spirit, as I yield my tongue to you, teach me how to refrain from evil communication and to fill myself with God's word so that what I put in comes forth with all purity and is pleasing to God. In Jesus' name, I pray. Amen.

Notes:

_____

_____

_____

_____

_____

_____

_____

_____

_____

Friday, Day 6

(188) When we focus on other's faults and *judge* them, but we wear rose-colored glasses in examining our own life, only seeing the positive in us, not the areas where we need to change, this is not only unrealistic but the scripture asks us: how can we even see the splinter in our brother's eyes when we ourselves have a log or beam in our own eye? Who are we to *judge? With the same standard of measure we use to pass out judgment, judgment will be measured back to us. We must get rid of our fault-finding glasses and rose-colored glasses, examine our own life, and leave the judging to God.

Read Scripture:

Matthew 7:1–4

Prayer:

Heavenly Father, I come to you with a heavy heart, knowing that I have spent more time fault-finding and judging others than I have in examining my own heart. Right now, as an act of my will, I examine my own heart and attitude of self-righteous superiority as though I have the right assuming the office of a judge. For this,

---

* *Judge*—criticize for doing wrong.

I repent. I am sorry. Now I ask you, Father God, to forgive me for the unjust and unfair judgments that I have made. I thank you for your forgiveness as I receive it now. Holy Spirit, I need you, and I am asking you to convict me whenever I am about to put on those faultfinding or rose-colored glasses again. All of this I pray, in Jesus' name. Amen.

Notes:

_____

_____

_____

_____

_____

_____

_____

_____

_____

Saturday, Day 7

(189) We all know how difficult it is to *trust* someone that we do not know. *Trust is having a firm belief in the integrity, ability, or character of a person. *Trust is having confidence or reliance and putting that *trust in that person. Many times, the Bible tells us to *trust in God. You will only *trust God to the degree that you know him because it's hard to *trust someone that you do not know. Like any relationships, it takes commitment. Getting to know God is an intimate time in his presence, worshipping him, studying his Word, getting to know him personally; and in doing so, you will have confidence in his reliability. He is dependable and trustworthy.

Read Scripture:

Psalm 31:14

Prayer:

Heavenly Father, I come before you now in the name of Jesus, asking you to forgive me for neglecting my personal relationship with you and for placing my trust in other things instead of putting my

---

* *Trust*—firm belief in the integrity, ability, or character of a person to have confidence in or reliance on.

trust in you. I thank you for your forgiveness as I receive it now. Holy Spirit, I need you, and I am asking you to help me to be mindful that my relationship with the Lord should be my greatest priority. Lord, I am desperate to know you, and I thank you that you are drawing me with your loving-kindness. As I seek you with my whole heart, I am developing a trust in you where I am confident in your reliability as I learn to depend on you and not my own strength, placing my full trust in you. For this, I thank you. In Jesus' name. Amen.

Notes:

_____

_____

_____

_____

_____

_____

_____

_____

Sunday, Day 1

(190) Hebrews chapter 11 is known as the heroes of faith chapter. By faith, through faith, in faith, and full of faith, these individuals subdued kingdoms, wrought righteousness, obtained promises, and stopped the mouths of lions. What examples they are for us to follow. You too are full of faith and power. By faith, through faith, in faith, and full of faith, you are empowered to *overcome* and set in motion to release that power to pray for others and see the same miracles, signs, and wonders.

Read Scripture:

Acts 6:8

Prayer:

Heavenly Father, I come before you in the name of Jesus, thanking you for your Word that reminds me of all those who by faith endured hardships, problems, and difficulties. What tremendous examples they were for us. Father, you said in your Word that faith comes by hearing and hearing by your Word. As I hear, read, and study your Word, it builds my trust in you, having full assurance

---

* *Overcome*—to succeed in dealing with a problem or difficulty.

and firm conviction that the same faith on the inside of me to see miracles, signs, and wonders because you are the same God yesterday, today, and forever. In Jesus' name, I pray. Amen.

Notes:

_____

_____

_____

_____

_____

_____

_____

_____

_____

Monday, Day 2

(191) Forgiveness is not an *option* for us as believers but rather it is a commandment. Jesus was the greatest example of forgiveness toward us when we were sinners. Remember at the cross, forgiveness was given to you. Extend forgiveness to others as well. Allow the Holy Spirit to bring to your remembrance those individuals who have hurt you, and to act on faith and forgive them for their transgressions against you.

Read Scripture:

Matthew 6:12

Prayer:

Heavenly Father, today, I come before you, asking that you would bring to my remembrance those individuals that I have not forgiven. Thank you for showing their faces before me now. As an act of my will, I choose by faith to forgive and release those individuals now just as Jesus has extended forgiveness to me. Thank you for your love and forgiveness as I receive it now. In Jesus' name. Amen.

---

* *Option*—the power or right to choose.

Notes:

_____

_____

_____

_____

_____

_____

_____

_____

_____

Tuesday, Day 3

(192) The Bible tells us that we should always pray without ceasing. That means it never stops, discontinues, comes to an end, halts, or passes away. Prayer never dies! Praying is our heavenly communication with our heavenly Father, God, and it stems from a relationship with him. Life gets busy, but we should never allow the busyness of our day to pull us away from our intimacy with God through time in his presence, studying his Word, praising and worshipping him, and communicating with him through prayer. Take time; make time. It should be a *priority* in our day.

Read Scripture:

1 Thessalonians 5:17

Prayer:

Heavenly Father, I come to you in the name of Jesus, asking you to forgive me for neglecting my intimate time with you. I thank you for your forgiveness as I receive it now. Holy Spirit, I need you. I am asking you to help me to cultivate my personal relationship with God by first focusing on setting this time aside to be in God's presence,

---

* *Priority*—something given special attention.

study his Word, praise and worship him, and communicate with him through prayer. Throughout the day, remind me that I can commune with him no matter what it is I am doing or where I am. I will practice his presence without ceasing. In Jesus' name. Amen.

Notes:

_____

_____

_____

_____

_____

_____

_____

_____

_____

Wednesday, Day 4

(193) *Strife** means violent or bitter conflict. It also means competition and rivalry. We are all part of one body. We should hurt when another hurts, and we should rejoice when another rejoices. There should not be any strife between us. "*Strife" is opposite of walking in agreement or being in harmony with one another. Even when we agree to disagree, we should never allow our differences to bring *strife and division between us because we are brothers and sisters in Christ.

Read Scripture:

Genesis 13:8

Prayer:

Father God, I come to you now, asking you to reveal to me if there is any strife in me which would cause division between me and my brothers or sisters in Christ. Thank you for showing me now. I ask you, Lord, to forgive me for allowing strife to divide and break this harmony between us. I thank you for your forgiveness as I receive it now. Holy Spirit, I need you, and I am asking you to put a check on

---

* *Strife*—angry or bitter disagreement over fundamental issues; conflict.

me whenever strife and division try to come in to divide us. Let there be no rivalry or competition rise up within my mind and heart, and let no disagreements rule over me; but let your love rule my heart. In Jesus' name, I pray. Amen.

Notes:

_____

_____

_____

_____

_____

_____

_____

_____

Thursday, Day 5

(194) That familiar song, "Amazing Grace," reminds us that we were once lost without Christ, but now we are found. We were in bondage to Satan and were *enslaved* in sin, but Christ Jesus has made us free! The Word of God encourages us to stand fast and not be entangled or twisted together in a tangled mass, or get involved in sin again once we have been set free. Stand in your liberty or freedom in Christ Jesus in which he has set you completely free!

Read Scripture:

Romans 3:24

Prayer:

Heavenly Father, in the name of Jesus, I come to you now, giving you thanks and praise for setting me free from the yoke of bondage from Satan's harness of slavery. Holy Spirit, I need you, and I am asking you to strengthen me today to stand firm in this liberty that Jesus Christ has so graciously given to me when he took my place at the cross. Help me to never take for granted the gift of my

---

* *Enslaved*—to make a slave or make subservient to force to submit.

freedom through Jesus Christ, my Lord and King. In Jesus' name, I pray. Amen.

Notes:

_____

_____

_____

_____

_____

_____

_____

_____

_____

Friday, Day 6

(195) As the spring season arrives, we see the beauty of the blossoms of the trees everywhere. Some trees are fruit-bearing trees, meaning that they will grow fruit on their branches in due season. The Bible tells us that a good tree cannot bring forth evil fruit, and neither can a corrupt tree bring forth good fruit. A tree will be known by its fruit, just as we know people by the fruit that they bear in their lives. As a believer, we should be bearing fruit after the kingdom of the God that we serve, and it should be *evident.* All who come across our path should notice that we are bearing fruit after the God kind.

Read Scripture:

Matthew 7:20

Prayer:

Heavenly Father, I come to you now, thanking you that you have purposed for me to be a person who bears fruit in my life of the kingdom of your Son, Jesus Christ. Holy Spirit, I need you in my life to assist me each day to present myself to God as a living sacrifice, holy and acceptable unto God, which is my reasonable service.

---

* *Evident*—capable of being seen and noticed.

I desire to be a tree that produces good fruit, and in order to do so, I know and understand that I must remain in right relationship with him. I must allow the transformation in my life through the renewing of my mind to God's Word, which is his will for my life, so that I will produce the fruit of God's likeness in my life. In Jesus' name, I pray. Amen.

Notes:

_____

_____

_____

_____

_____

_____

_____

_____

_____

Saturday, Day 7

(196) There is nothing more devastating to a child than being abandoned by his or her parents. "Abandonment" is the willful forsaking or forgoing of parental duties. A child often blames themselves for their parents' actions. They often feel that there is something wrong with them, and they carry this with them into adulthood. Nothing could be further from the truth. God is a God who will never *abandon* his children, and he is with you always. He will never leave you, and he will never forsake you.

Read Scripture:

1 Kings 8:57

Prayer:

Heavenly Father, I come before you now in the name of Jesus, thanking you that you said in your Word that you would never leave me, and you would never forsake me nor desert me. I thank you for never walking out on me like others have done. As an act of my will, I forgive all those who have abandoned me and left me. I do not hold this charge against them, and I release them by faith and forgive

---

* *Abandon*—to forsake completely; desert; leave behind.

them now. I renounce and break agreement with the fear and loneliness, shame, blame, and guilt that I carried because of it. I thank you for releasing your healing power in my life now, and bringing healing and wholeness to me as I accept your loving embrace. In Jesus' name. Amen.

Notes:

_____

_____

_____

_____

_____

_____

_____

_____

_____

Sunday, Day 1

(197) A messenger is one who carries a message. We are carriers of God's presence and of our Lord Jesus Christ, and the message which he preached while he was on this earth. His message was one of love, compassion, forgiveness, mercy, and hope. He brought the good news of the gospel, and we should also be one who is a good and faithful messenger, sharing this good news with all those who we come in contact with. We do not have to have eloquence of speech to be a good and faithful messenger. Sometimes, it is just in the sharing of your *testimony* and what God has done for you that others need to hear to give them hope.

Read Scripture:

> Proverbs 13:17

Prayer:

> Father God, I come before you, giving you thanks and praise for Jesus Christ who is the greatest example of your love, compassion, forgiveness, and mercy. He was a messenger of the good news everywhere he went, and he demonstrated it by his actions. Holy Spirit,

---

* *Testimony*—open declaration or profession, as of faith.

I need you, and I ask you to help me to be a faithful messenger who is not ashamed or afraid to share what God has done for me. Give me an intense desire to want to spread this hope wherever I go. Holy Spirit, I ask you to strengthen me with courage and boldness, yet with compassion and love, to share this blessed hope that is found only in Jesus Christ. All of this I pray, in Jesus' name. Amen.

Notes:

_____

_____

_____

_____

_____

_____

_____

_____

_____

Monday, Day 2

(198) We have all done it. We have said something without thinking about it first, and left a trail of destruction behind us. Speaking *thoughtlessly** comes natural to us and takes no effort to spew out what's on our mind. Rarely or never do we take time to think before we speak. Words are seeds that are sown, and the harvest of those words is something that we can expect an outcome, whether good or bad. We certainly do need God's grace to guard our lips. Our words should bring life to others and be a delight to God.

Read Scripture:

Proverbs 10:32

Prayer:

Father God, I come to you now, asking you to forgive me for every thoughtless word that has come forth out of my mouth. Forgive me for speaking my mind and not taking the time to think before I speak. I realize that my speech has not been upright or delightful to you, and for this, I am sorry. I thank you for your forgiveness as I receive it now. Holy Spirit, I need you, and I ask you to set a guard

---

* *Thoughtlessly*—inconsiderate of the feelings of others.

over my lips. I ask you, Holy Spirit, to be my filter who shows me and teaches me how to think before I speak, and when to speak and when to be silent. All of this I ask in Jesus' name. Amen.

Notes:

_____

_____

_____

_____

_____

_____

_____

_____

_____

Tuesday, Day 3

(199) Don't be duped. Adam and Eve were duped by the devil, but we don't have to be duped by the words of the wicked! "Duplicitous" means deliberate deceptiveness and that was the devil all the way. The word "duped" means when a person is easily deceived or is used to carry out the designs of another. There is no doubt that Adam and Eve were deceived and used to carry out the devil's plans for mankind. Thank God that he had a plan to redeem us from the plans of the devil. In order for us to not be duped, we must know what God's Word says to us in order to see if what people are saying to us lines up with the Word of God. We must continue in God's Word to be able to *discern* this evil world so that we are not duped by the devil.

Read Scripture:

Proverbs 10:32

Prayer:

Heavenly Father, I come before you now, thanking you that you have given to me your Word, which is your will for me. It is your Word which keeps me on the path of righteousness and guides my

---

* *Discern*—to see or realize; to notice.

steps. As I study your Word, I thank you for giving me the revelation and the wisdom that I need to stand against every lie of the enemy which is sent to deceive me from receiving the truth of your Word. I thank you, Holy Spirit that you are my help, and you guide me in truth always so that I am not led astray or duped by the words of the wicked. In Jesus' name, I pray. Amen.

Notes:

_____

_____

_____

_____

_____

_____

_____

_____

_____

Wednesday, Day 4

(200) We have all heard it said that we are a work in progress. After we give our life to God by accepting his Son, Jesus Christ, as our Lord, we become born again or consecrated, set apart for his sacred service. We are made the righteousness of God in Christ Jesus, but our minds and thought life must be *renewed* to his Word because his Word is God's thoughts and his ways. We become transformed and changed by the renewed mind and thought life. This renewing of our mind imparts God's thoughts and ways, and this new life and new way of living. God has begun a good work in us, and he is faithful to complete this work in us until the day of Jesus' return.

Read Scripture:

Philippians 1:6

Prayer:

Father God, in the name of Jesus, I come before you now, giving you thanks for making me a new creature in Christ Jesus and that I have been made righteous through him. I understand that your Word is your will for my life and that I must be transformed by

---

* *Renewed*—to make new again; restore.

renewing my mind and thoughts to what your Word says about me. Holy Spirit, I need you, and I am asking for your help. As you lead and guide me by drawing me to set time aside to study God's Word, give me the revelation of God's Word for my life, and show me how to apply and live it with corresponding action. In Jesus' name, I pray. Amen.

Notes:

_____

_____

_____

_____

_____

_____

_____

_____

_____

Thursday, Day 5

(201) The heart is the vital center and source of our being. The heart is the organ that helps supply blood and oxygen to all parts of the body. The heart is also the spirit of man by which we have received Jesus as our Lord. It has always been all about the heart as far as it concerns the Lord God. God looks at the heart, and God says to us in his Word that if we *seek* him with all of our heart and soul, we shall find him.

Read Scripture:

Deuteronomy 4:29

Prayer:

Heavenly Father, I come before you now in the name of Jesus, asking you to forgive me for not seeking you wholeheartedly. I thank you for your forgiveness as I receive it now. Holy Spirit, I need you, and I am asking you to show me my heart and the intents of my heart daily so that I may approach God with a pure heart. Help me to seek God so that I do it with all of my heart and soul, and not half-heartedly, but with all that is within me. In Jesus' name, I pray. Amen.

---

* *Seek*—to look, to pursue, and be after.

Notes:

_____

_____

_____

_____

_____

_____

_____

_____

_____

Friday, Day 6

(202) *Hope** is a virtue defined as the desire and search for a future good, difficult but not impossible to attain with God's help. The Bible says that hope deferred, postponed, withheld, or delayed can grieve you and make you sick at heart if you let it. Hold on to *hope tightly, and do not let it go until your dreams come true. Your prayers are answered because life's sweetness will satisfy your soul.

Read Scripture:

Proverbs 13:12

Prayer:

Heavenly Father, in the name of Jesus, I come to you, asking you to forgive me for allowing life's circumstances to take away my hope in you. I thank you for your forgiveness as I receive it now. Holy Spirit, I need you, and I am asking you to help me hold fast to hope and give me the desire to expect answers to my prayers, knowing that God hears and answers prayers. Holy Spirit, I am asking you to help me to exercise the fruit of patience that resides on the inside of me

---

* *Hope*—to desire and consider possible.

until I see the manifestation of my dreams and answered prayers. In Jesus' name, I pray. Amen.

Notes:

_____

_____

_____

_____

_____

_____

_____

_____

_____

Saturday, Day 7

(203) A promise is a declaration, assuring that one will or will not do something; it is a vow. We all know what it is like when someone makes a promise and breaks it by not following through. God is not slack or *negligent* concerning his promises. He is not lacking in care or attention, and he is a promise keeper, not a promise breaker. He can be trusted to do everything that he has promised to us.

Read Scripture:

> 2 Peter 3:9

Prayer:

Father God, I come to you in the name of Jesus, thanking you that you are not slack, negligent, or remiss in your promises toward me. I thank you that you are not lacking in care or attention to me or my life, and everything that you have promised me in your Word is good. I can trust you in all things because you are a God who keeps his promises to me. For this, I give you thanks and praise. In Jesus' name. Amen.

---

* *Negligent*—lacking care or concern.

Notes:

_____

_____

_____

_____

_____

_____

_____

_____

_____

Sunday, Day 1

(204) Water is a significant fraction of the human body, and the percentages of water are vital to our bodies. The benefits of drinking water are immeasurable. Jesus talked about the water that he gives us where we will never *thirst* and that it will be a well of water springing up within us that gives life throughout eternity. In order to receive this, we must come to Jesus, the giver of life eternal. Drink of the living water and receive all of its benefits.

Read Scripture:

John 4:14

Prayer:

Heavenly Father, I come to you today, giving you thanks and praise for eternal springs of living water within me and the benefits of this eternal life. I draw from the deep wells of the living water, and I will thirst no more. I come to Jesus, the giver of eternal life, and take rest in him. I am filled and satisfied as I receive this living water. In Jesus' name. Amen.

---

* *Thirst*—an eager longing, craving, or yearning.

Notes:

Monday, Day 2

(205) In times past, we used maps or an atlas for directions; but because of technology, we now have global positioning systems (GPS) applications on our phones to get us from point A to point B. The Word of God is our GPS. It will always lead and guide you in the right direction, and always gets you to your *destination* in God's time, if we take time to read, study, and follow it.

Read Scripture:

Psalm 119:105

Prayer:

Heavenly Father, I come before you now, thanking you for your Word, which you said is a lamp to my feet and a light to my path. I ask you to forgive me for not taking the time to study your Word, which is your will for my life. I thank you for your forgiveness as I receive it now. Holy Spirit, I need you. I am asking you to help me to make time to study the Word of God so that it brings light, showing me the way to go in the dark times of my life, and helps me to walk

---

* *Destination*—the ultimate end or purpose for which something is created or a person is destined.

in the direction that God has for me. All of this I ask in Jesus' name. Amen.

Notes:

_____

_____

_____

_____

_____

_____

_____

_____

_____

Tuesday, Day 3

(206) Scripture tells us that our words are like sword that is thrust or driven with force. Our words can stab and hurt others. With the same tongue, we can choose words of the wise that soothe and heal. It is hard to imagine that the tongue, being such a small muscular organ, can set the course for your whole day. With the tongue, you either speak life giving words or words of death. You have the power to kill or give life with that tongue, so choose to speak life and words that bring *healing.*

Read Scripture:

Proverbs 21:23

Prayer:

Heavenly Father, I come before you now, asking you to forgive me for every word that has come forth from my tongue that has brought death and not life. I thank you for your forgiveness as I receive it now. Holy Spirit, I need your help, and I am asking you to convict me when I am speaking words that are not life giving. I ask you, Holy Spirit, to help me to control my tongue instead of letting

---

* *Healing*—to ease or relieve emotional distress, soothing and comforting.

it control me. Help me to exercise the spirit of self-control over my tongue so that I speak life that brings healing to others and not death. In Jesus' name, I pray. Amen.

Notes:

_____

_____

_____

_____

_____

_____

_____

_____

_____

Wednesday, Day 4

(207) When you woke up this morning, you probably did not even give it a second thought that you woke up breathing, moving, and living. Sometimes, we can take things for granted, not even noticing the fact that we are blessed with the very first breath of the day. The ability to *breathe,* move, and do what you can comes from God, the Creator of life, so do not forget to give him thanks and praise today for giving you life and the ability to *breathe and move.

Read Scripture:

Psalm 150:6

Prayer:

Heavenly Father, I come before you today in awesome wonder that you are the God and Creator of all things. You are the Life Giver, and the One who grants me another day to live for you. I give you thanks and praise for every single breath that comes forth from me and for every part of my being. My very lungs are filled with life and the ability to bring in oxygen into my entire being and flush out carbon dioxide. What an amazing God you are who created me fearfully

---

* *Breathe*—to be alive; live.

and wonderfully, and with this breath, I give you thanks and praise. In Jesus' name. Amen.

Notes:

_____

_____

_____

_____

_____

_____

_____

_____

Thursday, Day 5

(208) God's Word is truth. It is not fictional or imaginary. By his Word, we obtain wisdom; and unlike the wisdom of man, this wisdom that comes from God gives us *insight* to who he is—his thoughts and his ways. This wisdom is far greater in value, and riches cannot even compare to it. As you study God's Word, ask him to give you revelation and insight, and ask him to show himself to you. Ask him for wisdom, knowledge, and understanding deep in your spirit.

Read Scripture:

Psalm 51:6

Prayer:

Father God, I come to you, asking you in the name of Jesus to open up my ears, mind, and heart to receive revelation, insight, knowledge, and understanding of your Word as I read and study it. I desire to know your thoughts, your ways, and your Word by the Spirit. I ask you for godly wisdom, and I ask you for an increased desire to know you in a deeper way as I give myself over to the study of your Word. I pray that I would desire truth in my inward parts,

---

* *Insight*—the ability to perceive or see clearly or deeply.

and in the hidden part, you shall make me to know wisdom. In Jesus' name. Amen.

Notes:

_____

_____

_____

_____

_____

_____

_____

_____

_____

Friday, Day 6

(209) It amazes me how we allow negative thoughts run *rampant* through our mind without taking control over them. We can work ourselves into a frenzy in no time when these negative thoughts take over. It takes practice to keep your mind focused on the Lord, and what God says in his Word, when those negative thoughts come. Today, purpose to keep your mind and thoughts directed to what God says in his Word. When you learn to trust him, then you can purpose to be peaceful.

Read Scripture:

Isaiah 26:3

Prayer:

Heavenly Father, I come to you now, asking you to forgive me for allowing negative thoughts, which are contrary to your Word, to run rampant in my mind, working me into a frenzy. I thank you for your forgiveness as I receive it now. Holy Spirit, I need you, and I ask you to help me in this area of my life. Assist me, Holy Spirit, when negative thoughts come to immediately take those destructive

---

* *Rampant*—unrestrained or violent in behavior, desire, or opinions.

thoughts and cast them down. Holy Spirit, bring to my remembrance what God's Word says so that I can replace those negative thoughts with what God says in his Word. In Jesus' name, I pray. Amen.

Notes:

_____

_____

_____

_____

_____

_____

_____

_____

_____

Saturday, Day 7

(210) When giving *counsel* to anyone or receiving *counsel as well, we should always represent God. Our opinion or advice cannot stand up to God's Word. Moses' father-in-law, Jethro, was an example of one who counseled Moses God-ward. You can never go wrong when giving *counsel according to the Word of God. Always give godly wisdom and *counsel over opinion or advice.

Read Scripture:

Exodus 18:19

Prayer:

Father God, in the name of Jesus, I come before you, asking you to forgive me for giving my opinion and advice when in fact, the one seeking counsel from me needs to hear about what you would say or do. I thank you for your forgiveness as I receive it now. Holy Spirit, I need you, and I am asking you to lead me when others come to me for counsel. I trust you, Holy Spirit, to give me what they need, and not what I think they need. I cannot nor will I give counsel without

---

* *Counsel*—to give advice, information, warning, direction, suggestion, and recommendation.

your leading, Holy Spirit, because with you, we can never go wrong. I thank you for leading me. In Jesus' name. Amen.

Notes:

_____

_____

_____

_____

_____

_____

_____

_____

Sunday, Day 1

(211) "Increase" means to become greater or larger, or to multiply or reproduce. The apostles asked Jesus to increase their faith. Jesus replied, "If you have even the smallest measure of *authentic* faith, it would be powerful enough to say to this large tree, 'My faith will pull you up by the roots and throw you into the sea,' and it will respond to your faith and obey you." Your circumstances will obey the smallest measure of your *authentic faith.

Read Scripture:

Luke 17:5–6

Prayer:

Heavenly Father, in the name of Jesus, I come before you now, asking you to forgive me for asking you to increase my faith when you said in your Word that the smallest measure of authentic faith will cause my circumstances to obey. I thank you for your forgiveness as I receive it now. Holy Spirit, I need you. I am asking you to help me exercise the smallest measure of authentic, undisputed, and genuine faith that can move mountains, and powerful enough to uproot

---

* *Authentic*—real, pure, true, and genuine.

the biggest tree by the roots and cast it into the sea. Thank you for the small measures of authentic faith that moves in my circumstances today. In Jesus' name. Amen.

Notes:

_____

_____

_____

_____

_____

_____

_____

_____

_____

_____

Monday, Day 2

(212) Whatever it is you're facing today, do not fear. Give it to God, and he will give you strength to go through. Scripture tells us to not be *dismayed* or be upset, distressed, or filled with dread. Ask God for his help today, and he said that he will help you and uphold or prevent you from falling or sinking. He will lift you, raise you upward, and support you. He is able to uphold you and take care of all that concerns you, and you do not have to do it alone because he is with you.

Read Scripture:

Isaiah 41:10

Prayer:

Father God, I come before you now, asking you to forgive me for allowing fear to overwhelm me in the situation that I am facing. I thank you for your forgiveness as I receive it now. Holy Spirit, I need you. I cannot do this without your help, and I am asking you to give me the strength of God that lifts me upward above the circumstances at hand. I ask you to sustain me, support me, and help me

---

* *Dismayed*—filled with depression, discouragement, apprehension, or alarm.

through this. I declare that I am not dismayed or in fear, and I do not dread the outcome because I put my trust in you today, my God, my Deliverer, my strength, and my help. In Jesus' name. Amen.

Notes:

_____

_____

_____

_____

_____

_____

_____

_____

_____

_____

Tuesday, Day 3

(213) God's thoughts toward you are good thoughts. His thoughts toward you are of peace and never evil. His plans for you are to give you hope and a bright **future.** In order to receive what God has for you, it is important to understand that God is a good God, and he is for you and not against you. When God sees you, he thinks good thoughts of you; and according to scripture, he has a great *future for you. Get ready to receive the good things in life that God has for you.

Read Scripture:

Jeremiah 29:11

Prayer:

Heavenly Father, I come to you, first of all, giving you thanks that according to Scripture, you are a good God who loves me, and your thoughts toward me are only good and never evil. Thank you, Father God, that the future that you have for me is bright and that I can expect good things to happen for me. You are my loving, caring, and faithful God who thinks the best for me and gives his best to me. For this, I am grateful. In Jesus' name. Amen.

---

* *Future*—your tomorrows.

Notes:

Wednesday, Day 4

(214) Whether you are a father, mother, wife, husband, child, employer, or employee, the Bible tells us to do all things without murmurings and disputes. We will be faced with disagreements and controversies that can lead to quarrels. But as a believer in Jesus Christ, Scripture tells us that we are supposed to shine like a star across the land, and we should not complain or *bicker* with one another. It takes a concentrated effort to do this, and we cannot do it on our own without God's help. Take time to examine your life and heart. Is your light dimming because of complaining or disputes among us?

Read Scripture:

Philippians 2:14–15

Prayer:

Heavenly Father, I come before you now as I have examined my own heart and life. I sincerely ask you to forgive me for my involvement in disagreements that have brought strife and division between me and others. I thank you for your forgiveness as I receive it now.

---

* *Bicker*—to argue or quarrel.

Holy Spirit, I need you because I know that I cannot do this on my own, so I am asking you to help me to be self-controlled when a disagreement happens. Lead me in these situations, and give me the words to diffuse the situation before it can get out of hand. Help me not to be quarrelsome but instead to be helpful in any disagreements, that I will help bring resolve and not conflict. In Jesus' name, I pray. Amen.

Notes:

_____

_____

_____

_____

_____

_____

_____

_____

_____

Thursday, Day 5

(215) Is it a coincidence or is it a God incidence? Sometimes in our lives, we have had things happen to us, and we will say that it was just a coincidence. A coincidence is a sequence of events that although accidental, seems to have been planned or arranged. A God incidence is an occurrence **influenced** by God's hand at work in your life for the good. Scripture tells us that we can be confident that God can orchestrate things in our lives to work toward something good when we live according to what he has planned for us. His will for you is his Word, and faith begins where you understand what his will or Word says for you.

Read Scripture:

Romans 8:28

Prayer:

Heavenly Father, I come before you in the name of Jesus, thanking you for your Word, which is your will for my life. When I live according to your will and your Word, I have the assurance that you will orchestrate everything for the good in my life, including the

---

* *Influenced*—to have an effect on the condition or development of.

smallest details. Holy Spirit, I need you. I ask you to help me to always take and make the time to study the Word of God so that I know without a shadow of doubt what God has for me. Unveil and reveal his Word to me, and give the understanding and the wisdom that I need to live by. In Jesus' name, I pray. Amen.

Notes:

_____

_____

_____

_____

_____

_____

_____

_____

_____

Friday, Day 6

(216) Scripture says that Adam was the first Adam and a living soul, and that Jesus is the second Adam, a quickening spirit. When the first Adam disobeyed and fell, I think about God's love for us while we were yet sinners, and he sent Jesus to redeem and buy us back, so to speak. What great love the Father has *lavished* upon us. He is indeed the God of second chances.

Read Scripture:

1 Corinthians 15:45

Prayer:

Father God, I come to you with a thankful heart today. I just want to say how much I love and appreciate Jesus Christ who took my place on that cross and paid the price to redeem me back to a right relationship with you. What a loving Father you are that you are mindful of me and all of mankind, and not leave us in that state but instead you sent your one and only Son. Thank you for being the God of second chances. I will ever be so grateful to give you all

---

* *Lavished*—to give in great amounts without limits.

of the honor and all of the praise that is due your magnificent name. In Jesus' name. Amen.

Notes:

_____

_____

_____

_____

_____

_____

_____

_____

_____

Saturday, Day 7

(217) The book of Proverbs is filled with words of wisdom by King Solomon. Many times, he spoke about our words and how the weight of our words produces results in our life. He instructs us to guard our words because it is like guarding our life, and if we do not have control over our tongue, it can *ruin* everything for us. In short, or to put it simply, he is telling us to watch what we say. Careful words make for a careful life, and careless words will leave us in a mess.

Read Scripture:

Proverbs 13:3

Prayer:

Father God, in the name of Jesus, I come before you, asking you to forgive me for not taking inventory of my own life and the words that have proceeded from my own mouth, which may very well be responsible for my failures and the non-productive seasons in my life. I take full responsibility for my actions. I repent and ask for your forgiveness, and thank you as I receive it now. Holy Spirit, I need you. I cannot do this on my own, and I realize that I need you in a big

---

* *Ruin*—to severely harm, damage, or spoil it.

way. I know now that the words that I speak carry the weight of my whole future, so I ask you, Holy Spirit, to check me and correct me when I am speaking words that are contrary to God's Word because his Word is his will for me. Thank you for helping me to bear good fruit in my life for the glory of God. In Jesus' name. Amen.

Notes:

_____

_____

_____

_____

_____

_____

_____

_____

_____

Sunday, Day 1

(218) The Bible says that the gifts in the body of Christ vary depending on the grace that has been poured out on each of us. Whether your gift is prophecy, serving, teaching, encouraging, mercy, or giving, the Scripture tells us that it is only by God's grace poured on us that we are able to do any of it. We should always remember that we cannot do it in and of ourselves for that would result in fleshly manifestations. But when we know and understand that it is by God's grace and that it is he that *enables* us to be all that has called us to be, and it is his grace that empowers us to do all that he has called us to do, then he will be glorified. His will be done in us and through us.

Read Scripture:

Romans 12:6–8

Prayer:

Father God, I come to you in the name of Jesus, thanking you for the wisdom and instruction that I glean from your Word. Thank you for the wonderful gifts that you give each of us in the body of

---

* *Enables*—to enable someone to do something means to give them permission or the right to do it.

Christ to build your kingdom. Thank you that every gift has a specific function and is beneficial for the growth and nourishment of your body. Thank you for revealing to me the grace gift that you have poured out upon me. Thank you for your grace that enables me to be all that you have called me to be and for your grace that empowers me to do all that you have called me to do. In Jesus' name, I pray. Amen.

Notes:

_____

_____

_____

_____

_____

_____

_____

_____

_____

Monday, Day 2

(219) Has someone ever told you that they were going to do something for you and your thoughts about it were, "We will see?" The Bible tells us that this happened to Moses, and the Lord said to Moses, "Is the Lord's power limited? Now you shall see whether my word will come true for you or not." Another translation says that God said to Moses, "Do you *doubt* me?" Do you question my power that I can do what I've said? Just watch—you'll see what will happen." So take it to heart and trust God to do what he says.

Read Scripture:

Numbers 11:23

Prayer:

Father God, I come to you with a repentant heart, asking you to forgive me for doubting that you would do for me what you have promised me in your Word. I thank you for your forgiveness as I receive it now. Holy Spirit, I need you, and I am asking you to help me. I know that faith comes by hearing, and hearing comes by the

---

* *Doubt*—if you doubt something, you believe that it might not be true or genuine or possible.

Word; so as I set time aside to hear and study God's Word, I expect faith to arise and all doubt to flee as I put my trust in God to do what he said that he would do for me. In Jesus' name, I pray. Amen.

Notes:

_____

_____

_____

_____

_____

_____

_____

_____

_____

Tuesday, Day 3

(220) Did you know that being in the sun has benefits? Sunlight triggers the release of hormones in your brain. Exposure to sunlight is thought to increase the brain's release of a hormone called serotonin, which is associated with boosting mood and helping a person feel calm and focused. At the same time, there is a hormone called melatonin that is released in the brain in the darker hours of the evening, which helps you rest. How marvelous that God provides us what we need by giving us both day and night. Scripture says that God is your sun and your shield. Scripture says that God will not *withhold* or keep back any good things from those who walk upright before him. You will never lack one thing that you need, for he provides it all!

Read Scripture:

Psalm 84:11

Prayer:

Father God, I come to you now as the one who provides for me without withholding any good thing from me. I examine my heart and ask you to forgive me for anything within me that hinders me

---

* *Withhold*—to refuse to give something that is desired by someone.

from walking upright and moral before you. I surrender my life. I give you my body, my mind, and my service as I realize that my ultimate need is to be able to walk before you in righteousness, knowing that you will always provide me everything that I need. I lack nothing, for in you, I have grace and favor, and everything that I need to live this life for you. In Jesus' name. Amen.

Notes:

_____

_____

_____

_____

_____

_____

_____

_____

_____

Wednesday, Day 4

(221) Scripture tells us that Abraham's faith was tried, meaning that he was being thoroughly *tested* and proved to be faithful. After he was proved, he received God's promise to him which was through his son, Isaac, his lineage would carry on his name. Likewise, when your faith is being tried, *tested, and proved that puts you on the receiving end of God's promises. Don't give up in the time of testing, but hold on firmly to God's promise until you have been proved. Then you will be on the receiving end of the promise as Abraham was.

Read Scripture:

Hebrews 11:17

Prayer:

Father God, I come to you in the name of Jesus, thanking you for giving me the strength through the trying of my faith in you. Just as Abraham was tested, proved, and trusted in you for the outcome, I look to you as the author and the finisher of my faith. Holy Spirit, I need you, and I ask you to help me through this time to help me to

---

* *Tested*—if an event or situation is a test of a person, it reveals their qualities or shows how one reacts.

lean on you for strength that will enable me to stand on the receiving end of God's promises, holding firm in my faith, standing on his promises. In Jesus' name, I pray. Amen.

Notes:

_____

_____

_____

_____

_____

_____

_____

_____

_____

Thursday, Day 5

(222) The word "grace" in Hebrew is "*charis*" (or khä'-rēs). It means the spiritual condition of one governed by the power of divine grace. Just as we were saved by grace, we should remember that every day is a gift of God's grace. Pure and simple, we should not go around *bragging** as if we are anything, for it is only by God's grace that we have been gifted with another day. What a precious gift to us from a good Father. Give him thanks for his grace upon your life today because without him, it would not even exist.

Read Scripture:

Ephesians 2:8–9

Prayer:

Father God, I come to you with a repentant heart, asking you to forgive me for taking your divine grace for granted. I thank you for your forgiveness as I receive it now. I realize that every day is a gift of your grace toward me and that it is only by your divine grace that I can live to face this day. I thank you, Holy Spirit, for being my

---

* *Bragging*—if you brag, you say in a very proud way that you have something or have done something.

Guide today, leading me through this day and everything that I will encounter in this day. Thank you for the grace to live the abundant life given to me by God's divine grace. In Jesus' name, I pray. Amen.

Notes:

_____

_____

_____

_____

_____

_____

_____

_____

Friday, Day 6

(223) Whether in the movies or real life, we have all seen when some-one is getting arrested and they are read their Miranda rights which starts like this" "You have the right to remain silent. Anything you say can and will be used against you in a court of law." Scripture tells us on judgment day that we will all be held *accountable* for every careless word that we have spoken. Our words will either acquit us or condemn us, and declare us either innocent or guilty, so we must choose our words wisely, knowing that we will have to give an account someday.

Read Scripture:

Matthew 12:36–37

Prayer:

Heavenly Father, I come before you with a heavy heart when I think about every thoughtless and careless word that I have spoken in my lifetime. If I would take inventory of every careless word that has come forth from my mouth, it would condemn me, and I would be found guilty as charged. I humbly ask you to forgive me for every

---

* *Accountable*—to account for one's acts; responsible.

single word that I have spoken that was careless, thoughtless, and irresponsible. I thank you for the blood of Jesus that washes and cleanses me now, and I thank you for your forgiveness as I receive it now. Holy Spirit, I need you in my life. I am asking you to help me to be aware that when I open my mouth to speak, every word will be words of life and not death. Holy Spirit, you are my help, and the guard over my lips that convicts me of those things that I say. Wave the red flag before me to get my attention before I say anything that is careless and does not glorify God. All of this I ask in the precious name of Jesus Christ. Amen.

Notes:

_____

_____

_____

_____

_____

_____

_____

_____

_____

Saturday, Day 7

(224) God is not against us having wealth and prosperity, but he does tell us that we should not put our trust in riches and that our trust should be in the God who blesses us with that wealth. When God blesses us with wealth and prosperity, we should not brag or boast and take advantage of others for more gain. Our hearts should never be so *attached* to our riches that we forget our God who is the one who gave us his blessings in the first place.

Read Scripture:

Psalms 62:10

Prayer:

Father God, I come to you in the name of Jesus, thanking you that wealth and prosperity is something that you desire for me. You are the God who gives me all things to enjoy, but more than that, to be a blessing to others and for your kingdom work. It is not by my own hand that these riches have come to me, but I acknowledge that it is you who has blessed me. I declare that I am only your vessel by

---

* *Attached*—emotionally connected, having strong feelings of affection or connection.

which you work through and that these blessings flow through me and are destined to go to fulfill your plans and purposes upon this earth. Give me your wisdom to steward the wealth and riches that you have blessed me with all the days of my life. In Jesus name, I pray. Amen.

Notes:

_____

_____

_____

_____

_____

_____

_____

_____

_____

Sunday, Day 1

(225) Before you were born, God planned your destiny in him and the good works that you would do. You were born to fulfill his plan and his purpose here upon this earth. He has the *blueprint* for your life, and he will order your steps to accomplish everything that he has planned for you. Look at it this way. It's not a setback; it's a set up. God has set you up to succeed and to accomplish great things for him. Seek after him and you will find him. He will reveal his *blueprint for your life to you one step at a time.

Read Scripture:

Ephesians 2:10

Prayer:

Heavenly Father, I am in awe as I come, knowing that you have already destined for me a plan for my life to fulfill the God-given things that you have prepared for me before I ever came to being upon this earth. I am the work of your hands, and you fashioned me and made me for your pleasure and for your glory. That is beyond anything I have ever imagined for my life. Father, you said that if I

---

* *Blueprint*—a detailed plan of action.

seek you with all of my heart, I would find you, and I am convinced that you will reveal the blueprint that you have for me and all that you have destined for me to do. I thank you that you have set me up to succeed and not fail, and that I can do everything through Christ who strengthens me In Jesus' name. Amen.

Notes:

_____

_____

_____

_____

_____

_____

_____

_____

_____

Monday, Day 2

(226) Jesus says, in Scripture, that the words he speaks are the words of the Father in him. Jesus has a tongue of one who is a *disciple* taught by the Father. He was teachable and eager to hear the Father in order to please and obey him. He was more than a replica, or carbon copy, of the Father, but he was one with the Father. Our desire is to be more like Jesus. To be one who is teachable, one who hears and listens to the Father, and one who obeys and carries out what the Father wants from us. To be one with the Father, we must be teachable. Hearing and obeying the Father is the heart of a true *disciple.

Read Scripture:

Isaiah 50:4

Prayer:

Heavenly Father, I come to you now, giving you thanks for Jesus Christ who showed us how much love he had for you by having a true heart of a disciple. Jesus was teachable in that he had a listening ear and submitted himself to the Father by learning to be obedient to him and pleasing him in all things. Holy Spirit, I need you as much

---

* *Disciple*—one who embraces and assists in spreading the teachings of another.

as I need the air that I breathe. I ask you to help me to be one with the Father as a teachable disciple given over to God's teaching. Help me to hear and to obey my Father God, just as Jesus did. In Jesus' name, I pray. Amen.

Notes:

_____

_____

_____

_____

_____

_____

_____

_____

_____

Tuesday, Day 3

(227) We are told in scripture that above all, or most importantly, we are to take the shield of faith, which is part of the armor of God to protect us from weapons that are hurled or thrust at us. We have an adversary who is Satan, who wants to steal, kill, and destroy. He wants to divert you or make you turn aside from the course that you are on, and he is always trying to *hijack* your faith and take control. God has given us that shield of faith with the promise that when we use it, the fiery darts that the enemy throws, hurls, or thrusts at us will be quenched and put out; and we would overcome. Raise your shield of faith.

Read Scripture:

Ephesians 6:16

Prayer:

Father God, in the name of Jesus, I come to you, asking, first of all, to forgive me for becoming lax in using the armor of God that you have given me. I thank you for your forgiveness as I receive it now. Holy Spirit, I need you. I am asking you to show me and give

---

* *Hijack*—to take over and take control.

me insight into the spirit realm to know and discern when I am under attack and when the enemy's darts are being thrown at me so that I can raise the shield of faith to put out every dart that is targeted at me. Thank you for disarming and counteracting the lies of the enemy with the truth of your Word, and when the shield of faith is raised and lifted up heavenward above the lies, I overcome the attack of my enemies. In Jesus' victorious name. Amen.

Notes:

_____

_____

_____

_____

_____

_____

_____

_____

_____

Wednesday, Day 4

(228) No one enjoys going through the furnace of affliction, but it has its purpose in God. The fiery trials that you go through are not to break you but to burn up the flesh and prove you, to establish the truth or validity that you are God's. God has held back his wrath and is patient with us. He is corrective and not destructive, and it is he who **refines** us so that the beauty of his grace would be seen in us as a pure reflection of the Father. So do not despise the fiery trials in the furnace of affliction that you are going through but rather accept this refining process which is for our everlasting good and for God's glory.

Read Scripture:

Isaiah 48:9–10

Prayer:

Heavenly Father, I come humbly before your throne of grace, asking you to forgive me for resisting the process of refining, instead of embracing it. Forgive me for complaining and murmuring, which grieves your heart. I thank you for your forgiveness as I receive it now. Thank you that you are corrective and not destructive in your

---

* *Refine*—improve or perfect by pruning or polishing and removing impurities.

purposes and that this fiery trial that I am going through is not meant to destroy me, and I will not be burned or be destroyed by it. I accept that it is purposed to refine me and remove any impurities in my life. Thank you that the more I am pressed by affliction, the sweeter the smell of your grace that rises to meet our nostrils, and the more you are fashioning the inward spiritual life that you have purposed for me. In Jesus' name, I pray. Amen.

Notes:

_____

_____

_____

_____

_____

_____

_____

_____

_____

Thursday, Day 5

(229) God has placed inside of you dreams, visions, and plans for you to succeed in them. But instead of them coming to fruition, they laid dormant in you. They are not dead because when God purposes something, it cannot die. It is time for you to *prophesy* to those dreams just like God had Ezekiel speak to the dry bones of Israel. If God can lay sinews upon dry, dead bones, and bring up flesh upon it, and cover it with skin, and put breath into it so that it lives, surely he can restore and revive those dreams and plans that he put on the inside of you. Begin to prophesy to those dormant dreams and command them to life.

Read Scripture:

Ezekiel 37:6

Prayer:

Father God, I come to you, thanking you for every single dream, plan, and vision that you have placed on the inside of me. I thank you that what you have purposed cannot ever die. Holy Spirit,

---

* *Prophesy*—if you prophesy that something will happen, you say that you strongly believe that it will happen.

as an act of my will and with your help, I begin now to prophesy to those God-given dreams, plans, and vision that are lying dormant; and I call them to come forth in the name of Jesus. I speak life and purpose to every dream, plan, and vision to be activated within me as God gives me his wisdom and leads me to walk in everything that he has purposed for me. I speak forth out of my lips that every dream, vision, and God-given plan that he has given me will come to full fruition from this day forth. I vow to give you, God, all the glory, honor, and praise for it. In Jesus' name. Amen.

Notes:

_____

_____

_____

_____

_____

_____

_____

_____

_____

Friday, Day 6

(230) The Bible tells us that God is the healer of the broken hearted and is close to those who have a repentant heart. When we express with all sincerity to God our *remorse* or bitter anguish; regret for our misdeeds, wrongdoings, or sins; and cry out to God for his help, he always hears us and delivers us. When was the last time you experienced deep sorrow for sinning against God? God will never despise or look down on one with contempt who has a broken and contrite spirit. It is time for examination of the heart.

Read Scripture:

Psalm 34:18

Prayer:

Father God, I come to you now, thanking you for showing me the condition of my own heart and for giving me the opportunity to confess my sin before you. After examination of my own heart, I realize that I have not always acknowledged my wrongdoings, misdeeds, or sins against you. You said in your Word that if I confess my

---

* *Remorse*—a strong feeling of sadness and regret about something wrong that you have done.

sins, you are faithful and just to forgive me and cleanse me from all unrighteousness. So I come before you now, asking you to forgive me for every misdeed, sin, and wrong-doing that I have committed before you in your sight and for omitting those sins as well. Holy Spirit, you are my help. I need you to always bring to my attention every misdeed, wrong-doing, and sin that I need to repent of; and help me to resist them before I commit them. All of this I ask in Jesus' name. Amen.

Notes:

_____

_____

_____

_____

_____

_____

_____

_____

_____

Saturday, Day 7

(231) Godly wisdom is the ability to discern or judge what is true and right. Scripture tells us that wise people are builders. They build families, businesses, and communities; and they are intelligent. They also have insight, and what they *accomplish* is established and lasts. Wise people are skilled in leadership, and their hearts are filled with the treasures of wisdom and pleasures of spiritual wealth. Wisdom can make anyone into a mighty warrior, and revelation-knowledge increases strength. Godly wisdom is something that God desires to give us, but it does not come without seeking to know him personally.

Read Scripture:

Proverbs 24:3–5

Prayer:

Heavenly Father, I come to you today, thanking you for showing me in scripture that it is your will for my life to give me godly wisdom as I seek to know you more personally and intimately. Holy Spirit, you always lead and guide me into all truth, so I am asking for you to help me to discern God's Word in every aspect of my life.

---

* *Accomplish*—to bring to a goal or successful conclusion; carry out; finish.

I ask you to direct me in decisions that will build according to God's kingdom principles so that everything that I do is established on a firm foundation and will endure, last, and stand the test of time. I receive your guidance, Holy Spirit, from this day forward. In Jesus' name, I pray. Amen.

Notes:

_____

_____

_____

_____

_____

_____

_____

_____

_____

Sunday, Day 1

(232) Faith is an unquestionable belief in God, and it is absolute certainty in the trustworthiness of God. In Hebrews chapter 11, known as the faith hero hall of fame, we see how living by faith is a way of life. Faith opened Noah's heart to receive revelation and *warnings* from God about what was coming, even things that had never been seen. But he stepped out in reverent obedience to God and built an ark that would save him and his family. By his faith, the world was condemned, but Noah received God's gift of righteousness that comes by believing. Living by faith in God is a way of life.

Read Scripture:

Habakkuk 2:4

Prayer:

Father God, I come to you, asking you to forgive me for my lack of faith and trust in you. I thank you for your forgiveness as I receive it now. Holy Spirit, I need you, and I am asking you to help me to live by faith for it is written in God's Word that the righteous shall live by it. I thank you that faith comes by hearing and hearing

---

* *Warnings*—to give notice or caution.

by the Word of God. So as I read, hear, and study God's Word, faith comes, faith rises, and faith moves with corresponding action and with complete trust in God. For this, I thank you. In Jesus' name. Amen.

Notes:

_____

_____

_____

_____

_____

_____

_____

_____

_____

_____

Monday, Day 2

(233) The Bible tells us that if Christ did not resurrect, then the preaching of the Word is done in **vain** or is fruitless, without success. It even goes so far to say that our faith in God and his message would be worthless and in *vain as well. But I tell you the good news, and that good news is Jesus Christ has been raised from the dead. Our preaching and faith is not in *vain because he is the risen Lord!

Read Scripture:

1 Corinthians 15:14

Prayer:

Heavenly Father, I come to you now, shouting praises and giving you thanks for my risen Lord Jesus Christ! Because of your resurrection power that raised Jesus from the dead, I know now that whenever we preach or hear the preached message that you raised Jesus from the dead, we can rejoice in this truth. Our faith in you is not in vain, and if you can raise Jesus from the dead, then you can

---

* *Vain*—if you do something in vain, you do not succeed in achieving what you intend.

and will move in my life with that same power. For this, I thank you. In Jesus' name. Amen.

Notes:

_____

_____

_____

_____

_____

_____

_____

_____

_____

Tuesday, Day 3

(234) Whenever we get bad news, it often feels like the very breath within us is taken away. We are left in utter shock, we lose hope, and our emotions can take over if we let them. It is a discipline to turn to the Word of God in these situations because we do not automatically feel like picking up the Bible, and we certainly do not feel like speaking what the Word says. It is easier to focus and speak about the problem that we are facing. God tells us in his Word that his word is our comfort in times of *trouble,* and it will revive us. Start practicing the discipline of turning to the Word of God for comfort, solace, and revitalization.

Read Scripture:

Psalm 119:50

Prayer:

Father God, I come before you now. First of all, I ask you to forgive me for allowing my circumstance to dictate and control my emotions, which always leads me to stay focused on my problem and causes despair. I thank you for your forgiveness as I receive it now.

---

* *Trouble*—a distressing or difficult circumstance or situation.

Holy Spirit, I need you, and I am asking you to give me comfort and draw me to a place of surrender and discipline to look to God's Word for the answers to what I am going through. I thank you that when engulfed in God's Word and not the problem, I find comfort, strength, and peace; and I am not easily moved by my feelings or circumstances, but am fully trusting in God. For this, I thank you. In Jesus' name, I pray. Amen.

Notes:

_____

_____

_____

_____

_____

_____

_____

_____

_____

_____

Wednesday, Day 4

(235) When you have accepted Jesus Christ as your Lord and Savior, you are accepted by God. You become justified and **validated* by him. Imagine this as Scripture tells us that God places a garment of salvation on you and wraps around you a cloak or robe of righteousness. We are moved out of the place of obscurity to being seen as a bride, and just as a groom would put on a tux and a bride her jeweled tiara, he then walks with us and puts us in places, and brings righteousness into full bloom. He makes praise visible before the nations to display his splendor.

Read Scripture:

Isaiah 61:10–11

Prayer:

Heavenly Father, I come before you in humble adoration, knowing that I have been justified and validated by you. Words cannot even begin to express how much I feel loved and accepted by you. It is you who has clothed me in the garment of salvation and the robe

---

* *Validated*—to prove or confirm that a person is valuable or worthwhile and to accept and approve them.

of righteousness. I am honored to represent you, my King, as your righteous one, to make your praise glorious in all the earth before nations and to display your splendor, your majesty, and your glory in the name of my Lord and Savior, Jesus Christ. Amen.

Notes:

_____

_____

_____

_____

_____

_____

_____

_____

_____

Thursday, Day 5

(236) The Bible tells us that we should never get tired of doing what is right and what is good. As a matter of fact, it tells us that we should *persist* or hold firmly and steadfastly to our purpose despite the obstacles or setbacks that we may face. Often, the tiring comes when we begin to do things in our own strength, which will wear us out. When do it in God's strength, we know that we will indeed reap the harvest.

Read Scripture:

Galatians 6:9

Prayer:

Father God, I come to you now, thanking you for your Word which has encouraged me to not grow weary but to hold fast and continue doing what is true and right in your sight, and that I will reap a harvest if I do not faint or grow weak. Holy Spirit, I need you, and I know that I cannot do this without you. As an act of my will, I submit to your leading; and my dependence is upon you for your

---

*   *Persist*—if you persist in doing something, you continue to do it even though it is difficult or other people are against it.

strength and your ability to stand fast and not grow weary, knowing that in doing this, there will be a reaping and yielding of a wonderful harvest. For this, I am grateful. In Jesus' name. Amen.

Notes:

_____

_____

_____

_____

_____

_____

_____

_____

_____

Friday, Day 6

(237) Work, home life, social life, extracurricular activities, charity work, etc. can make you *weary* or physically and mentally exhausted. There is also a weariness that comes naturally through the aging process. However, it is God who gives strength and vitality or physical, mental vigor and energy to the weary. There is one prerequisite and that is you must come to him first. Are you *weary? Come to God who is able to strengthen you today.

Read Scripture:

Isaiah 40:29

Prayer:

Father God, I come to you today, acknowledging that it is you who gives my weary body and soul strength when I am physically and mentally drained. Holy Spirit, you are my help, and I need you. I cannot do this without you, so as an act of my will, I submit my whole being to you. I am asking you to give me the strength of God today and revive me from the inside out. I receive strength, vigor,

---

* *Weary*—physically or mentally tired.

energy, and newness of life today; and I thank you for it. In Jesus'
name. Amen.

Notes:

_____

_____

_____

_____

_____

_____

_____

_____

_____

Saturday, Day 7

(238) A Christian who has a devoted heart to God is one who understands that their life is set apart to God and for God. They live a consecrated life, a dedicated life. This is a person who has learned to judge his own self. All believers should *confess* their sins to God when he is aware of them, and we should do it every time that God has uncovered us in the time of exposing. For if we do this, when sudden storms of life overwhelm us, we will be kept safe.

Read Scripture:

Psalm 32:6

Prayer:

Heavenly Father, I come before you with a heart of remorse and repentance. I ask you to forgive me for not taking the time daily to judge my own thoughts and actions. I thank you for your forgiveness as I receive it now. Holy Spirit, I need you. I am asking you to convict me and show me my own thoughts and actions that separate me from God and help me to have a penitent heart so that I can confess

---

* *Confess*—if someone confesses their sins, they tell God about their sins so that they can be forgiven.

my sin and receive God's forgiveness. Holy Spirit, I desire to live a consecrated and devoted life to God, but I cannot do it without you. So as an act of my will, I yield my will to you today, and I ask you to help me to live a life that is pleasing to God. All of this I pray in Jesus' name. Amen.

Notes:

_____

_____

_____

_____

_____

_____

_____

_____

_____

_____

Sunday, Day 1

(239) You are designed by God, and each member has been placed in the body of Christ to function as he desires. As individuals, we should not ever *compare* ourselves with others in the body of Christ. When we compare ourselves to others, we begin to examine the similarities or differences. It is not a competition. We should not strive against another, or others, to attain a goal, or outdo another for acknowledgment, advantage, or victory. That in itself produces defeat. Instead, we should recognize, appreciate, respect all members of the body of Christ and connect, join, associate, or link together in unity and function in the way God intended for us.

Read Scripture:

1 Corinthians 12:18

Prayer:

Father God, in the name of Jesus, I come before you now. And as an act of my will, I ask you to examine my heart. Show me my own heart and see if there is anything in me where I have competed or compared myself with other members of the church body. I repent

---

* *Compare*—to examine to see if you are equal or alike to others.

for doing so, and I thank you for your forgiveness as I receive it now. Holy Spirit, I need you, and I am asking you to help me in this area. Show me how to appreciate, respect, and honor all my brothers and sisters in Christ and to understand that we have different gifts and functions that God has blessed us with so that we are able to be unified, building the kingdom of God. In Jesus' name, I pray. Amen.

Notes:

_____

_____

_____

_____

_____

_____

_____

_____

_____

Monday, Day 2

(240) When we are going through difficult times in life and no one really knows what we are going through, we have the tendency to think that no one cares, not even God. We can feel so alone and swallowed up by the problem at hand. The truth is that God is continually, without interruption, steadily, and constantly with us, extending his mighty righteous right hand to save us. Go ahead and take his right hand that is extended to you now, and *hold* on tightly to it. God won't ever let go of your hand, and he doesn't want you to let go of his either.

Read Scripture:

Psalm 73:23

Prayer:

Heavenly Father, I come to you in the midst of the storm and the loneliness that I am experiencing right now. As an act of my will, I reach out my hand to your mighty right hand that is extended to me now, and I take hold of it as you pull me close to you during this

---

* *Hold*—to have and keep in one's grasp and to keep from falling or moving; support.

time. Thank you for never letting go of me, and thank you for helping me through this time. I thank you that I am not alone in this but
that you are with me every step of the way. In Jesus' name. Amen.

Notes:

_____

_____

_____

_____

_____

_____

_____

_____

_____

Tuesday, Day 3

(241) We have all heard the saying, "God does not make junk." God loves you. You are special to him. God sees you as an asset, meaning you are *_valuable_* or useful; and you are not a liability, burden, or nuisance. Any other voice that tears you down and makes you feel bad about yourself is a lie, and it is not God's voice. It is time for you to fight back the lies, and the way that you do that is with truth. God's word is truth, and through the Bible, you can find out what God says about you and who you are in Christ.

Read Scripture:

Isaiah 43:4

Prayer:

Heavenly Father, I come to you now, asking you to forgive me for giving ear to the lies, and for believing the voices and lies of the enemy instead of your word. I thank you for your forgiveness as I receive it now. Holy Spirit, you are my help, and I need you. I am asking you to help me to replace the lies, and as an act of my will, I submit my will to the will of God for my life by making the time to

---

* _Valuable_—important, worthy, priceless, and precious.

read and study God's Word, which promises to give me insight and revelation as to who I am in Christ Jesus. I thank you for this. In Jesus' name. Amen.

Notes:

_____

_____

_____

_____

_____

_____

_____

_____

_____

Wednesday, Day 4

(242) Jesus spoke to us in the Gospels that in this world, we would have trouble, but to be of *good cheer* because he overcame the world. What that means is that Jesus overcame every distressing situation that he faced and so can we. Jesus did this by submitting his will to the will of the Father, and he desired to please the Father. Yes, we will have troubles in life, but you can overcome them the same way that Jesus did when he said, "Nevertheless, Father, not my will but yours be done."

Read Scripture:

John 16:33

Prayer:

Father God, I come to you now, giving you thanks and praise for Jesus who by living example showed me how to overcome the trouble that is in this world. Holy Spirit, you are my help, and I cannot do this without you. As an act of my will, I submit and yield my will to you now, and I declare that I will be of good cheer just as Jesus said. I stand in full agreement with the will of God in humble

---

*   *Good cheer*—cheerful or courageous spirit.

submission saying, "Nevertheless, Father, not my will but yours be done." In Jesus' name. Amen.

Notes:

_____

_____

_____

_____

_____

_____

_____

_____

_____

Thursday, Day 5

(243) We live in a day and age where we have evolved into fast food places being all around us. At every corner, you can turn and almost be sure to see one. We have grown *accustomed* to getting our food fast and easy. Sad to say we want microwave results in life and that is how we can be with God. We should never treat God like a fast food restaurant, going to him for a quick and easy result. It has always been about covenant relationship, and this relationship with him is personal and intimate. We should take our time in his presence, communing with him.

Read Scripture:

Revelation 3:20

Prayer:

Heavenly Father, I come before you asking for your forgiveness. I repent for the times in my life where I may have treated you as if you were a microwave kind of God, expecting quick results from you instead of spending quality times of devotion to you. I thank you for your forgiveness as I receive it now. Holy Spirit, I need you. I am

---

* *Accustomed*—being in the habit of something.

asking you to help me live a devoted and disciplined life of worship, studying the Word of God, and praying and communicating with God in a personal and intimate way. I pray in Jesus' name. Amen.

Notes:

_____

_____

_____

_____

_____

_____

_____

_____

_____

Friday, Day 6

(244) Have you ever greeted someone and asked them how their day was, and they replied, "It's just another day." God helps us to never have the attitude that "it is just another day." With God on your side, it is never just another day. It's a promising day, a yes and amen day! It's a blessed day, and if God is determined to stand with you, then who can stand *against* you. It's a good day, and a God day!

Read Scripture:

Romans 8:31

Prayer:

Father God, I come before you now, thanking you that today I woke up and inhaled fresh air. I woke up in my right mind, and it is not just another day, but it is a day of promise. It is a good day because I do not face this day alone, but you are with me, standing for me. With you on my side, who can stand against me? I just want to thank you, Lord, for giving me this day, and I declare that it is a blessed day. In Jesus' name. Amen.

---

* *Against*—opposed to or in conflict or disagreement with.

Notes:

_____

_____

_____

_____

_____

_____

_____

_____

_____

Saturday, Day 7

(245) In the summer months, there is nothing as good as a ripe, sweet fruit. We never see the process that this fruit has to go through to grow and become ripe and ready for the consumer to buy and eat, but we savor every bite of sweetness when we eat it. The Bible talks about the fruit of righteousness that is supposed to be manifested through our life and recognized as such. This only happens through the process of maturity, right standing with God, and right doing being evident in our life so that others would desire this *abounding,* full, rich, abundant life in Jesus Christ.

Read Scripture:

Philippians 1:11

Prayer:

Father God, I come to you, thanking you for your Word which instructs me on how I should be filled with fruits of righteousness, which is right standing and right doing that comes through Jesus Christ, my Lord, and not of my own doing. He is sweet Jesus, the Anointed One, who enables me to be fruit bearing, making him

---

* *Abounding*—to have abundance or plenty of.

attractive to others so that others are drawn to him by my life and desiring the abounding, full, and rich abundant life that he provides for us, and that which brings glory and honor to you. All of this I pray in the precious name of Jesus Christ. Amen.

Notes:

_____

_____

_____

_____

_____

_____

_____

_____

_____

Sunday, Day 1

(246) We all have a family member or know someone who is so against everything you believe in as far as God is concerned. At times, they have personally attacked you for being outspoken about your love, faith, and belief in Jesus Christ. Always remember that God's arm is not too short to save the hardest of persons, and no one is beyond his reach. No matter what it looks like, when we pray for them, our prayers are *effective.* Remember to pray for that family member or someone who has not accepted Jesus as their Lord and Savior, yet.

Read Scripture:

Isaiah 59:1

Prayer:

Father God, I come before you today, thanking you for your love and your compassion for my family who does not know you as Lord and Savior. Holy Spirit, I need you, and I am asking you to give me the heart of the Father and the compassion for my loved ones who are not saved. I thank you, God, that you willed that they

---

* *Effective*—producing an intended result or having a successful or desired result.

not perish but that they come to everlasting life. I ask you, Father, to send labors into their path who would speak the truth to them and that you would draw them with your loving-kindness. I pray that the heart of my loved ones would be softened and prepared to receive the truth of the gospel and that they would accept Jesus as Lord and be saved. In Jesus' name. Amen.

Notes:

_____

_____

_____

_____

_____

_____

_____

_____

_____

Monday, Day 2

(247) Have you ever sat in church listening to a sermon and all of a sudden, your mind went into thinking about what you're going to make for lunch, or you thought about all the things that you had to do the upcoming week? All of that would be called a *distraction* to draw your attention away from hearing the Word. Faith comes only one way and that is by hearing the Word of God. It takes discipline to tune in to hear the Word of God. Don't let the distractions get in the way.

Read Scripture:

Romans 10:17

Prayer:

Father God, I thank you for your Word today. You said that faith comes by hearing and hearing by the Word of God. As an act of my will, I submit my hearing to your Word today, and I prepare my heart to receive your Word every time your Word is preached. I declare that I will not be distracted and pulled away from hearing

---

* *Distractions*—if you are distracted, you are not concentrating on something because you are worried or are thinking about something else.

your Word, but I will be disciplined in my life to tune in to hear your Word that are words of life for me. For this, I thank you. In Jesus' name. Amen.

Notes:

_____

_____

_____

_____

_____

_____

_____

_____

_____

Tuesday, Day 3

(248) Love is who God is, and by constantly using our faith, the life of Jesus is released on the inside of us and that love is the root and source by which everything we do flows from. Love is the very basis or foundation of everything that we are and everything that we do. As we are rooted and *grounded* in him, then the love, which is the very heart of God, is received by us in depths, lengths, and widths to live full lives in him. We then can express that same love of God that we have received to others around us.

Read Scripture:

Ephesians 3:17

Prayer:

Heavenly Father, as I come to you, I acknowledge you as God, and you are love. There are depths of your love that I desire to know. I declare that as my faith in Jesus is released on the inside of me, the more I know you and your love. You become the very source by which everything I do and become flows so that I can express your very love to those around me. Thank you for the extravagant dimen-

---

* *Grounded*—to be firmly established.

sions of your love that we can experience to live the fullness of life in you. In Jesus' name. Amen.

Notes:

_____

_____

_____

_____

_____

_____

_____

_____

_____

Wednesday, Day 4

(249) Scripture tells us that the sword of the Spirit is the Word of God. As a believer in Jesus Christ, we have been given the Word of God as a weapon that slices the enemy into pieces. What this means is that we have the power, or *jurisdiction,* and the territorial range of authority or control in our lives over all the power of the enemy. Our minds are transformed and renewed by the Word, and we can pray effectively. The question is: how sharp is your sword?

Read Scripture:

Ephesians 6:17

Prayer:

Heavenly Father, I come before you now, asking you to forgive me for the lack of knowledge that I have concerning your Word and the armor that you have given me. I repent before you now, and I thank you for your forgiveness as I receive it now. Holy Spirit, I need you, and I am asking you to give me the hunger and desire to study the Word of God that prepares me for life's battles. Teach me, Holy Spirit, as my mind is renewed by the study of the Word and

---

* *Jurisdiction*—the territorial range of authority or control.

covered by the helmet of salvation against the lies of the enemy; let my life be transformed. Holy Spirit, I ask you to give me the revelation and understanding as I study the Word of God. Teach me about the authority and jurisdiction that God has given to me over all the power of the enemy so that I can stand against him effectively. In Jesus' name, I pray. Amen.

Notes:

_____

_____

_____

_____

_____

_____

_____

_____

_____

Thursday, Day 5

(250) There is no doubt that everyone enjoys a holiday and especially when they get the day off work with pay. We should thank God for those times that are recognized as such because it is a blessing. Scripture says that Jesus is the *resurrection* and the eternal life; and whoever believes in, adheres to, trusts in, and relies on him, although he may die, yet he shall live. As a believer in Jesus Christ, we should be so thankful that Jesus is not a holiday, but the *resurrection and the life, and we shall live with him eternally.

Read Scripture:

John 11:25

Prayer:

Father God, I come to you in the name of Jesus Christ, the One who died and resurrected, and is seated at your right hand. I thank you that because of Jesus, I can live the abundant life while here on this temporal earth. But when I die, I will live with you forever in the eternal place that you have prepared for me. Today, I rejoice in the

---

* *Resurrection*—when a dead person comes back to life.

God of my salvation and in Jesus Christ, who is the resurrection and life eternal. Amen.

Notes:

_____

_____

_____

_____

_____

_____

_____

_____

Friday, Day 6

(251) Everyone desires a *promotion** on their job at some time in their life. *Promotion usually comes with more responsibility and an increase in pay as well. The definition of *"promotion" is an act of rising in rank or position. As a believer, there is a *promotion that the Bible talks about, and it does not come from the east or from the west, but from God. God is the judge. He will put down one, and he will set up or promote another. Be encouraged today. In all that you do, do it as unto the Lord to please him. He will promote you in due season.

Read Scripture:

Psalm 75:6–7

Prayer:

Heavenly Father, thank you for giving me the ability to do what I do. I pray that in everything that I do, I would remember to do it as unto you. Holy Spirit, I need you. I am asking you to help me to always portray the characteristics of God by being on time and completing tasks to the best of my ability, knowing that as I do this unto

---

* *Promotion*—to elevate, upgrade, and move up.

you, that it is you that will promote me in due season. All of this I pray in Jesus' name. Amen.

Notes:

_____

_____

_____

_____

_____

_____

_____

_____

_____

Saturday, Day 7

(252) Scripture tells us that God loves us, and Jesus told us that because we love him and believed that he came from God, that the Father himself loves us. We are validated by God through Jesus Christ, and the validation of our worthiness or *legitimacy** does not come from others or by how many likes you get on social media. It comes from God alone, and you are accepted by him.

Read Scripture:

John 16:27

Prayer:

Heavenly Father, I thank you that I am legitimately accepted by you because of Jesus Christ, your Son, as I have accepted him as my Lord and Savior, and that you see me through his eyes. I do not look to the world, others, or social media to validate me because I am deemed worthy because of the price that Jesus paid to redeem me back to a right relationship with you. I have been justified and made righteous in your sight, and for this, I am eternally grateful and give you thanks and praise. In Jesus' name. Amen.

---

* *Legitimacy*—undisputed credibility.

Notes:

Sunday, Day 1

(253) The Bible tells us that we should not allow unwholesome talk come out of our mouths. Unwholesome talk is detrimental to physical or moral well-being. When we speak, we should not be tearing others down; but instead, we should be building others up according to their needs so that it is beneficial and not *harmful* to them. Encourage someone today because the world already tears them down. Be a minister of God's grace today.

Read Scripture:

Ephesians 4:29

Prayer:

Heavenly Father, in the name of Jesus I come before you now, asking you to forgive me for any unwholesome talk that has come forth from my lips, and for the harm and injury it has brought to the hearer. I thank you for your forgiveness as I receive it now. Holy Spirit, I need you, and I am asking you to help me. As an act of my will, I submit my heart to you because I know that it is a heart issue, as it is out of the abundance of the heart that my mouth speaks.

---

* *Harmful*—causing injury, damage that is hurtful.

Remove those things in the depths of my heart such as anger, bitterness, and anything else that is rooted within me that is unlike God. Fill me with his unfailing love, mercy, and grace so that my words will reflect the heart of God. In Jesus' name, I pray. Amen.

Notes:

_____

_____

_____

_____

_____

_____

_____

_____

_____

Monday, Day 2

(254) Fitness is a very important aspect of our life. It is not unusual for us to take an hour of our day to go to the gym or even go for a long *walk** for exercise. There is so much technology these days that even helps us to count how many steps we take in any given day. When we *walk with God, we are in fact taking it one faith step at a time. God sees all of our ways, and he counts all our steps. Make your steps count for him today by walking according to his Word, his plan, and his purpose for your life.

Read Scripture:

Job 31:4

Prayer:

Father God, I come to you in amazement at how you see all of my ways and count my steps. Thank you that my walk with you consists of a disciplined life when I take the time to worship you, study your Word, and live by faith in your Word, which is your will for my life. My steps matter. Lead me every step of the way in conduct and behavior as I put my trust in you to step into fulfilling your plan,

---

* *Walk*—to conduct oneself or behave in a particular manner; to advance.

your will, and your purpose on this earth. In Jesus' name, I pray. Amen.

Notes:

_____

_____

_____

_____

_____

_____

_____

_____

_____

Tuesday, Day 3

(255) Goodness, or God's kindness and generosity and his mercy or disposition of *compassion,* goes with you wherever you go. His faithful protection and loving provision will pursue you, and it never leaves you. It follows you all of the days of your life on this earth. When you leave here to be with him, you will dwell with him forever and ever for all of eternity.

Read Scripture:

Psalm 23:6

Prayer:

Heavenly Father, I worship you today and give you thanks for your goodness, kindness, and mercy that follow me all the days of my life. Thank you for your protection and your provision that pursue, follow, chase, and capture me and will never leave me. Because of your great compassion, I am well cared for by you. When I leave this earth at the appointed time, I will be with you forever for all eternity; and for this, I am exceedingly grateful. In Jesus' name. Amen.

---

* *Compassion*—deep awareness of the suffering of another accompanied by the wish to relive it.

Notes:

_____

_____

_____

_____

_____

_____

_____

_____

_____

Wednesday, Day 4

(256) If you have ever walked through a tree farm with fruit trees all around, you will notice that any fruit that is found on the ground left for any period of time will rot. The fruit on the tree that is still on the branch is a better quality of fruit for consumption. Our relationship with God is such that we are to remain attached to him and *abide* in him because without him, we can do nothing. He is the vine and we are the branches. Stay connected to the vine and bear fruit after the God kind.

Read Scripture:

John 15:5

Prayer:

Heavenly Father, I come to you with a heart of repentance today. I realize that I have not been abiding in you and have been doing things apart from you, and for this, I am sorry. I ask you to forgive me. I thank you for your forgiveness as I receive it now. Holy Spirit, I need you. I am asking you to help me because apart from you, I can do nothing. Help me to abide and remain in him by nur-

---

* *Abide*—to dwell with, to remain, stay, and continue.

turing my personal relationship in his presence, worship, and study of the Word so that I will bear the God kind of fruit in my life. In Jesus' name, I pray. Amen.

Notes:

_____

_____

_____

_____

_____

_____

_____

_____

_____

Thursday, Day 5

(257) The Bible tells us that we have a new and better covenant established on better promises and that Jesus was the *mediator,* or the go between, who reconciled us back to a right relationship with God. Because of this, we don't just know him by the book, but we know him by the Spirit. This plan of action that he has for our lives is no longer a letter written in ink on paper, but it's written with his Spirit on our spirit, his life on our lives poured out by him.

Read Scripture:

2 Corinthians 3:6

Prayer:

Father God, thank you for opening up my understanding to know that Jesus established for me a new and better covenant by reconciling me back to you. Thank you the plan you have for my life is not a letter written on paper with ink, but it is your Spirit being poured out to my spirit, enabling me to live the life that you have planned for me. It is by your Spirit that I can do all things through you. I receive by the spirit all that you have for me in this day, and

---

* *Mediator*—a go between, intercessor, and advocate.

I am filled with expectancy today to see and experience all that you have for me. For this, I give you thanks and praise. In Jesus' name. Amen.

Notes:

_____

_____

_____

_____

_____

_____

_____

_____

_____

Friday, Day 6

(258) There is so much doubt and unbelief in this day and age that we live in. Have we become a "I will believe it when I see it" kind of generation instead of having faith in God? Faith is when you stop believing the things you see and start believing the things you don't see. Jesus told doubting Thomas that there are those who have never seen him with their eyes but have believed in him with their hearts, and that they will be blessed even more. It is time to *believe* that God meant what he said, and God said what he meant.

Read Scripture:

John 20:29

Prayer:

Father God, I come before you, asking you, first of all, to please forgive me for walking in doubt and unbelief instead of faith in you. I thank you for your forgiveness as I receive it now. Holy Spirit, I need you, and I am asking for your help. I know that faith comes by hearing and hearing by the Word, so as an act of my will, I submit to your leading and take the time to hear the Word of God without dis-

---

*   *Believe*—to accept as true and real.

traction. Because faith comes by hearing and hearing by the Word, I am asking for revelation to flow and for divine, supernatural disclosure where God makes known to me his revealed Word. I declare that with my heart, I believe what God says to be the truth, the whole truth, and nothing but the truth. So help me, God. Amen.

Notes:

_____

_____

_____

_____

_____

_____

_____

_____

Saturday, Day 7

(259) Everyone in the body of Christ is considered *co-laborer* with God. We are God's fellow workers, working together for one purpose, his purpose. There is only one foundation that has already been laid, and that foundation is Jesus Christ. Metaphorically speaking, whether or not you are the architect who designed the blueprint, the one picking out the materials, the one putting up the walls, or the one doing the cleanup, we must always remember, that there is only one foundation, the one that is already laid—Jesus Christ. What we do should be built on Jesus' life and example when he was on this earth.

Read Scripture:

1 Corinthians 3:9

Prayer:

Heavenly Father, I come to you acknowledging that I am a co-laborer in your kingdom, working together alongside other believers, with Jesus Christ being the foundation of everything that which we do is built on. His life and example that he lived on the earth was

---

* *Co-laborer*—one who labors with another; an associate in labor.

to always please you. God, I pray that my desire would always be to please you in everything that I do, always reflecting your love, compassion, mercy, and grace wherever I go and in all that I do. In Jesus' name, I pray. Amen.

Notes:

_____

_____

_____

_____

_____

_____

_____

_____

_____

Sunday, Day 1

(260) One of the enemy's strategies that he uses against a believer is our past. When we get **stuck** in the past, then it is very difficult to move ahead, and we accomplish nothing. Process is a forward movement, a course of action intended to achieve a result. It is time to stop going over old history and yield to the process of moving forth into new things that are waiting for us on the road to progress forward, onward, and upward.

Read Scripture:

Isaiah 42:9

Prayer:

Heavenly Father, I come to you now, asking you to forgive me for reliving the past and bringing up old history. I thank you for your forgiveness as I receive it now. Holy Spirit, I need you, and I am asking for your help. As an act of my will, I submit my will to you, and I take it one step at a time to get unstuck from the past. I willingly progress forward into all things new that await me in the

---

* *Stuck*—if something is stuck in a particular position, it is fixed tightly in this position and is unable to move.

walk of faith in God, and I thank you for taking the lead. In Jesus' name. Amen.

Notes:

_____

_____

_____

_____

_____

_____

_____

_____

_____

Monday, Day 2

(261) Love, it's not an option. God commands us as a *mandate* and decree that we should present ourselves as a true specimen of his love in the same way that he has loved us. We must be willing to lay down our selfish ways and be willing to put others before us just as Jesus Christ did, which was a full expression of his love for the Father. It is time to take inventory of our own life and examine whether or not we are a lover of God. We can only love others when we fully understand how much the Father loves us.

Read Scripture:

John 13:34–35

Prayer:

Heavenly Father, I come before you with sorrow in my heart as I have examined my own heart and life, and have notably seen where I have not always fulfilled your mandate to love one another as you have loved me. For this, I repent and ask you to forgive me. Thank you for your forgiveness as I receive it now. Holy Spirit, I need you, and I am asking for your help concerning this love walk. As I spend

---

* *Mandate*—an authoritative command that is to be obeyed.

time in God's presence, worship, and studying his Word, I ask you to shed God's love in my heart for others so that I will be a demonstration of God's love and will be his representation here upon the earth. In Jesus' name, I pray. Amen.

Notes:

_____

_____

_____

_____

_____

_____

_____

_____

Tuesday, Day 3

(262) A woman of good judgment that does what is true and right according to what Scripture says is a wise woman. A wise woman is one who builds her home with her words and does not tear it down brick by brick. She is one who encourages her family. She edifies and builds them up instead of speaking words that are *demeaning* and destructive. A woman can only be a wise woman when she knows the only wise God who is all wisdom.

Read Scripture:

Proverbs 14:1

Prayer:

Father God, in the name of Jesus, I come before you with godly sorrow that leads to repentance, and I want to say I am sorry for the foolish things that I have said which are contrary to what you tell me I should do in scriptures. I thank you for your forgiveness as I receive it now. Holy Spirit, I cannot do this without your help. I yield myself over to your leading as I make the time to spend with God in his presence, worshipping him and studying his Word. Help me to get to

---

* *Demeaning*—to intentionally make one feel less by putting him or her down.

know him for myself so that his characteristics are formed in me; and I become a wise woman who does what is true, right, and just in his eyes in building my home for the Lord. In Jesus' name, I pray. Amen.

Notes:

_____

_____

_____

_____

_____

_____

_____

_____

_____

Wednesday, Day 4

(263) Sometimes, when we go through difficult times, we sit in utter silence as if we have been abandoned by everyone, including God; but that is so far from the truth. If God was able to redeem us from the *consequences* of sin, he is also able to free us from what distresses us. He is not shorthanded that he can't save you. He is a great Deliverer, and his hand is always reaching. Take hold of his hand today and let him lift you up.

Read Scripture:

Isaiah 50:2

Prayer:

Heavenly Father, I come to you now, asking you to forgive me for allowing my difficult circumstance to separate me from you. I thank you for your forgiveness as I receive it now. Holy Spirit, I need you, and I am asking you to teach me how to reach out to God when I am in distress. I know that I cannot do this without you; so as an act of my will, I submit my spirit, my will, and my mind over to you,

---

* *Consequences*—the aftermath, outcome, or result of something that someone has done.

535

putting my trust in God. I declare that God is my deliverer and the one whose hand is always reaching for me. I reach back and take his hand with all confidence that I am indeed in good hands, and for this, I say thank you. In Jesus' name. Amen.

Notes:

_____

_____

_____

_____

_____

_____

_____

_____

_____

Thursday, Day 5

(264) Why is it that we have no trouble telling others of all the horrible things we go through, but rarely do we tell them the good things that God has done for us? Testify means to declare publicly or make known. It also means to acknowledge openly. In the old testament, Moses met with his father-in-law, Jethro, and they both asked how each other was doing when Moses began to tell him the whole story of what they had been through, the misery and the tribulation. But he also testified and told him everything that God had done for them and how God had rescued them from Pharaoh and the Egyptians. Take time to *reflect* on the good things that God has done for you, and tell someone today about it.

Read Scripture:

Exodus 18:7–8

Prayer:

Heavenly Father, in the name of Jesus, I come to you with a heart of repentance, asking you to forgive me for focusing and speaking only of all the negative things in my life, and rarely or never

---

* *Reflect*—when you reflect on something, you think deeply about it.

telling about your goodness and all the good things that you have done for me. I thank you for your forgiveness as I receive it now. Holy Spirit, I need you, and I am asking you to help me. Holy Spirit, I thank you that you bring to my remembrance all the good things that God has done for me and for the opportunities throughout the day to tell someone about God and all the good that he has done for me. I will testify and make known the goodness of my God today. In Jesus' name. Amen.

Notes:

_____

_____

_____

_____

_____

_____

_____

_____

Friday, Day 6

(265) Have you ever heard a believer say, "It's hard living for God in this world that we live in"? On the contrary, Scripture tells us that every believer has the conquering power on the inside of them to live for God and win over the world's ways. Jesus overcame the world, and instead of us being subject to the world and its ways, having *dominion* over us, we can make the world subject to us and bring it to its knees, so to speak. The person who wins over the world's ways is simply the one who believes Jesus is the Son of God. Our continuous, persistent faith in Jesus Christ causes us to already have the victory, and we are just walking it out.

Read Scripture:

1 John 5:4–5

Prayer:

Heavenly Father, I come to you in the name of Jesus, thanking you that as a believer in Jesus Christ, your Son, I have the power on the inside of me to overcome the ways of the world. The world does not have dominion over me because of my continued faith in Jesus.

Dominion—dominance or power through legal authority.

Jesus has already obtained the victory for me, and I am walking it out in my life daily. Holy Spirit, you are my help and my strength, and I can depend on you to help me to overcome and defeat the worldly ways that I once lived. I make it subject to the name of Jesus and the overcoming power on the inside of me to rise above it and live according to God's ways, plans, and purpose that he has for me. For this, I am thankful. In Jesus' name. Amen.

Notes:

_____

_____

_____

_____

_____

_____

_____

_____

_____

WEEK 38

Saturday, Day 7

(266) Being self-centered or *selfish* is when we are seeking or concentrating on one's own advantage, pleasure, or well-being without regard for others. Ouch! If that hurt you, then there is a strong possibility that you have been more concerned about your own interests and never giving a thought about others' interest. Jesus abandoned every display of selfishness when he chose to lay down his life for us at the cross. Take interest in someone else and do something good for someone without expecting something in return.

Read Scripture:

Philippians 2:4

Prayer:

Father God, I come to you today, and as I have reflected on my actions, I ask you to forgive me for spending too much time on my own interests and never looking to the interests of others. I thank you for your forgiveness as I receive it now. Holy Spirit I need your help, and I am asking you to help me concerning this. Reveal to me the times when I am being self-absorbed and uncaring toward others,

---

* *Selfish*—when one cares about himself or herself and not about other people.

and help me to have a heart that is genuinely caring for others so that my giving to others becomes a life style and not just a selfish act to appease my own guilt. Cultivate in me a heart of true caring and giving as Jesus did. All of this I pray in his name. Amen.

Notes:

_____

_____

_____

_____

_____

_____

_____

_____

_____

Sunday, Day 1

(267) Have you ever went on and on about your job and complained about it nonstop to someone? And then you happen to pass someone who is totally incapacitated and unable to do the very things that you are able to do and would be glad to do the very things that you are complaining about, and you feel horrible for being so *ungrateful?* Consider the fact that you have all your limbs, you woke up breathing, and that you do have a job. Don't complain about having to work, but thank God that you can. An attitude of gratitude will change your attitude. Give thanks to the Lord, for his mercy endures forever.

Read Scripture:

1 Chronicles 16:34

Prayer:

Heavenly Father, I humbly come before you, acknowledging my sin before you. I have been so ungrateful, and instead of being thankful for my job and the ability to do my job, I have complained

---

* *Ungrateful*—unappreciative; not displaying gratitude; not giving due return or acknowledgment.

constantly. Please forgive me for murmuring, complaining, and being so ungrateful. Thank you for your forgiveness as I receive it now. Holy Spirit, I need you to help me with this attitude of resentment, displeasure, and grumbling. I take full responsibility for my negative feelings of dissatisfaction, and I willfully make the decision to stop the complaining and grumbling. I choose to give thanks for my job, for having full use of my faculties, and for the ability to do my job. I choose to give God thanks in all things and for all things. In Jesus' name, I pray. Amen.

Notes:

_____

_____

_____

_____

_____

_____

_____

_____

_____

Monday, Day 2

(268) Scripture tells us that Jesus is the Good Shepherd. A good shepherd takes care of his sheep and will go so far as to lay down his life for them just as Jesus did. Likewise, a sheep who knows the shepherd will hear and *respond* to his voice and obey his commands willingly, following him wherever he leads. God speaks to us through his Word, the Bible, and even through all the noise, you can turn to God and his Word. You can hear his voice leading and guiding you to green pastures where you are well cared for and protected.

Read Scripture:

John 10:27

Prayer:

Father God, I come to you, thanking you that the Bible is your thoughts and your ways, and that I can find guidance and direction for my own life through the pages as I read and study your Word, spend time in your presence in worship, and hear what you are saying to me. I give you thanks for Jesus who is the Good Shepherd. I hear

---

* *Respond*—to answer with words, a reaction, gesture, etc.

his voice, obey his voice, and follow his voice with all clarity; and the voice of a stranger I will not follow. In Jesus' name, I pray. Amen.

Notes:

_____

_____

_____

_____

_____

_____

_____

_____

_____

Tuesday, Day 3

(269) You have the fruit of *patience* that was given to you as one of the fruits of the Spirit when you were born again, and trust me that you will have the opportunity to exercise it more than once. When your faith is tested and challenges come your way, just know that under that kind of pressure, your faith-life is forced into the open, and it will show its true colors. It will bring out things in you that you did not know were there. The trying of your faith will blossom under pressure and teach you true *patience as you endure.

Read Scripture:

2 Corinthians 6:4

Prayer:

Heavenly Father, I come to you with a repentant heart, knowing that I have not always exercised the fruit of patience under the pressure of my difficult circumstance; and for this, I am sorry. I ask you to forgive me. Thank you for your forgiveness as I receive it now. Holy Spirit, I need you not just today but every day. Help me to put actions to exercising the fruit of patience. As I am tested and

---

* *Patience*—being able to stay calm and not get annoyed.

challenged, show me those things on the inside of me that need to be changed. Help me to submit to the process with endurance, and perseverance so that I become well-developed, not deficient in any way, but a mature believer. In Jesus' name, I pray. Amen.

Notes:

_____

_____

_____

_____

_____

_____

_____

_____

_____

Wednesday, Day 4

(270) In the Bible, we know that time and time again, the Pharisees tried to *entrap* Jesus. They conspired against him to discuss how they can lure him into their trap. Today, we must avoid those who try to entangle us in their conspired criticism and gossip. To be entangled means to get wrapped up and twisted together. Be watchful and careful not to get entangled in criticism and gossip or anything else that is unlike our God, but pray instead.

Read Scripture:

Matthew 22:15

Prayer:

Father God, I come to you now, repenting for the times that I have allowed myself to get entangled in criticism of others, gossip about others, or any other behaviors that is unlike you. I am sorry for the harm that I have caused because of it. I thank you for your forgiveness as I receive it now. Holy Spirit, I need you, and I am asking you to help me with strength to resist the temptation to speak evil

---

* *Entrap*—to trick or deceive someone and make them believe or do something wrong.

of others and to convict me when I am about to do so. Help me to guard my thoughts and tongue so that I do not get tangled, wrapped up, and twisted together in any actions that are unlike you. In Jesus' name, I pray. Amen.

Notes:

_____

_____

_____

_____

_____

_____

_____

_____

_____

Thursday, Day 5

(271) The storms of life come and go, and you have the power within you to be *calm* through it. You have the authority in Jesus' name to rebuke the anxious thoughts and stress that tries to take you under in your circumstances. Jesus boldly did this when he was with the disciples, showing them by his actions how to deal with the raging storms that may come. Speak to the storm with your God-given authority and command it to cease in Jesus' name.

Read Scripture:

Luke 8:24

Prayer:

Heavenly Father, I come to you now, admitting that through the storms of life, I have not taken the God-given authority that you have given to me through Jesus Christ. Instead, I have succumbed to its overpowering force, and I ask you to forgive me. I thank you for your forgiveness as I receive it now. Holy Spirit, I thank you that you are my help. I am not ashamed to say that I need you daily. I am asking you to bring to my remembrance the God-given authority that

---

* *Calm*—a calm person does not show or feel any worry, anger, or excitement.

I have through Jesus Christ when the storms of life come. Teach me how to use this commanding authority which has the power over all the forces of evil, yet having power within me to be calm through it all. In Jesus' name, I pray. Amen.

Notes:

_____

_____

_____

_____

_____

_____

_____

_____

_____

Friday, Day 6

(272) We have all experienced when someone has called us out of our name. Whether intentional or not, we can get annoyed and may feel as if they do not know us at all if they can't get our name right. It may even make you feel insignificant or not important. With God, you are *significant* and worthy of notice. As a matter of fact, he knows you so well that he knows the number of hairs that are on your head. You are marked by him, and he takes notice of you even when others around you don't.

Read Scripture:

Matthew 10:30

Prayer:

Heavenly Father, I must admit that today, as I stand here in your presence, I am overwhelmed by the truth that you would even take notice of me. Thank you that you count me worthy of being noticed. To know that you even know the number of hairs that are on my head is fascinating to me. Thank you for showing me that even though others may have little regard for me, I am significant

---

* *Significant*—being important and having meaning or purpose.

to you. Today, I declare that I see myself as you see me and that I no longer see myself as inadequate not good enough, or incapable, but as important, loved, and accepted by you. For this, I thank you. In Jesus' name. Amen.

Notes:

_____

_____

_____

_____

_____

_____

_____

_____

_____

Saturday, Day 7

(273) The battle is on, and God is on your side. He is for you and not against you. He has not left your side, but he is your impenetrable and solid shield. He is your *strength** or source of power that helps you overcome resistance or opposition and overthrows it on your behalf. Trust him with all of your heart, with unwavering confidence in him that he is there to help you. Begin to praise him and thank him for his presence that is there with you right now. He is your help.

Read Scripture:

Psalm 28:7

Prayer:

Father God, I come to you with shouts of praise and thanksgiving because you are not only my source of power and strength when opposition comes against me, but you are also my ever present God who is with me always. You have not, nor will you ever leave me, but you are my impenetrable shield in whom I put my whole trust in. Thank you for reminding me that you are for me and not against

---

* *Strength*—someone's strength in a difficult situation is their confidence or courage.

me, and you are not only on my side, but you are by my side through everything that I go through. For this, I shout hallelujah and amen.

Notes:

_____

_____

_____

_____

_____

_____

_____

_____

_____

Sunday, Day 1

(274) Did you know that it is God's desire to give us richly all things to enjoy? It is God who prospers us, and he is not against us being wealthy and prosperous. But what he commands us is that we not get so wrapped up in those riches that we become prideful and begin to *rely* on those riches instead of relying on him. It is God who lavishes on us all good things, meeting our needs and giving all things to enjoy and to share with others. No riches could ever compare with God. It is in God we trust and in God we *rely on, always.

Read Scripture:

 1 Timothy 6:17

Prayer:

 Heavenly Father, I thank you for showing your lavish love to me through the scripture today. Your Word says that it is you who gives us all things to enjoy and that it is you who gives us riches to meet our needs and to enjoy life. Holy Spirit, I ask you now to help me to always remember to put my trust in God and not the riches that he

---

* *Rely*—if you rely on someone, you need them and depend on them in order to live or work properly.

has blessed me with. Help me, Holy Spirit, to never be high-minded, lofty, or prideful, but to always remain humble and grateful, knowing that it is God and God alone that I put my trust in. Holy Spirit, you are my Guide, and I am asking you to lead me and teach me the ways of God so that I can be a good steward of the riches that he has put me in charge of. In Jesus' name, I pray. Amen.

Notes:

_____

_____

_____

_____

_____

_____

_____

_____

_____

Monday, Day 2

(275) "I'm only human," "I can't help it," or "The devil made me do it," are sayings and definite signs that we are allowing our fleshly nature to dictate to us; and we are being a carnal Christian. Yes, we have a human nature, and the tendencies to let it rule in our lives lead us further away from God. A practicing Christian will *incline* his or her heart to the Word of God to hear and then follow through with corresponding actions. We depart from evil and are no longer workers of iniquity.

Read Scripture:

Psalm 141:4

Prayer:

Heavenly Father, I humble myself before you now, and I come, asking you to forgive me for the times where I have allowed my fleshly nature rule over me and yielding to its desires. And in doing so, I have let it pull me away from you. I thank you for your forgive-

---

* *Incline*—to turn and bend one's ear to hear. If you incline to think or act in a particular way, or if something inclines you to it, you are likely to think or act in that way.

ness as I receive it now. Holy Spirit, I need you in my life, and I am asking you to help me to yield myself to the Greater One who lives on the inside of me. As an act of my will, I incline my ears to hear your word, "oh God," and I incline my heart to do your will and to depart from evil. In Jesus' name, I pray. Amen.

Notes:

_____

_____

_____

_____

_____

_____

_____

_____

_____

Tuesday, Day 3

(276) You have heard it said that you are a soldier in the army of the Lord. Scripture tells us that we are to be like good soldiers passing through the difficulties and to endure or carry on despite hardships and sufferings. A good soldier does not *quit* when the going gets tough; but they endure, face, and withstand adversity with courage. They hold up, bear up, and stand up, knowing whose they are. Be that good soldier of Christ that he has purposed you to be.

Read Scripture:

2 Timothy 2:3

Prayer:

Father God, I come to you today, standing in your presence with boldness and courage as a good soldier who endures through hardships and sufferings. I declare that you are my strength and my shield, and my very present help in time of trouble. I stand in full stance as a good soldier to carry out your command until the very end, knowing that you will hold me up and bear me up in your hand to stand as a good soldier for your name's sake. In Jesus' name. Amen.

---

* *Quit*—to depart, leave, or give up.

Notes:

Wednesday, Day 4

(277) Sometimes, we can be our own worst critic. We can forgive others, but when it comes to forgiving ourselves, we can find that very difficult to do. Unforgiveness toward our self is destructive, and having or making no allowance for error or *weakness* in ourselves is not of God. Have you been holding unforgiveness toward yourself for the things that you have done in the past? If God has forgiven you and does not even bring it to his or your remembrance, then why haven't you?

Read Scripture:

Psalm 85:2

Prayer:

Heavenly Father, I want to say thank you for forgiving me for not only some, but all of my sins, past, present, and future. You have showed me how great your love is for me and how the same forgiveness you gave to me is the same forgiveness that I need to extend to myself. So as an act of my will, I forgive myself for all my mistakes, wrongs, shortcomings, and sins. I no longer stand condemned, but

---

* *Weakness*—a flaw or imperfection, feeble or frail.

forgiven and washed clean because of the blood of Jesus Christ. For this, I give you thanks and praise. In Jesus' name. Amen.

Notes:

_____

_____

_____

_____

_____

_____

_____

_____

_____

Thursday, Day 5

(278) When your child is exhibiting bad behavior, that does not make them a bad person. Your words have power, and telling them that they are bad is not only hurtful but it affects them deeply. You can address their bad behavior without telling them that they are bad, lest they eventually believe it and act it out. After addressing their bad behavior, speak words of *affirmation.* Speak life over your child; they are your precious seed.

Read Scripture:

Proverbs 18:21

Prayer:

Father God, I ask you to forgive me for speaking words to my child that are hurtful to them. I ask you to help me to think before I speak and that you would remind me of scriptures that would build them up and not tear them down. Holy Spirit, I ask for your help to address their bad behavior without resulting in saying that they are bad, and help me to speak words that line up with scripture and what

---

* *Affirmation*—to say something positive that supports another.

God says about them. Give me the heart of God to always see them as he sees them. In Jesus' name. Amen.

Notes:

_____

_____

_____

_____

_____

_____

_____

_____

Friday, Day 6

(279) According to Scripture, Jesus is the only way to God. We were *estranged* from God through one act of Adam and Eve, disobedience; but through one act of obedience, Jesus reconciled or brought us back together with God. Your ministry is that of reconciliation. You now are able to reconcile those who are estranged from God back to him by telling them about Jesus Christ. He is the only bridge back to God for them to cross over.

Read Scripture:

2 Corinthians 5:18

Prayer:

Heavenly Father, how I give you the glory, honor, and praise today for Jesus Christ who has reconciled me back to a right relationship with you, bringing us back together again. There is no other place that I would rather be than right here in your presence. Thank you for showing me that my ministry is to be more like Jesus Christ and to share your love to those who are estranged from you in hopes that they will be reconciled back to you through accepting Jesus

---

* *Estranged*—separated and living apart from someone.

Christ as their Lord and Savior. Jesus, I thank you for your obedience to the Father and the opportunities today to share the love of God with the help of the Holy Spirit. In Jesus' name. Amen.

Notes:

_____

_____

_____

_____

_____

_____

_____

_____

_____

Saturday, Day 7

(280) Charity means love directed toward God first, then to others who are objects of God's love. Charity does not always mean giving money to others, although that is one of the major ways that we do to bless others. You really do have so much more to give than you think you do. A smile, a laugh, a hug, a listening ear, an encouraging word, a prayer for someone else is giving of one's self. One act of *kindness* can really bless someone's day. Be a blessing to someone today.

Read Scripture:

2 Peter 1:7

Prayer:

Father God, I come to you first of all, asking for your forgiveness. Please forgive me for seeing charity as only monetary donations given to others or organizations. I thank you for your forgiveness as I receive it now. Thank you, Father, for opening my eyes to see that there is so much in me to give away to others. Holy Spirit, I need you. I am asking you now to give me a tender heart and a listening

---

* *Kindness*—the quality of being gentle, caring, and helpful, warmhearted and considerate.

ear to be aware today of others around me who may need a smile, a hug, or an encouraging word. Show me in creative yet simple ways that I can be a blessing to God by giving of myself to others. In Jesus' name, I pray. Amen.

Notes:

_____

_____

_____

_____

_____

_____

_____

_____

_____

Sunday, Day 1

(281) As the years come and go, there is great anticipation to begin a new year or a fresh start, and we look forward to putting the previous year behind us. We look ahead trying hard to forget all of the past year's challenges we faced, and we also reminisce on the good things that took place. Scripture tells us that there are *pioneers* who blazed the way for us, and they are cheering us on to run the race and finish our course. Jesus never lost sight of where he was headed. He plowed through everything on his way to the cross to finish well and to please the Father, and we should do likewise.

Read Scripture:

Hebrews 12:1–3

Prayer:

Father God, I come to you now, thanking you for the pioneers of faith that came before me who ran their race and finished their course, and for Jesus who is my ultimate example of the one who was in the same race as I am. He stood the course and pushed through

---

* *Pioneer*—to be the first to open or prepare a way. Founders, leaders, and trail-blazers.

every obstacle and difficulty he faced. Holy Spirit, you are my Guide and my help. I ask that you would strengthen me in my inner being so that I would run my race and finish my course just as Jesus did with one thing in mind, and that was to please the Father by his obedience. All of this I ask in the name of Jesus. Amen.

Notes:

_____

_____

_____

_____

_____

_____

_____

_____

_____

Monday, Day 2

(282) It is true that we have an outward man, and we have an inward man. We should spend time taking care of our outer man the best that we can even though Scripture tells us that our outward man is changing and aging daily and that it gradually wears out. Our inner man should also be nourished by spending time in God's presence, in worship, studying the Word, and praying. Your inner man will never wear out, and it is being renewed day by day. Our inner man is *revitalized* with new life, vitality. It is strong, active, and full of energy.

Read Scripture:

2 Corinthians 4:16

Prayer:

Father God, I come before you, giving you the thanks and praise for both my outer man and my inner man. Give me the wisdom to care for my outer man to the best of my ability. I thank you that the renewing and revitalizing of my inward man is daily infused with your power and your strength to live my life for you in fullness of joy. I thank you that I do not faint at the aging of my outward man

---

* *Revitalized*—restored to new life and vigor.

but that I have the ability to let the inward man have predominance over my outer being, and I glorify you in it. In Jesus' name. Amen.

Notes:

_____

_____

_____

_____

_____

_____

_____

_____

_____

Tuesday, Day 3

(283) Scripturally speaking, you are a *vessel* or a container, and you have a deep significant purpose on this earth to be a carrier of God's presence that he can use to pour out to others. Did you know that you are called by his name? It means that it is by Jesus and him alone that you were called to the Father, but more than that, he created you and is shaping and molding you for his purpose. He takes personal interest in you to fashion and form you into a beautiful *vessel for his profound glory.

Read Scripture:

Isaiah 43:7

Prayer:

Heavenly Father, I thank you that you have called me by your name and that you have a significant purpose for my life. As an act of my will, I submit to the Holy Spirit who always leads me and guides me into all truth. I yield myself as clay in the Potter's hands to fashion, form, and mold me into the created vessel that you have desired to make of me for the significant purpose that you have so that you

---

* *Vessel*—a person regarded as an agent or vehicle for some purpose or quality.

can pour out of this vessel into the lives of others upon this earth and to bring about your profound glory. To you be all the glory. In Jesus' name. Amen.

Notes:

_____

_____

_____

_____

_____

_____

_____

_____

_____

_____

Wednesday, Day 4

(284) We have been told in Scripture that in this world we will have trouble. Sometimes, it may seem as if you are the only one facing difficult circumstances, but there are other brothers and sisters who are facing trouble the same as you. You can make a decisive stand against the enemy and resist his every attack with your strong and *vigorous* faith. Be encouraged because God will get the last word, and he will restore and reestablish you to the original condition that he intended for you.

Read Scripture:

    1 Peter 5:9–10

Prayer:

    Father God, I come to you now in the name of Jesus, thanking you that you have given me the power to resist every attack of the enemy that comes against me. I declare that I am strong in the Lord and in the power of his might. I declare that I will not falter, faint, or fall, for my God is bearing me with his right hand in his strength to stand above the trouble. I will magnify the Lord and not the cir-

---

* *Vigorous*—strong, powerful, robust, strong, healthy, and full of energy.

cumstance, and declare his goodness and his faithfulness toward me. God is on my side, and he will get the last word and will restore and reestablish me to the original condition that he intended for me. In Jesus' name. Amen.

Notes:

_____

_____

_____

_____

_____

_____

_____

_____

_____

Thursday, Day 5

(285) A *tsunami* is a high, long sea wave caused by an underwater earthquake and can cause damage and loss of life, but have you ever imagined a spiritual *tsunami? Imagine a wave of God's Spirit, just one breath from the Almighty God can bring created life upon the earth. Surely, with one breath of his Spirit, he can restore you, heal you, and strengthen you. Are you ready for God's spiritual *tsunami in your life? Get ready because here it comes!

Read Scripture:

Psalm 104:30

Prayer:

Father God, I stand here in your presence today, ready for your spiritual tsunami wave to come and wash over me with your mighty power, bringing new strength to me, and touching me with your healing power from head to toe. I breathe in your presence right now, allowing it to permeate my entire being. I declare now that by the very breath of your Spirit, I am restored and made whole, renewed, and revived in spirit, soul, and body. In Jesus' powerful name. Amen.

---

* *Tsunami*—a sudden increase in or overwhelming number or volume of.

Notes:

_____

_____

_____

_____

_____

_____

_____

_____

Friday, Day 6

(286) In dire circumstances, fear may come; and many times, we let that fear rule over us. Instead of ruling over it, we place ourselves under it. This should not be so. Scripture tells us that we should bless the Lord at all times. "All times" means even in dire circumstances. It is an act of faith to open your mouth and say it aloud, "I will bless the Lord at all times, and his praise shall continuously be in my mouth!" Shout it out because in doing so, it is magnifying the Lord over your problem; and in your seeking him, he will *deliver* you from all your fears.

Read Scripture:

Psalm 34:1–4

Prayer:

Heavenly Father, I come to you now, and as an act of my will, I bless you, Lord, even in this circumstance that I am in. Again, I speak with my mouth aloud, "I will bless the Lord at all times, and his praise shall continually be in my mouth!" "I magnify your name, Lord, above this problem!" Thank you, Father God, that my praise

---

* *Deliver*—if someone delivers you from something, they rescue or save you from it.

arises in the midst of problems, and instead of being under the problem, I rise above it. In seeking you above all else, I declare that you have delivered me from all my fears. For this, I give you the glory, the honor, and all of the praise. In Jesus' name. Amen.

Notes:

_____

_____

_____

_____

_____

_____

_____

_____

_____

Saturday, Day 7

(287) In the Old Testament, we read about God's people, the Israelites. God did wonders for them time and time again, yet they continued to sin against him. They flattered God with their mouths and lied to God with their lips. Their hearts were so far from him, meaning that they did not keep covenant with God. They did *lack* faithfulness, and their hearts were not devoted to him even though God showed his great love for them and he protected and provided for them. Let us not give God lip service, but let us keep the covenant to serve him wholeheartedly.

Read Scripture:

Psalm 78:36–37

Prayer:

Heavenly Father, I come before you after the examination of my own heart and life, and I confess that I have not been fully devoted to you. Like the Israelites, I have oftentimes worshipped you with my

---

* *Lack*—if you say that someone or something lacks a particular quality or that a particular quality is lacking in them, you mean that they do not have any or enough of it.

mouth, but my heart was not in it. I repent for this, and I am asking you to forgive me. Thank you for your forgiveness as I receive it now. Holy Spirit, you are my help, and I need your help in my life. As an act of my will, I submit my will to you and ask that you would teach me wholeheartedly to seek God with a heart that is devoted, committed, and faithful to him so that my mouth, lips, and heart become one with him. In Jesus' name, I pray. Amen.

Notes:

_____

_____

_____

_____

_____

_____

_____

_____

_____

Sunday, Day 1

(288) Life is much like a book. There are chapters of our life that we would soon rather forget and others that we would like to live in forever if we could. There are chapters that we would like to rewrite all over again if we could, but you will never move ahead or complete your mission and see what the outcome is if you don't turn the page. You cannot change what was in the past, so *forget about it and focus on what is ahead. It is time to turn the page and **forge** ahead by faith into the next chapter of your life.

Read Scripture:

Isaiah 43:18

Prayer:

Father God, I thank you that you are the Author and the Finisher of my faith. I thank you that you see the beginning, you see the end, and you even see the chapters of my entire life and everything in-between. I thank you that there is nothing in my past that can compare to what you are going to do for me now and in the future. As an act of my will, I turn the page and forge forward, placing my full trust in

---

* *Forge*—to move at a steady and persevering pace and increase speed.

you, knowing that what you have for me is extravagant, lavish, abundant, and without limitation. I receive it all in the precious name of Jesus. Amen.

Notes:

_____

_____

_____

_____

_____

_____

_____

_____

Monday, Day 2

(289) Are you experiencing *turmoil* on the inside? Is there a violent disturbance going on inside your mind? Has there been an interruption of your peace by utter confusion? Is there such commotion going on in your life that you are on edge all the time and you feel uneasy? You-yes, *you* have the power on the inside of you to speak peace to whatever it is that is causing you unrest. You have the power to be calm. Go ahead, speak it again and again. "Peace. Be still. I receive calmness." Command it with your God-given authority to cease.

Read Scripture:

Mark 4:39

Prayer:

Heavenly Father, I come before you now, thanking you for the authority that you have given me through Jesus Christ my Lord. Just as Jesus spoke to the atmosphere and the storm that was raging and he commanded it to be still, I use that same authority. I speak to the raging storm going on in the inside of me. I command every dark

---

* *Turmoil*—a state of confusion, disorder, uncertainty, or great anxiety.

and demonic force that is at work to cease in its operations against me. "I remind you that all authority has been given to me. I declare that you are stripped of your authority. You are rendered null, void, and powerless against me." I now receive the peace of God and calmness in my mind and heart. In Jesus' powerful name. Amen.

Notes:

_____

_____

_____

_____

_____

_____

_____

_____

_____

_____

Tuesday, Day 3

(290) The Bible tells us that a nation who chooses God is blessed. Pray for your leaders today that they will choose the Almighty God. Pray for the leaders of our nation to hear and obey God. Pray for the leaders of our nation to call upon the Holy Spirit to help them lead our nation. A nation and its people who put their trust in God will receive the **favor** of God. We desire a nation that will have God's favor and stay in the FOG. (Favor of God).

Read Scripture:

Psalm 33:12

Prayer:

Father God, I come to you now, and I pray for the leaders of our nation. I pray that you would draw them with your loving-kindness to yourself. I pray for their salvation and that labors would be sent forth to speak the gospel to them and that they would respond to your love by accepting Jesus as their Lord and Savior. I pray that you would pour out your Spirit upon them and give them godly wisdom

---

* *Favor*—an act of kindness beyond what is due or usual; or gaining approval, acceptance, or special benefits; or blessings.

in all of their decisions for our nation. Let them always look to you for guidance, putting their trust in you and not in man. Thank you for your divine protection over them and for the favor that they have with you. In Jesus' name, I pray. Amen.

Notes:

_____

_____

_____

_____

_____

_____

_____

_____

_____

Wednesday, Day 4

(291) Did you know that God never slumbers or sleeps? He never ever dozes off or is in an inactive state when it comes to watching over you and caring for you. He watches over you; and he keeps awake to guard, *protect,* or attend to you. So why are you losing sleep over trivial matters? Lay your head down and rest peacefully. God is your keeper, and he is never slack or negligent. He is and keen in fully watching over you. You are in good hands. You are in God's hands.

Read Scripture:

Psalm 121:3–4

Prayer:

Heavenly Father, I come to you in awe of your amazing love for me. What an absolute comfort it is to know that you never slumber or sleep concerning me, and that you are lovingly and caringly watching over me twenty-four hours a, day, seven days a week. You are a good Father who faithfully guards, protects, leads, and guides me; and I can trust you whole-heartedly. At the same time, I can rest peacefully without concern for my life because I am in your hands.

---

* *Protect*—to cover or shield from exposure, injury, damage, or destruction.

For this, I say thank you for being such a good God. In Jesus' name, I pray. Amen.

Notes:

_____

_____

_____

_____

_____

_____

_____

_____

Thursday, Day 5

(292) Every single day is precious and a gift from God. As you unwrap this gift called today and you watch it unfold in your life, make sure to share the beauty of it with others. Others need to hear what God is doing in your life to show them that there is so much to be thankful for. As you share your blessings, they will then be encouraged to look at today as a gift from God and that each day has blessings of heavenly proportions. *Proclaim* the goodness of the Lord, and bless his name while it is still called today.

Read Scripture:

Psalm 96:2

Prayer:

Heavenly Father, I give you thanks for the gift of today. There are some who did not make it to see another day, but I woke up breathing; and for this, I give you all of the praise! Today is a glorious day, and I will take time to share the beauty of this day with others that I come in contact with. I will remind them of your goodness and your kindness, and the very fact that they woke up to see another

---

* *Proclaim*—to praise or glorify openly or publicly.

day is in itself one of the greatest blessings that you have given to us. For this, we should show gratitude and thanks, and partake of the blessing that you have bestowed on us. All this we pray in the name of Jesus. Amen.

Notes:

_____

_____

_____

_____

_____

_____

_____

_____

_____

Friday, Day 6

(293) Whenever you face an obstacle or challenging circumstance, many times, discouragement will come and try to stare you down; and it will camp out if you let it. You can **deflect** it by considering and thinking carefully about all that the Lord has done for you in times past. Remembering how he brought you through the last trial and his faithfulness to you will remind you of why you put your trust in him. He has never failed you yet, and he never will.

Read Scripture:

   1 Samuel 12:24

Prayer:

   Father God, I come before you now. I have considered my ways, and I can see the times where I have allowed discouragement to camp at my place. I am sorry for allowing this to happen, and I ask you to forgive me. Thank you for your forgiveness as I receive it now. I stand in awe and reverence as I reflect back on what you have done for me in times of trial and great distress. You are indeed the true and faith-

---

* *Deflect*—if you deflect something, such as criticism or attention, you act in a way that prevents it from being directed toward you or affecting you.

ful God who has always been faithful to see me through, and never once have you failed me. For this, I thank you. In the mighty name of Jesus, I pray. Amen.

Notes:

_____

_____

_____

_____

_____

_____

_____

_____

_____

Saturday, Day 7

(294) As a believer in Christ Jesus, there may be times where others will say things to you that can be hurtful and make you feel excluded. They may tell you that you are too *extreme* about your faith, but in reality, we should not be too surprised because Jesus went through the same thing. He was persecuted to the *extreme for his convictions, and if others tell you that you are too *extreme, just lift your hands and thank the Lord. Be extreme for Jesus. After all, he went to the cross for you, and that is extreme.

Read Scripture:

Philippians 2:8

Prayer:

Heavenly Father, I come to you, giving you thanks for Jesus and his extreme love for me. Holy Spirit, help me to always remember that when others exclude me or persecute me because they feel that I am too extreme in my faith, that Jesus experienced the same thing. But all he wanted to do was please the Father, and he went all the way to the cross to accomplish the will of the Father despite being

---

* *Extreme*—utmost or exceedingly great in degree.

rejected, spit on, beaten, and killed. I thank you, Jesus, for going to the extreme for me and obeying the Father to the point of death. Amen.

Notes:

_____

_____

_____

_____

_____

_____

_____

_____

Sunday, Day 1

(295) Scripture tells us that anyone who remains devoted to the Lord, is committed, and has faith and confidence in him from the inside of his inner-most being will flow continual, uninterrupted rivers of living water. The definition of "river" in the dictionary is any abundant stream or flow that is smooth, graceful, and steady. These rivers are not just refreshing but are life giving, just as our Lord God is. Lay hands on your belly and *stir up** the river, for out of your belly will flow rivers of living water.

Read Scripture:

John 7:38

Prayer:

Father God, you said that if I am devoted and committed to you, and have faith and confidence in you that out of my inner-most being will flow rivers of living water. As an act of my will, I yield myself over to the Holy Spirit who is my help. Holy Spirit, teach me to be totally surrendered and given over to God's presence, worship, and the Word without limitations so that this life-giving water would

---

* *Stir up*—to move around, especially briskly; be active.

continually, without interruption, flow through me as a life source, so that I may bless the life of others as well. In Jesus' name, I pray. Amen.

Notes:

_____

_____

_____

_____

_____

_____

_____

_____

_____

Monday, Day 2

(296) Have you ever experienced a time growing up when someone bigger than you was picking on you, and your older brother or sister stepped in and took care of that bully for you? When the enemy sends the big bully of *fear,* just know that you have a Big Brother who is on your side; and when fear comes knocking on your door, he answers the door. Fear trembled and ran. God fights for you.

Read Scripture:

Deuteronomy 3:22

Prayer:

Father God, I come before you now, in awe of you, knowing that you are for me and not against me. And when the enemy comes against me, it is you that fights for me. I will not be afraid of those who come against me for your name's sake because you are my shield that stands in front of me, protecting me from all harm. When fear comes knocking, it is you who answers. Fear stands, trembles, turns,

---

* *Fear*—a fear is a strong emotion that something unpleasant might happen or might have happened.

and runs because of your magnificent power and authority. I will not fear because you are fighting for me. In Jesus' name. Amen.

Notes:

_____

_____

_____

_____

_____

_____

_____

_____

_____

Tuesday, Day 3

(297) Have you ever heard someone say that they are standing on the Word? What that means is they are standing upright, they are stable, and they are resisting being taken down and are resisting successfully, *withstanding* the storm or circumstance. They believe the Word; and are reading, and meditating on the Word and confessing the Word out of their mouth to the circumstance, confronting it fearlessly. They are standing in the wisdom of God. In order to be able to stand on the Word, you have to stay in the Word.

Read Scripture:

2 Chronicles 9:7

Prayer:

Heavenly Father, I come to you with a repentant heart, asking you to forgive me for standing in my own strength and not on your wisdom and strength that comes by reading, meditating, confessing, and believing your Word. I thank you for your forgiveness as I receive it now. Holy Spirit, I need you daily. I am asking you to help me. Be

---

* *Withstanding*—to stand up against or oppose with firm determination and to resist successfully.

my teacher and show me how to study the Word. Help me to meditate on it until it gets in my spirit so that I will begin to speak it in all circumstances and be able to stand on the Word of God, which is his will for my life. In Jesus' name, I pray. Amen.

Notes:

_____

_____

_____

_____

_____

_____

_____

_____

_____

Wednesday, Day 4

(298) A believer's walk is one where we trust God and obey his voice. It is a life where we desire to please God, and we do this by walking by faith. Every step with God is a step into a life that is good. Father does know best. When we refuse to listen and obey our Father, and we follow the plans of our *stubborn* heart, then we are stepping backward and not forward. It is one thing to say that you trust God, and it's another to actually trust him. Do you trust God?

Read Scripture:

Jeremiah 7:23–24

Prayer:

Heavenly Father, I come to you now, asking you to forgive me for the stubbornness of my heart in doing things my way instead of hearing and obeying your Word. I thank you for your forgiveness as I receive it now. Holy Spirit, I need you today and every day. As an act of my will, I submit and yield my will to you because you always lead me and guide me into all truth. I desire to move forward in God

---

* *Stubborn*—someone who is stubborn or who behaves in a stubborn way is determined to do what they want and is very unwilling to change their mind.

with God rather than letting my stubborn heart rule and take me backward. As I step forward, I am hearing and obeying God's Word, which is his perfect will for my life. In Jesus' name. Amen.

Notes:

_____

_____

_____

_____

_____

_____

_____

_____

_____

Thursday, Day 5

(299) When Jesus prayed, he desired that God's kingdom would come and his will be done upon this earth just as it is in heaven. How powerful is that? Jesus was God's *representative,* and when he spoke, he released heaven on this earth. God's Word is powerful and authoritative. You also are God's *representative here are the earth. When you know who you are in Christ and the authority of speaking God's Word, you are releasing heaven upon the earth, and God's kingdom is being established.

Read Scripture:

Matthew 6:10

Prayer:

Father God, I come to you in reverential fear, and I repent, first of all, for not seeing, knowing, and understanding that I am your representative here on the earth. I thank you for your forgiveness as I receive it now. Holy Spirit, you are my help, and I need you in my life. Show me who I am as a kingdom of God citizen and the legal

---

* *Representative*—standing or acting for another especially through delegated authority.

rights that have been given to me. Teach me about my God-given authority and reveal to me how to operate in this authority so that when I speak forth God's Word, his kingdom is being established here upon the earth. All of this I ask in Jesus' mighty name. Amen.

Notes:

_____

_____

_____

_____

_____

_____

_____

_____

_____

_____

Friday, Day 6

(300) Jesus has made an investment in you by his death and resurrection. When you accept him as your Lord and Savior, you are in fact investing your entire life by placing yourself in his hands. You are safe and secure, and he seals you with the Holy Spirit by placing the spirit of holiness on the inside of you. Guard this treasure on the inside of you and *invest* in the Spirit daily, where the returns are greater than great.

Read Scripture:

  2 Timothy 1:12–14

Prayer:

  Father God, I come to you, giving you thanks and praise for investing in my life by sending Jesus to pay the price for my sin and for my redemption and salvation that places me safely in your hands. Thank you for the precious Holy Spirit that resides on the inside of me and always reveals who you are and enables me to be all that you have called me to be. Holy Spirit, I treasure my relationship with

---

* *Invest*—if you invest time or energy in something, you spend a lot of time or energy on something that you consider to be useful or likely to be successful.

you, and I am asking you to show me who you are more and more as I invest in my time with you. Thank you that you reveal yourself to me in a greater way. I pray in Jesus' name. Amen.

Notes:

_____

_____

_____

_____

_____

_____

_____

_____

_____

Saturday, Day 7

(301) Jesus performed many miracles during his time here on the earth. There was **evidence** of these healings everywhere he went, yet there were critics all around him and Jesus faced harsh judgments. They were unbelieving, fault-finding, and skeptical people who were denying and doubting the true miracles of Jesus even though they saw it with their own eyes. God help us to not walk in unbelief and be like some who don't believe in miracles until they need one. Jesus is still the miracle worker.

Read Scripture:

John 12:37

Prayer:

Father God, I come before you now in all humility, asking your forgiveness for being skeptical and walking in unbelief, which is doubting you and is the opposite of faith. I thank you for your forgiveness as I receive it now. Holy Spirit, I need you. I am asking you to help me and show me how to walk in faith and by faith in God

---

* *Evidence*—evidence is anything that you see, experience, read, or are told that causes you to believe that something is true or has really happened.

because he is the same yesterday, today, and forever. He is a miracle worker today just as much as he was, through Jesus, when he walked the earth performing miracles. Holy Spirit, draw me to the Word of God because faith comes by hearing, and as I hear, faith comes and believes in the miracle working power of Jesus Christ, my Lord. Amen.

Notes:

_____

_____

_____

_____

_____

_____

_____

_____

Sunday, Day 1

(302) Many times, children are told not to *cry and that big boys and girls don't *cry. If you have been told this, I encourage you to let that lie go and release it now. The Bible tells us that we should *cry out* to God, meaning to verbalize; and even when we can't put it into words and we can't articulate clearly, then we can *cry out to God with a shout. Every single time we are in trouble, we should *cry out to God and call on him, not just on a 911 basis, but daily. Don't hold it in any longer. Go ahead and *cry out to God.

Read Scripture:

Psalm 86:3–7

Prayer:

Heavenly Father, I come to you now in sorrow, asking you to forgive me for believing the lie as a child that big boys and girls don't cry. I reject, renounce, and denounce that lie now in Jesus' name. Father God, your Word is truth, and you tell me in your Word that I can come to you daily if I am in trouble. I can cry out to you and that

---

* *Cry out*—if you cry out, you call out loudly because you are frightened, unhappy, or in pain. A shout, scream, or wail.

you bend your ear to hear me and answer me. Thank you for being my Father and that I can expect to hear from you when I cry out to you. In Jesus' precious name. Amen.

Notes:

_____

_____

_____

_____

_____

_____

_____

_____

_____

Monday, Day 2

(303) When negative emotions are in control, it is our flesh that is ruling, and not our spirit. When our spirit is ruling, we are in *communion* with God's Spirit, and we begin to operate by Christ's Spirit, thinking his thoughts and perceiving by the Spirit all things. We can only have the mind of Christ when we perceive by the Spirit, when we are guided by his thoughts and purpose, and when we possess his insight. It is spirit to Spirit.

Read Scripture:

1 Corinthians 2:16

Prayer:

Father God, I come to you now, giving you thanks for your Word which tells me that I have the mind of Christ. I also ask your forgiveness for allowing my flesh to override my spirit and be in control with negative emotions. Thank you for your forgiveness as I receive it now. Holy Spirit, I need you. I am asking for you to guide me into all truth as it is by my spirit communing with God's Spirit so that I can perceive and understand the mind of Christ and where my

---

* *Communion*—intimate fellowship.

thoughts begin to align themselves to his thoughts to possess all that
he has purposed for me in this life. In Jesus' name. Amen.

Notes:

_____

_____

_____

_____

_____

_____

_____

_____

_____

Tuesday, Day 3

(304) Do you have a heavy heart, or are you experiencing a great deal of sadness? Even in the dry spells that we go through in life, God sees us, and he reminds us that you will **reap** a harvest in joy for the tears that you have sown. It is all right to cry those tears unto God. Every tear that is sown is counted by him. God will bring rain to your drought-stricken circumstances, and you will reap his blessings. You will be able to laugh again and experience his joy.

Read Scripture:

Psalm 126:5–6

Prayer:

Heavenly Father, I come to you today, and I cry out to you with literal tears. But with every tear that falls, I thank you that the sadness falls with it. You take account of every tear that I shed, and as I release them to you, I thank you that you are going to bring life-giving rain to my drought-stricken circumstances. I receive this rain now, and I thank you that with it is the harvest of joy in place of every tear that I have cried. I declare that I will laugh again and experience the full-

---

* *Reap*—to get as a return, recompense, or result.

ness of joy as you have promised me in your Word. In Jesus' name. Amen.

Notes:

_____

_____

_____

_____

_____

_____

_____

_____

_____

Wednesday, Day 4

(305) Being a witness means to testify to the truth or genuineness of something. You are a living witness that God is the true and living God, and that there are no other gods before him or after him. Your very life is evidence, or proof, and an example to others around you. God has chosen you for a special purpose, and you attest, or affirm, that God is true and genuine by your very life becoming saved and becoming a new creature in him. All can see the *transformation** of your life. Can I get a faithful witness?

Read Scripture:

Isaiah 43:10

Prayer:

Heavenly Father, I come to you as a believer, admitting to you that I have not always been a faithful witness, and for this, I repent and ask for you to forgive me. I thank you for your forgiveness as I receive it now. Holy Spirit, you always testify of the Father, and only say and do what you hear him say and do. Holy Spirit, I am asking you to help me to live my life as proof of the new creature that God

___

* *Transformation*—change in form, appearance, nature, or character.

has made of me when I accepted Jesus as Lord and Savior. Let the transformation of the inward man be seen in outward actions in all that I say and do so that the true and living God will be evident to everyone that I come into contact with. In Jesus' name, I pray. Amen.

Notes:

_____

_____

_____

_____

_____

_____

_____

_____

_____

Thursday, Day 5

(306) Why is it that God always gets a bad rap, so to speak, when bad things happen in life? Why do we tend to place a negative, undeserved reputation on him when we go through challenges in life? What it comes down to is we have embraced and believed a lie instead of the truth. Scripture tells us that everything that God does is right. He is holy, and all of his ways are just. He is *gracious* and kind in all of his ways, and all of his works are stamped with love because that is who he is.

Read Scripture:

Psalm 145:17

Prayer:

Father God, I come in humility to your throne of grace today, asking you to forgive me for believing lies about you when I go through trying circumstances. I renounce, denounce, and reject the lie that I have believed and received about you that is causing bad things to happen to me. I render the lie to be null, void, and power-less in my life. Thank you for your forgiveness as I receive it now. I

---

* *Gracious*—merciful or compassionate.

declare your goodness and your kindness; and that all of your works are right, just, true, and good because that is who you are. You are a good God, and I worship you today. In Jesus' name. Amen.

Notes:

_____

_____

_____

_____

_____

_____

_____

_____

_____

Friday, Day 6

(307) Through the gospel or good news, the righteousness of God is revealed to us, or it is laid out in open view and made known to us. It comes from faith, and it *unveiled* to us in ways that stirs up and awakens even more faith. The righteous, honest, true, and faithful One, which is you, is living by faith, in faith, and through faith. We are obtaining true life by faith. I'm just living by faith. What about you?

Read Scripture:

Romans 1:17

Prayer:

Father God, I thank you that faith is not a singular event that happens just once, but it is a way of living. I was made righteous by faith in Jesus Christ; therefore, I shall live by faith. I thank you that you take me from faith to faith, and that you are revealing yourself and manifesting yourself to me as my faith in you is lifted upward. Holy Spirit, help me to always pursue the true and righteous God

---

* *Unveiled*—made evident or manifest or proved without doubt or question.

without drawing back or retreating from him, but let my faith in him be stirred and awakened. In Jesus' name, I pray. Amen.

Notes:

_____

_____

_____

_____

_____

_____

_____

_____

_____

Saturday, Day 7

(308) When someone has been *disloyal* to us, we must be careful not to look at God the same way. God is not like man, and he is loyal and unwavering in his love and affection toward us. He will not desert you. Neither will his loving-kindness for you cease. He will not turn a deaf ear to your prayer because your prayer and his mercy always go hand in hand.

Read Scripture:

Psalm 66:20

Prayer:

Heavenly Father, I come to you with a heart of repentance for all the times that I have unjustly felt as if you had let me down, or when I accused you of not hearing or answering my prayer. I thank you for your forgiveness as I receive it now. Holy Spirit, I need you, and I am asking you to teach me to draw near to God and to know him as the God that is loyal and unwavering in his love for me. Teach me, Holy Spirit, to know deep within me that when I do pray to

---

*   *Disloyal*—not loyal or faithful; deserting one's allegiance or duty.

God, his mercy, compassion, and kindness that he shows me is real and true. Show me how to receive it. I pray in Jesus' name. Amen.

Notes:

_____

_____

_____

_____

_____

_____

_____

_____

_____

Sunday, Day 1

(309) We are told in Scripture that Jesus is the light of the world. The world is a very dark place, and we need Jesus to *illuminate* our way. How does he do this? It really begins when we watch and observe, when we pursue and adhere or listen to his teaching, and when we go in the same direction as him. When we do this, we are enlightened spiritually and are given insight and clarity. We are able to understand and made aware of what is really going on instead of being in the dark, murky, unknown, and dark hidden things. Jesus *illuminates my whole day. Do you have the light of life?

Read Scripture:

John 8:12

Prayer:

Heavenly Father, I thank you that in this dark world that I live in, you have given to me Jesus who is the Light of life. Holy Spirit, I am asking you to help me. Give me a hunger and desire to study the

---

* *Illuminate*—if you illuminate something that is unclear or difficult to understand, you make it clearer by explaining it carefully or giving information about it.

scriptures and to know Jesus in a more intimate and personal way so that I know him and hear him in a greater way. I pray for the spirit of revelation to unveil the hidden things so that I am aware of what is really going on and that I know how to pray and proceed as Jesus illuminates my way. Amen.

Notes:

_____

_____

_____

_____

_____

_____

_____

_____

Monday, Day 2

(310) You are the *beneficiary* of all the benefits of God, but unless you see yourself as the or recipient of his blessings, you will never be able to receive them. When Jesus died, he willed everything to you, and the only conditions to receiving all that he left you is that you must know that you are the designated one that these benefits belong to. You must know what these benefits are, and you must receive them by faith because they are legally yours.

Read Scripture:

Psalm 68:19

Prayer:

Heavenly Father, I come to you, thanking you for your Word which says that you are the God of my salvation that loads me down with your benefits every single day. Because of my faith in what Jesus has done for me through salvation, I am the designated recipient, or receiver, of all of your benefits. Holy Spirit, I need you, and I am asking you to show me as I study the Word of God all the benefits and

---

* *Beneficiary*—the beneficiaries of a will are legally entitled to receive money or property from someone when that person dies.

promises that are written in God's Word that legally belong to me as his child. I thank you for every one of those benefits as I receive them by faith. In Jesus' name. Amen.

Notes:

_____

_____

_____

_____

_____

_____

_____

_____

_____

Tuesday, Day 3

(311) Are you burdened today with something that is emotionally difficult to bear? Are you loaded down with difficulties or responsibilities that are taking a toll on you, mentally, emotionally, and physically? It is time to *discard,* reject, and let loose of that burden, and place it on God's shoulders. Give those burdens to God. Once you have done that, then he will pull you up and hold you upright again. He will not allow you to be shaken. He will not let you slip and fall.

Read Scripture:

Psalm 55:22

Prayer:

Heavenly Father, I come running to you today with every single burden that you never intended for me to carry, and I throw it down at your feet. I let it all go, and I lose it from me now. I place it upon your shoulders as my burden bearer. Thank you for the release of all stress, anxiety, and worry as I have given the heavy load to you. Thank you for standing me upright on my feet again. I can trust in you that you will not allow me to be shaken or to slip and fall as long

---

* *Discard*—to cast aside or dispose of; get rid of.

as I am bringing all those burdens to you. For this, I say thank you.
In Jesus' name. Amen.

Notes:

_____

_____

_____

_____

_____

_____

_____

_____

Wednesday, Day 4

(312) When you are ill and the doctors say that what you have is *incurable* and they have done all that they can for you, do not lose heart. Those things that are impossible with man are possible with God. Jesus, who was wounded for your transgressions, bruised for your iniquities, and the chastisement of your peace was upon him, it is by his stripes that he took for you that you are healed. Don't be afraid to ask God to heal you, but when you do, be willing to read, study, meditate, and speak the scriptures daily as you would take the prescription medicine that the doctors would give you.

Read Scripture:

Luke 18:27

Prayer:

Heavenly Father, I come to you now in the name of Jesus. You said in your Word that the things that are impossible with man are possible with you. So right now, I come to you, thanking you that Jesus redeemed me from the curse. This sickness on my body is a

---

* *Incurable*—not likely to be changed or corrected and to be fatal, terminal or inoperable.

curse, so I speak according to your Word that it is by the stripes of Jesus Christ that I am healed. I renounce, denounce, and reject sickness and disease. I command it to leave my body. Holy Spirit, as I study the Word of God, meditate on it, and speak it over my body, I thank you that you are working a cause and effect of healing in my body and that your Word is medicine to all of my flesh. I declare this by faith. In the name of Jesus. Amen.

Notes:

_____

_____

_____

_____

_____

_____

_____

_____

_____

Thursday, Day 5

(313) Peace means freedom from disturbance. It also means *tranquil-ity,** calmness, and freedom from disquieting or oppressive thoughts or emotions. Peace means having harmony in personal relations; and freedom from quarrels and disagreements. Today, I say to you. "Peace be with you."

Read Scripture:

   Psalm 122:8

Prayer:

   Heavenly Father, I come to you, giving you thanks and praise for your perfect peace today. I declare that your peace on the inside of me quiets all thoughts and emotions that are oppressive and that do not line up with your Word, which is your will for me. As an act of my will, I determine today that my personal relationships will be free from quarrels and disagreements and that perfect peace on the inside of me will cause me to walk in harmony with others. I thank you, Father, for your peace today. In Jesus' name. Amen.

---

* *Tranquility*—a disposition free from stress or emotion.

Notes:

Friday, Day 6

(314) The heroes of faith that the Bible talks about in Hebrews *subdued* kingdoms, and this is a testimony to their faith in God and an example for us to follow. When you fasten your faith to the promises of God, you can accept abundant royal promises. The word "fasten" means to become attached, fixed, or joined; so when you join your faith or attach yourself by faith and fix yourself firmly to the promises of God for you that are written in the Bible or Word of God, then you can obtain or succeed in possessing every promise that God has given you.

Read Scripture:

Hebrews 11:33

Prayer:

Heavenly Father, I thank you for the heroes of faith who were godly examples of those who walked by faith. By faith, they subdued kingdoms, stopped the mouths of lions, and obtained your promises. I come to you now by faith and in faith, and I attach myself to every

---

* *Subdue*—to bring under control by physical force, persuasion, or other means; overcome.

promise that you have for me in your Word, which is your will for me. I declare that I am strong in faith, and that I walk by faith and not by sight. I fix myself firmly to your promises and possess them now. In Jesus' name. Amen.

Notes:

_____

_____

_____

_____

_____

_____

_____

_____

_____

Saturday, Day 7

(315) Many times in Scripture, it tells us that God is our help. The definition of help is "to give material or financial aid." It means to provide relief. It also means to alleviate the *burden* by giving assistance. To help also means to give aid to you to make something easier for you. When we understand that God is there to help us, we can rejoice and offer him songs of joy and delight. What more can be said except that God is your help, if you ask him and if you let him.

Read Scripture:

Psalm 63:7

Prayer:

Father God, I come before you today, first of all, asking you to forgive me. I did not realize how many times in Scripture you say that you are my help, and because of that, I have not come to you, asking you for your help. Forgive me for doing things on my own when you were always there to help me. I thank you for your forgiveness as I receive it now. Holy Spirit, I need you in my life, and I am asking you for your help. Teach me how to ask God for help when I

---

* *Burden*—something that is emotionally difficult to bear or carry.

need his help, and show me how to receive God's help, knowing that he wants to and will help me when I come to him and ask him. In Jesus' name, I pray. Amen.

Notes:

_____

_____

_____

_____

_____

_____

_____

_____

_____

Sunday, Day 1

(316) The Bible tells us that God is love. God's love is transmissible by direct or indirect contact, and it can be transmitted or sent from one person to another. It can be imparted to others with your words or even a kind gesture. If you are a believer who truly loves God, then you are a *contagious* Christian, and the infectious love of God is being spread by you wherever you go. God is love and love is you.

Read Scripture:

    1 Corinthians 8:3

Prayer:

    Heavenly Father, I come to you now in the name of Jesus, thanking you for your love toward me while I was yet a sinner. You sent Jesus Christ to die for me and to redeem me from the previous state of sin that I was in. I thank you that because you are love and you are in me, that same love that you showed me I can show to others. I declare that your love is shed abroad in my heart and that this love cannot be contained within me, but it must be released to others. In Jesus' name. Amen.

---

*   *Contagious*—transmitted by direct or indirect contact.

Notes:

_____

_____

_____

_____

_____

_____

_____

_____

_____

Monday, Day 2

(317) In the beginning, Adam and Eve lived in a very perfect world without sin, lack, sickness, disease, poverty, danger, etc. But when they disobeyed God, a *curse* was placed upon the earth and everything in it. If you have accepted Jesus as your Lord and Savior, then you have been redeemed, and Jesus has set you free from the *curse. In other words, you have been pardoned or released from punishment, wrongdoing, fault, or disfavor from God. You are forgiven, and you are no longer under the *curse because of Jesus Christ. Thank him for redeeming you from the curse.

Read Scripture:

Galatians 3:13

Prayer:

Heavenly Father, I come before you now with a heart of gratitude and unending praise because of what you have done for me. I declare with my mouth that Jesus is indeed my Lord and my Savior, and he has redeemed me from the curse and anything under the curse. Jesus has pardoned me from the punishment of my sin and

---

* *Curse*—a source or cause of evil and to afflict with great evil.

took it upon himself and paid my debt for me. Thank you, Jesus, that you hung on that cross and took from me sickness, disease, lack, poverty, fear, shame, guilt, and disfavor. Because of you, I have favor with God again. Amen.

Notes:

_____

_____

_____

_____

_____

_____

_____

_____

_____

Tuesday, Day 3

(318) As for God, he is *perfect,* and all of his ways are *perfect and without defect or blemish. He is faultless and excellent in all respects. What a mighty God you serve. His Word has been tested, tried, and proven true. He is your shelter, and when you turn to him and hide yourself in him, he will wrap himself around you, giving you full shelter, protection, care, and security. How perfect is that?

Read Scripture:

Psalm 18:30

Prayer:

Father God, I come to you now, in awe of your goodness and your kindness to me. You are glorious and magnificent in all of your ways, and there is no one else like you. Your Word has been tested, tried, and proven true; and I know that I can rely and depend on you. As an act of my will, I yield and surrender to the Holy Spirit and trust him to lead and guide me into all truth. Thank you, Father God, that you are my strong shield and buckler, and when I turn to you and hide myself in you, I am protected, cared for. You wrap yourself

---

* *Perfect*—being without defect or blemish, flaw, or imperfection.

around me and cover me on all sides, and I am secure in you. For this, I thank you. In Jesus' name. Amen.

Notes:

_____

_____

_____

_____

_____

_____

_____

_____

Wednesday, Day 4

(319) Scripture tells us in Luke chapter 18 that there was a rich ruler who asked Jesus how he could inherit eternal life. Jesus told him to sell everything he had, give it to the poor, and follow him instead. The man was very sorrowful because he did not want to give up his riches. Jesus said it was hard for the rich to enter into heaven, but that it was not impossible. God is not against you being rich for he is the one who gives you the ability to succeed. However, do not let riches *rule* over your heart and separate you from God but rather build his kingdom with the use of your riches.

Read Scripture:

Luke 18:18–24

Prayer:

Father God, I come to you, giving you thanks and praise for your many blessings. I know and understand that you have given me the ability to succeed in all that I do and that it is only by your grace that I have indeed been blessed. Holy Spirit, I need you, and

---

* *Rule*—if something rules your life, it influences or restricts your actions in a way that is not good for you.

I am asking you to always be the center of my life. Lead and guide me in every decision that I make concerning the wealth that God has blessed me with. I pray that you would remind me to always seek first God's kingdom and his righteousness, and lead me in all investments made for the sake of the kingdom of God and for his glory. In Jesus' name, I pray. Amen.

Notes:

_____

_____

_____

_____

_____

_____

_____

_____

_____

Thursday, Day 5

(320) Scriptures give us warning that we are not to believe every spirit but that we are to try the spirits whether they are from God or not because many false prophets have gone out into the world. Scripture goes on further to tell us that every spirit that does not confess that Jesus Christ has come in the flesh is not of God—and this is the spirit of *antichrist.* Know that you have the Greater One living on the inside of you, and he is greater than he that is in the world. Do not fear what is to come but rather get to know God. Get to know him by his Word.

Read Scripture:

1 John 4:3–4

Prayer:

Father God, I come to you now, thanking you for Jesus who is the Greater One that lives on the inside of me and for the Holy Spirit who is the one who leads and guides me always into all truth. Help me, Holy Spirit, to rely and depend on you in these last days. Help

---

* *Antichrist*—a disbeliever in Christ or one who actively denies or opposes Christianity.

me to correctly test and try every spirit, whether it be of God or not, and give me the discernment to know the difference. I declare that I do not have to fear for great is my God who lives and resides on the inside of me. In Jesus' wonderful name. Amen.

Notes:

_____

_____

_____

_____

_____

_____

_____

_____

_____

Friday, Day 6

(321) Be careful when trying circumstances come your way and your faith in God is tried. Do not allow a pessimistic attitude where you expect only bad outcomes to happen. Do not let the circumstances dictate to you and take you out of faith. Do not allow your thoughts to run rampant and take you away from hope to *hopelessness.* You have the strength of God to make it through, and you have everything to live for. So shake off that pessimistic Eeyore syndrome of gloom and doom.

Read Scripture:

Job 6:11

Prayer:

Heavenly Father, I come before you now, asking you to forgive me for thinking thoughts that are pessimistic where I expect the worst outcome in difficult circumstances. Thank you for your forgiveness as I receive it now. I shake off all pessimism and doom and gloom right now, renounce it, and break all agreement with it. Holy

---

Hopelessness—the despair you feel when you have abandoned hope of comfort or success.

Spirit, I need you, and I am asking you to help me draw on God's strength during this time. I choose to hope and believe in God and for the best outcome according to my faith in God alone. I trust him in this and through this; and I put my trust, faith, and hope in him. In Jesus' name. Amen.

Notes:

_____

_____

_____

_____

_____

_____

_____

_____

_____

Saturday, Day 7

(322) Are you walking with God? The Bible tells us that how can two walk together unless they have agreed to meet. The word "meet" means to make arrangements to come into another's presence. So first of all, have you placed yourself in his presence? He is there, waiting. Second is the word "*agreement." This word is powerful when you understand it. The word *agreement" means to be in harmony or one accord. It is a covenant between you and God. Are you in *agreement* with God and his Word? The power of agreement with God is not him agreeing with you, but you agreeing with him. After all, he is God. How can you walk with him, in step with him, together if you do not agree to meet and align yourself with him and his Word?

Read Scripture:

Amos 3:3

Prayer:

Heavenly Father, I come to you now in all humility, asking you to forgive me for saying that I am walking with you, but not fully

---

* *Agreement*—a covenant between God and his people in which God makes certain promises and requires obedience in return.

understanding what that means until now. I thank you for your forgiveness as I receive it now. Holy Spirit, I need you, and I am asking you to help me to make it a priority to come into God's presence, worshipping him, thanking him, and studying his Word, which is his will for my life. Holy Spirit, help me to align my life with God and his Word. As I meditate on God's Word, give me revelation, knowledge, and understanding so I can align my words and my life to his Word, to be in covenant and harmony with him, so that I am walking with God in unity and one accord. In Jesus' name, I pray. Amen.

Notes:

_____

_____

_____

_____

_____

_____

_____

_____

_____

Sunday, Day 1

(323) We are told that we have an adversary or an opponent, enemy or foe, who attacks us. His name is Satan; and he comes only to kill, steal, and destroy. But Jesus defeated him, making a public spectacle of him. Now get this picture in your mind; Jesus victoriously made our adversary, or Satan, to crawl on his hands and knees, laid him low to the ground, and paraded him around like a whipped puppy as a defeated enemy. Now it is up to you to set the devil straight by enforcing the Word of God over your adversary because he is subject to the *authority* of the Word of God. All power and *authority has been given unto you. Know your authority in Jesus Christ.

Read Scripture:

Luke 10:19

Prayer:

Father God, I come before you, declaring that you have given unto me the power and the authority over the adversary who comes only to kill, steal, and destroy. I thank you for the authority that is in the name of Jesus. So in the name of Jesus Christ, I take authority

---

* *Authority*—the right to command and control.

right now over Satan, and the demons, principalities, powers, and wickedness in high places. I declare every one of your plots, plans, and schemes against me are rendered ineffective. I remind you that Jesus, the Son of God, was manifest to destroy your works so you are defeated; and I remind you of that defeat as I plead the blood of Jesus Christ that defeated you over my home and my family, over my call, and over my life and the life of my loved ones. I take my seat of authority over you, Satan, and I command you to take your hands off me, my family, and all that God has blessed me with. In Jesus' powerful name. Amen.

Notes:

_____

_____

_____

_____

_____

_____

_____

_____

_____

Monday, Day 2

(324) God keeps covenant with the upright that walk before him wholeheartedly. In the heavens, upon the earth, or even beneath the earth, there is no one like him. God always keeps covenant and will never break it. We must be *determined* in our heart to continue to keep covenant with God and walk upright before him. Love on both parts is what binds us in this covenant with God. There is no one like our God.

Read Scripture:

  1 Kings 8:23

Prayer:

  Father God, I come to you now, thanking you for your continued love for me and for always keeping your covenant. I am asking you to forgive me for the times where I have half-heartedly walked with you and have not wholeheartedly walked upright before you. Thank you for your forgiveness as I receive it now. Holy Spirit, I need you, not just today but every day. Teach me and reveal to me

---

* *Determined*—if you are determined to do something, you have made a firm decision to do it and will not let anything stop you.

this wonderful covenant with God that I may understand it with my whole heart so that I may decisively walk before him in true covenant with him. In Jesus' name, I pray. Amen.

Notes:

_____

_____

_____

_____

_____

_____

_____

_____

_____

Tuesday, Day 3

(325) The Bible tells us that God's grace is *sufficient,* meaning it is adequate or that it is enough. God's grace is when he enables you to be all that he created you to be and when he empowers you to do all that he has called you to do. No matter what difficulty you are going through right now, just remember that before you were formed in your mother's womb, you were loaded with God's grace to make it through your entire life. God already knew what you would go through, and he provided enough of his grace for you to get through it. His grace is enough.

Read Scripture:

2 Corinthians 12:9

Prayer:

Heavenly Father, I come before you now, giving you thanks and praise for your sufficient grace. Thank you that you gave me what I needed to make it through every single day, hour, and minute of my life no matter what I go through. You have enabled and empowered

---

* *Sufficient*—if something is sufficient for a particular purpose, there is enough of it for the purpose.

me to be all that you have called me to be and to do all that you have created me to do. For this, I will be eternally grateful. Thank you for your grace that is sufficient for me. In Jesus' name, I pray. Amen.

Notes:

_____

_____

_____

_____

_____

_____

_____

_____

_____

Wednesday, Day 4

(326) When you pray, do you know that it is Father God's delight and that it pleases him greatly? For those of you who have children, we know how proud we are when they do or get acknowledged for something they did, or when they receive a reward, trophy, medal, etc. for finishing well. We *delight* in our children, pat them on the back, and shout it from the rooftops that this is our child. Every time that you pray, remember how pleasing it is to your Father God and that you are his delight.

Read Scripture:

Proverbs 15:8

Prayer:

Father God, I come to now in prayer and communicate with you my heartfelt desire, which is to please you. Father, I desire to see your will be done on earth as it is in heaven. I pray for your will, plan, and purpose in my life; and I set myself in total agreement with your Word, which is your will for my life. Holy Spirit, I need you, and I am asking you to teach me how to pray for the will of the Father

---

* *Delight*—extreme pleasure or satisfaction.

according to his Word. Establish my heart in total agreement with God and his Word in order to see his kingdom come. In Jesus' name, I pray. Amen.

Notes:

_____

_____

_____

_____

_____

_____

_____

_____

_____

Thursday, Day 5

(327) Scripture tells us that no weapon that is forged, whether fraudulently, counterfeit, falsified, or formed against the righteous will prosper or succeed and that every tongue that rises up against them in the seat of judgment shall be proven to be in the wrong. People may use their tongue as a weapon against you, but it will not prosper. God will *vindicate* you, so do not take matters into your own hands but let God handle it.

Read Scripture:

> Isaiah 54:17

Prayer:

Father God, in the name of Jesus, I come before you now, thanking you that no weapon that is formed against me shall succeed, and every tongue that rises against me to judge me that is counterfeit will not prosper and will be proven to be in the wrong. Thank you that vindication comes from you alone, Lord; and you will clear me of all accusation, blame, suspicion, or doubt with proof. Therefore, I give

---

* *Vindicate*—to clear of accusation, blame, suspicion, or doubt.

it all to you, knowing that you represent me and will bring vindication for me. In Jesus' name. Amen.

Notes:

_____

_____

_____

_____

_____

_____

_____

_____

WEEK 47

Friday, Day 6

(328) Draw near to God, hear all that God shall say, and speak forth what God says, not what we feel or what we think, but what his Word tells us. Speak for that which he says. Not one single word of his will fall to the ground without it producing his destiny in your life or in the life of others. God's Word has power to bring into *fruition** his plans and his purpose. His words are life producing, so speak forth God's word and let them drop like seeds everywhere you go.

Read Scripture:

Deuteronomy 5:27

Prayer:

Father God, as I spend time in your Holy Word and draw near to hear what it is you have to say, I declare that your Word become living and active on the inside of me, discerning my thoughts and the intent of my heart. Your Word shows me the areas of my life where I need change, allowing you to make the adjustments as I yield to the Holy Spirit. I thank you, Holy Spirit, for showing me truth always,

---

* *Fruition*—if something comes to fruition, it starts to succeed and produce the results that were intended or hoped for.

for developing within me the seeds of God's fruitfulness, and for giving me the boldness and grace to speak forth his word, which produces life and sows seeds of goodness wherever I go. In Jesus' name, I pray. Amen.

Notes:

_____

_____

_____

_____

_____

_____

_____

_____

_____

Saturday, Day 7

(329) The more time that you spend in getting to know God by spending time in his presence, praising and worshipping, studying the Word, and living according to it, his word becomes so ingrained on the inside of you that his word can't help but *emerge* from your mouth. It changes you internally and will manifest outwardly. The psalmist David said that the eternal God spoke through him. This comes from a very personal and intimate relationship with God. Loving God, knowing him, hearing him, and obeying him makes you a likely candidate for God to speak through you. What you put into you will eventually come out.

Read Scripture:

2 Samuel 23:2

Prayer:

Heavenly Father, I come to you now, giving you thanks and praise for your amazing faithfulness toward me. Thank you for the Holy Spirit who is my help. Holy Spirit, I am asking you to help me. Give me a hunger and a desire in my heart to make time and be

---

* *Emerge*—to come forth into existence to radiate.

with God's presence, praising, worshipping, studying the Word, and praying, so I may be drawn to a place of deep intimacy with him. I pray that this deep relationship with God transform me internally to a degree that his Word pours forth from my lips, continually speaking of him so that he may speak through me. In Jesus' name, I pray. Amen.

Notes:

_____

_____

_____

_____

_____

_____

_____

_____

_____

Sunday, Day 1

(330) Have you ever needed *help* in your life and you reached out to others, but no matter who you called, no one answered or was available? And then just when you were about to give up, that one person called you back, and it was the right person with the encouragement or *help that you needed. You then thought to yourself how glad you were that he or she was the one who answered your call. Scripture tells us that our help is in the name of the Lord. His name is Jesus, and all you have to do is say that name. When no one else answers your call for *help, you can call on his name, Jesus, and he will send *help your way.

Read Scripture:

Psalm 124:8

Prayer:

Heavenly Father, I come to you now, thanking you for Jesus. Thank you that in situations that seem hopeless, all that I have to do is call on the name of Jesus, and he is there to help me in any and all

---

* *Help*—to save, rescue, or assist. To do something with or for someone that he cannot do alone.

circumstances. When no one is there to take my calls or is available to help, I can cry out to Jesus, and I can depend on that wonderful name of Jesus who is my help. He will send assistance to me whenever and wherever I am, and for this, I give you thanks and praise. Amen.

Notes:

_____

_____

_____

_____

_____

_____

_____

_____

_____

Monday, Day 2

(331) A *secret* is something that we may be able to keep others from knowing and can hide it well within ourselves, but with God, he knows all things, including the secrets of our heart. Sometimes, these *secrets can really bring us harm as we walk around as an undercover Christian, as this *secret eats us up on the inside. Since there is nothing that is hidden to God or from God because he is omniscient and knows all anyway, why not come out from under the covers and willingly bring it to God so that he can deliver you from any and all *secrets that are hidden?

Read Scripture:

Psalm 44:21

Prayer:

Heavenly Father, I come before you now with my whole heart, and I am asking you to reveal and uncover those secret or hidden things within me that are harmful and not beneficial for my life. I willingly submit all of those things that you reveal to me that were hidden within me, and I ask you for your forgiveness as I receive it

---

* *Secret*—something that is kept private to oneself and is hidden from others.

now. Thank you that there is nothing hidden that won't be revealed and brought to the light. Any and all darkness that has tried to hide from you is now exposed to the light, and I am set free and delivered from its affects. I thank you for never rejecting me, but instead you have set me free. In Jesus' name. Amen.

Notes:

_____

_____

_____

_____

_____

_____

_____

_____

Tuesday, Day 3

(332) Many of you already know the scripture in Psalm 37:23, which says, "The steps of a good man are ordered by the Lord." But we are going to take it one step further. When God's Word is in your heart or spirit by consistent time studying, meditating, and speaking the Word of God, which is his will for you, then you become surefooted. This means that you are designed to hold well to the road or path. You will not swerve or turn aside from the straight path and change course when trouble comes, but you will remain steady. Not one of your steps will falter, slip, or slide from God's ways. There will be no side stepping or *backsliding* when God's Word is engraved on your heart.

Read Scripture:

Psalm 37:31

---

* *Backsliding*—a return to former bad habits or vices from a state of virtue and failing to do something they promised or agreed to do, or have started again doing something undesirable that they had previously stopped doing.

Prayer:

Father God, I come before you now, asking you to forgive me for allowing distractions and other things to draw me away from time with you and time in studying your Word. I thank you for your forgiveness as I receive it now. Holy Spirit, you are my help, and I am asking you to help me to prioritize the things of God that are vitally important to daily living. As an act of my will, I take time to study God's Word without interruption or distraction because it is his Word, which is his will for me. I desire for God's will to be accomplished in my life so that instead of an unstable Christian, I become a surefooted Christian whose steps are firm, secure, and unwavering. I will not falter, fail, slip, or backslide. In Jesus' name, I pray. Amen.

Notes:

_____

_____

_____

_____

_____

_____

_____

_____

_____

Wednesday, Day 4

(333) God cannot and will not ever violate his covenant with you. He has given you his word, his Holy Word, and he cannot ever take back the words he has already spoken. He cannot alter or change a single word that he has uttered from his lips. He has given you his precious promises, and he cannot and will not ever withdraw even one of them. His promises are non-negotiable and are not even open to discussion to be modified or changed. He cannot break covenant with you because he is not a promise breaker, but a promise keeper. He is a covenant keeping God, and everything that he has promised you is *irrevocable* and rightfully belongs to you. Receive! "Receive" means to be the person who gets (something sent or transmitted) to take, to accept, to have.

Read Scripture:

Psalm 89:34

Prayer:

Heavenly Father, I come before you now, giving you thanks and praise for the covenant God that you are! Every word that you have

---

* *Irrevocable*—cannot be changed or reversed.

spoken has been established and cannot be changed. Your promises for me are absolute and are not to be doubted or questioned. Your word is free from limitations, and I place no restrictions on them. By faith, I set myself in agreement with your Word, and I am positioned to receive every one of your promises for me. I thank you that I can expect everything that you have said will come to pass in my life because you are a promise keeping God. For this, I thank you. In the name of Jesus, I pray. Amen.

Notes:

_____

_____

_____

_____

_____

_____

_____

_____

_____

Thursday, Day 5

(334) The Bible says that not one of God's thoughts or even his purposes can be restrained. The definition of "purpose" is "the reason for which something is done or created or for which something exists." When you were born, God intended a desired and good result for you. Scripture says that none of God's purposes can be restrained. However, you can inhibit or prevent his purposes in your life when you try to control, limit, or when you don't take the liberty or make the choice to follow his lead. Realize and *attain* his purpose for you.

Read Scripture:

Job 42:1–2

Prayer:

Heavenly Father, I come before you now, humbled by the truth of your Word that tells me that I was born for a reason and that you intended me to fulfill your good purpose. As an act of my will, I submit to the Holy Spirit and take off the limits by following his leading

---

* *Attain*—to reach in the course of development or growth, and to reach and be successful.

into the full purpose that you have for me, and to obtain and attain to my God-given purpose this day. In Jesus' name. Amen.

Notes:

_____

_____

_____

_____

_____

_____

_____

_____

Friday, Day 6

(335) If you know that sin is in your heart, and you do not repent and turn from it, you do absolutely nothing about it, and you *ignore* it altogether, it will surely keep the Lord from hearing you. Don't close your eyes to your sin or cozy up to it, but instead, our sin must be acknowledged by us. We must then confess it to God, repent, turn, and walk away from it with the intent of never doing it again.

Read Scripture:

Psalm 66:18

Prayer:

Father God, I come to you now with a heart that is ready to acknowledge my sin before you. I repent for my sin against you, and I ask you to forgive me for ignoring my wrong-doing. I confess it before you now, and I thank you for your forgiveness as I receive it now. I turn my heart back to you, God. I ask for the Holy Spirit to help me recognize and bring to light any sin that I need to acknowledge and repent on a daily basis so that it does not separate me from

---

* *Ignore*—to fail or refuse to notice.

you. I thank you for your love, your mercy, and your forgiveness, and for never giving up on me. In Jesus' name, I pray. Amen.

Notes:

_____

_____

_____

_____

_____

_____

_____

_____

Saturday, Day 7

(336) We live in a day and age where people give to many charities with either monetary support or volunteering their time, skills, and resources to the cause that they believe in. The Bible tells us that when you take up the Lord's righteous cause by living morally, just, and right, and to be honest, pure, ethical, and virtuous, that the Lord himself takes pleasure in your prosperity. It is a " *cause-and-effect*" relationship. When we take up his righteous cause, we reap the effect, and God cannot help but bless us.

Read Scripture:

Psalm 35:27

Prayer:

Heavenly Father, I come to you, giving you thanks and praise for your grace that enables me to have a right relationship with you. I also thank you that it is the same grace that you give to me that I can live morally, ethically, honest, pure, and right before you, upholding your righteous cause daily. I thank you for giving to me the precious

---

* *Cause and effect*—a "cause and effect" relationship is a relationship in which one event, the cause, makes another event happen, the effect.

Holy Spirit who helps me by guiding me, leading me, and showing me your truth, and who empowers me to live upright before you. In Jesus' holy name. Amen.

Notes:

_____

_____

_____

_____

_____

_____

_____

_____

_____

Sunday, Day 1

(337) The world's standards say that crying is a weakness, yet the Bible tells us time and time again that anytime you are experiencing deep sorrow, *suffering,* or pain, you can and should cry out to God. God hears you when you cry out to him, and he answers those cries. Don't be ashamed to cry out to God in your distress.

Read Scripture:

Psalm 18:6

Prayer:

Heavenly Father, I come to you now, asking you, first of all, to forgive me for being ashamed and embarrassed, and thinking that crying is a weakness according to the world's standards. I thank you for your forgiveness as I receive it now. I come to the realization that I am not to live according to the world's standards but according to your Word, which is your perfect will for me. I thank you that you are a God who hears me when I cry out to you in my distress and that in you, I can find comfort, relief, peace, and strength. I ask you, Holy

---

*   *Suffering*—pain, agony, hardship, misery, anguish, torture, discomfort, affliction.

Spirit, to help me to continue to turn to the true and living God who always hears and answers my cries. In Jesus' name, I pray. Amen.

Notes:

_____

_____

_____

_____

_____

_____

_____

_____

_____

Monday, Day 2

(338) Many times when we **falter,** fall, or fail, we are so inclined to give up and turn away from our faith. Scripture tells us that the just man may fall seven times, the number 7 being perfect and complete, and we fall short from being perfect. Nevertheless, we rise up again and again and again. If you are in that state right now where you have fallen, or failed, and you are about to quit, I speak to you. "Rise up!"

Read Scripture:

> Proverbs 24:16

Prayer:

> Heavenly Father, I come to you now, thanking you that you alone are the one who gives me the strength when I have faltered, fallen, or failed. According to Scripture, you said that a just man falls seven times, and he rises again. So as an act of my faith, I take your hand that reaches out to me now, and I pull myself up and rise up out of every failure, every mistake, and every imperfection that has

---

* *Falter*—to lose strength or momentum. When you lose your confidence and stop doing something or start making mistakes.

tried to keep me down. I rise again, depending on your grace to get me through. In Jesus' name, I pray. Amen.

Notes:

_____

_____

_____

_____

_____

_____

_____

_____

_____

Tuesday, Day 3

(339) As a believer, many times we have asked God to reveal himself to us as if he was going to appear and show himself right before us with our natural eyes that we see with. God is the invisible God that we cannot see, but when he reveals himself to us, it is usually through his Word, which is his perfect will for us. *Revelation* is when God takes what he has and makes it known to us, and it is not taught by man. He gives us insight into his own nature and purpose for mankind. *Revelation comes from encounters or meetings with God. Take time to meet with God.

Read Scripture:

Galatians 1:12

Prayer:

Heavenly Father, I come before you, first of all, repenting for my negligence in not taking the time to come into your presence, spend time in worship, study your Word, pray, and get to know you as you would like me to. I thank you for your forgiveness as I receive

---

* *Revelation*—a divine revelation is a sign or explanation from God about his nature or purpose.

it now. Holy Spirit, I am asking you to help me to be sensitive when I am being drawn by the Father's loving-kindness to spend time with him because he does want to make himself known to me in a very intimate and personal way. Thank you that I can expect him to reveal himself and give me insight into his character, his nature, and also for him to show me his purpose, not just for me, but for all of mankind. In Jesus' name, I pray. Amen.

Notes:

_____

_____

_____

_____

_____

_____

_____

_____

_____

Wednesday, Day 4

(340) In the scriptures, Jesus was talking to the Jews; and as he was speaking, there were many who believed him. That means that they believed that he was the Son of God and that they believed that the Father had sent him. He told them that if they continued in his Word, they were indeed his disciples and the truth would make them free. Free from what? From their sin, and free from the *religiosity* that kept many of the religious Jews bound and from seeing that he was sent by the Father. If you believe that Jesus is the Son of God and the Father sent him, and you continue in his word, then you are free indeed.

Read Scripture:

John 8:36

Prayer:

Father God, I come to you now in the name of Jesus, the one and only Name by which man can be saved. I believe that Jesus is the Son of God and that he was sent by you, Father, to set me free from

---

* *Religiosity*—if you refer to a person's religiosity, you are referring to the fact that they are religious in a way that seems exaggerated and insincere or hypocritical.

my sin. I believe that Jesus is the only way, the only truth, and the life. As I continue in your word, Father God, I am set free from man's religiosity that keeps man bound, and from knowing you as the truth and I am free indeed. I thank you for setting me free in the wonderful name of Jesus Christ, my Lord. Amen.

Notes:

_____

_____

_____

_____

_____

_____

_____

_____

_____

Thursday, Day 5

(341) The hand of the Father is continually on your life. Because of his loving-kindness for you and toward you, he will never abandon you. God will work out the plans that he has for your life, so do not be *concerned* that he will walk away from the wonderful things that he has started in your life. He remains faithful to complete what he has started. If he can strike your foes with one hand and save you with his other hand, know that he will work out every detail of your life and will work it all out for you. Be secure in his love for you.

Read Scripture:

Psalm 138:8

Prayer:

Father God, I come to you now in full surrender, knowing that you will perfect those things that concern me or that I am worried or troubled about. I thank you that you will never abandon or leave me or give up on me and that you will work out the plans for my life that you have destined for me. According to Psalm 138:8, you are the God that can strike my foes with one hand and save me with the

---

* *Concerned*—uneasy or anxious. Worried or troubled.

other hand. I can rest assured that I am secure in you, knowing that you will bring to a completion all the wonderful things that you have started in me. And for this, I give you thanks and praise. In Jesus' name. Amen.

Notes:

_____

_____

_____

_____

_____

_____

_____

_____

Friday, Day 6

(342) Because of misunderstandings, we can allow the enemy to come in through strife and confusion, and bring discord. Sometimes, you can be put in a position where you feel like you have to defend yourself, but it is a wise move to take a step back from the situation and look to God. You don't have to say a word to defend yourself because God is your *defender,* and in the end, the truth will come out and you will be vindicated. Ask God to give you the wisdom to handle the situation the way that he would want you to and that his outcome would prevail over the enemy's scheme.

Read Scripture:

Psalm 5:11

Prayer:

Heavenly Father, I come to you in total submission, asking you to help me to look within and examine my own self, and to repent for any part that I have played in allowing the enemy to bring discord in the body of Christ. For this, I am truly sorry, and I ask you to

---

* *Defender*—to support in the face of criticism and to keep you safe from danger, attack, or harm.

forgive me. I thank you for your forgiveness as I receive it now. Holy Spirit, I need your help. I am asking you to help me to exercise the fruit of self-control and give me the wisdom to know when to speak and when to step back, allowing God to work through the situation to bring about the resolve that he would desire. Give me the strength to hold fast to God and to respond the way that he would want me to, knowing that there is an outcome that can be totally directed by him, bringing about his result to the situation and his peace. In Jesus' name, I pray. Amen.

Notes:

_____

_____

_____

_____

_____

_____

_____

_____

_____

Saturday, Day 7

(343) Every one of us has done things that has brought guilt, embarrassment, and *shame* on us. One of the greatest lies of the enemy is when he reminds us of it, making us feel ashamed all over again as if it was something that we have just committed. In times like this, remember that Jesus took all that shame on himself and crucified it on the cross and that now you can look up and place all of your hope in God, as he is the Glory and the One who has lifted you up out of that shame forever.

Read Scripture:

Psalm 3:3

Prayer:

Heavenly Father, God, I come to you boldly in the name of Jesus, declaring that you are the Glory and the lifter of my head! Jesus has taken all shame, embarrassment, and guilt upon himself for me and has crucified it when he died on the cross for me. So I take the

---

* *Shame*—a painful emotion caused by the belief that one is or is perceived by others to be inferior or unworthy of respect because of one's actions, thoughts, circumstances, or experiences.

authority over shame; and I renounce, denounce, and break all agreement with it. I render it powerless in my life and the life of my children and my children's children. In Jesus' redeeming name! Amen.

Notes:

_____

_____

_____

_____

_____

_____

_____

_____

_____

Sunday, Day 1

(344) We all have heard it said that God is love. The very essence of his being is love for mankind. The same love which we heard of was what drew us to him when we first accepted Jesus as our Lord and Savior, and it is the same love that lives on the inside of us that emanates from us. The love of God on the inside of you is what draws people to him. God's love *abounds* and abides in you, so give them his love the same way that he loved you.

Read Scripture:

1 Thessalonians 3:12

Prayer:

Heavenly Father, I come to you now, giving you thanks for your precious, unconditional love toward all of mankind. I declare that your abounding love is on the inside of me as I live for you. It flows through me and spills over into the lives of others. Today, I will allow myself to share your love with those that I come into contact with by acts of kindness and gestures that will demonstrate your love toward them. In Jesus' name, I pray. Amen.

---

* *Abound*—to be rich or well supplied with.

Notes:

Monday, Day 2

(345) The God of all creation, the One who made the land and sea, and created everything in it from the smallest of creatures to all of humankind is able to care for you. There is nothing that you are going through that he does not understand; he is able to care for you. Your *problem* is not too big for God. If he made the heavens and the earth, don't you think that he is able to handle all of your problems?

Read Scripture:

Jeremiah 32:17

Prayer:

Father God, you are the almighty and powerful God, the Creator of all creation. You made the heavens and everything in it, and you made the earth and all that is in it, including mankind. According to your Word, there is nothing too hard for you; therefore, I bring all of my problems to you, knowing that you are more than able to resolve anything that I am facing. As an act of my will, I choose to take all of the problems that I have been trying to deal with on my own, and I

---

*   *Problem*—a matter or a situation regarded as unwelcome or harmful and needing to be dealt with and overcome.

lay them down before you and release them into your hands. I thank you for your perfect peace that keeps me from taking it all up again, putting my full trust in you. In Jesus' name. Amen.

Notes:

_____

_____

_____

_____

_____

_____

_____

_____

Tuesday, Day 3

(346) *Faithfulness* is one of the greatest values in any relationship. Without it, many are left feeling betrayed, abandoned, and forsaken. When trust is broken, relationships are destroyed because of unfaithfulness. Our God, however, is faithful to us even when we are not faithful to him. Scripture tells us that his *faithfulness* toward us is great and that his faithfulness to us is new every morning.

Read Scripture:

Lamentations 3:23

Prayer:

Heavenly Father, I come to you, giving you thanks and praise for your faithfulness that is new toward me every single day. Every morning, when I rise to see another day, you are there for me, and with me, to face the day. You are my reliable God, and I can depend on you to be unchangeable toward me despite of my shortcomings. Thank you for your unconditional love that remains the same for me day after day. For your faithfulness, I am very grateful. In Jesus' name. Amen.

---

* *Faithfulness*—dependable, reliable, and loyal.

Notes:

Wednesday, Day 4

(347) You are stronger than you think you are! Scriptures tell us that you are strong in the Lord and in the power of his might. Apart from him, you can do nothing; but when you are in union with the Lord Jesus, you are supernaturally **infused* with his power flowing in and through you. You can stand through any force of warfare that you are facing from evil forces. Draw your strength from him today and allow his supernatural strength to rule your life and walk in victory.

Read Scripture:

Ephesians 6:10

Prayer:

Father God, I speak forth your word according to Ephesians 6:10 declaring, "I am strong in the Lord and in the power of his might." Even though all the forces of evil have come against me, I am infused and filled with your supernatural power and strength to stand against these forces of evil. I overcome by the blood of Jesus Christ and my testimony, which is that Jesus has defeated my enemy,

---

* *Infused*—to fill or cause to be filled with something or permeated to flow throughout.

making a public spectacle of him. So I stand firm in my position of victory that was won for me through Jesus Christ, my Lord. Amen.

Notes:

_____

_____

_____

_____

_____

_____

_____

_____

_____

Thursday, Day 5

(348) When you are lacking physical strength, you are faint and lacking in vigor or mental strength, and you are feeling fragile, there is no better time for you to turn to God's Word. The Word of God will *uphold* you when you're weak in your knees. God's Word will speak to your mind and your heart; and it will take you by your arms and lift you up, strengthen you, and elevate you above any hopeless situation that you are facing. He will keep you from sinking or falling.

Read Scripture:

Job 4:4

Prayer:

Heavenly Father, I come before you now. Although I have been hit hard and am being whirled about and in danger of falling from the blow, but as an act of my will, I come to you, and I look to your Word which strengthens my feeble knees right now. I declare that your Word speaks truth to my mind and stirs up within me faith to therefore reach out and lift my arms to you, knowing that you will lift me up to rise above this hopeless situation. I speak to my feeble

---

* *Uphold*—to prevent from falling or sinking. To lift up and keep elevated.

knees and command them to be strong. I confess that my God is able to keep me from falling and sinking, and he causes me to stand elevated above it all. For this, I give you thanks and praise. In Jesus' name. Amen.

Notes:

_____

_____

_____

_____

_____

_____

_____

_____

_____

Friday, Day 6

(349) God has promised you that he will enlarge the path beneath your feet, making your feet so *secure** that you will be able to stand firmly and tread safely on paths of testing and trouble. Your feet will not slip under you because every step will be securely fixed and fastened so that you will not fall. Keep on trusting in God and stepping on because each step you take is one more step into your victory.

Read Scripture:

Psalms 18:36

Prayer:

Heavenly Father, I come before you now, thanking you that according to your word in Psalm 18:36, you have made my feet firm and secure in you and that through times of testing and trouble, you enlarge and broaden my path so that I will not slip and fall. Thank you that my steps are protected and guarded by you from danger and attacks, and in very step that I take, I trust you and declare the victory in my life. In Jesus' name. Amen.

---

* *Secure*—firm; not liable to fail. Protected and guarded. Free from danger or attack.

Notes:

_____

_____

_____

_____

_____

_____

_____

_____

_____

Saturday, Day 7

(350) We have seen how time changes all things around us. One of the greatest sayings you will hear from our elders is, "Back in the day." "Back in the day" refers to how things were for them then, and now all they have is the precious memories to remind them of how it was. Although this is true of the way things change year by year and from generation to generation, one thing remains the *same* and never changes. His name is Jesus. Then, now, and tomorrow, he is the same.

Read Scripture:

Hebrews 13:8

Prayer:

Father God, according to Hebrews 13:8, Jesus is the same yesterday, today, and forever. I thank you that he is the one person whose character is unquestionable throughout all generations. Everything about him is constant, consistent, and eternally changeless, always. I thank you because I find great comfort in the name of Jesus. Amen.

---

* *Same*—being one without addition, change, or discontinuance. Unchanged in character, condition, etc.

Notes:

Sunday, Day 1

(351) When we place high expectations on ourselves, or others, and fail to meet those expectations, you would be considered a *perfectionist.* A *perfectionist is one who is nit-picky and a stickler, always looking for flaws, demanding no mistakes from self and others. Perfectionism causes one to have unrealistic expectations and often looks to man for approval instead of looking to God and live to please him who is himself perfect. God certainly knows that you are not perfect, so how can you expect that from others?

Read Scripture:

Psalm 18:32

Prayer:

Father God, I come before you now, asking first for your forgiveness for having a perfectionist attitude and placing unrealistic expectations upon myself and others to perform or be perfect, when you yourself are the only perfect one. I thank you for your forgiveness as I receive it now. Father, I thank you for your great love and

---

* *Perfectionist*—someone who is displeased with anything that is not perfect or not meeting quite often impossible standards.

for sending Jesus into a sinful, imperfect world to redeem us and save us from our self and from eternal death. I am blameless in your sight because of Jesus and not of anything I have done, for you are just and perfect in all of your ways. For this, I am grateful. In Jesus' name. Amen.

Notes:

_____

_____

_____

_____

_____

_____

_____

_____

_____

Monday, Day 2

(352) God's Word is his resume. You can look back at what he did for the Israelites and stand in awe of how God walked with them, talked to them, and moved on their behalf with many miracles. Yet they refused to rely on him, trust in him, and obey him. Why? Because they were a *stubborn* and rebellious generation who did not prepare their heart to know and follow God, and their spirit was not faithful to God. God never poured out his entire wrath on them because it would have destroyed them. God showed his mercy toward them time and time again. Because of Jesus Christ, we do not have to encounter wrath from God, only his mercy and his compassion. However, you can legally open the door to the enemy and let him in when you become stubborn and rebellious against God. Satan comes to kill, steal, and destroy. Is the door wide open for the enemy to attack you? Then repent for being *stubborn and rebellious, and shut that door.

Read Scripture:

Psalm 78:38

---

* *Stubborn*—someone who is stubborn or who behaves in a stubborn way is determined to do what they want and is very unwilling to change their mind. They are unreasonably or perversely unyielding.

Prayer:

Heavenly Father, God, I come to you now in the name of Jesus, and I bow before you in all humility. I am grieved by my attitude and my actions. I repent to you now, asking for you to forgive me for rebelling against you as my forefathers did by not putting my confidence in you and not keeping your Word, but doing things my own way independently and apart from you. I thank you for your mercy, compassion, and forgiveness as I receive it now. I boldly renounce, denounce, and break agreement with the spirit of rebellion and my own stubbornness right now; and I render it null, void, and powerless. I shut the door on it now, declaring that it no longer has the legal right to operate in my life. Holy Spirit, you are my help, and I need you now to help me to live a devoted life to God who wants the best for me. As an act of my will, I yield and surrender to you, Holy Spirit, as my Guide, my Teacher, and my help to incline my ears to the words of my God with a teachable heart, willing to learn with the intent to obey and live according to God's Word which is his will for my life. In Jesus' name, I pray. Amen.

Notes:

_____

_____

_____

_____

_____

_____

_____

_____

Tuesday, Day 3

(353) We can all agree that standing fast in the Lord is not a challenge when things are going good in your life. The real test to stand firm in your belief in God really comes to light when you are faced with trouble that tries your faith in God. Faith comes by hearing and hearing by the Word of God. You must give yourself over to the Word of God continually because it causes you to grow in faith. When your faith becomes strong, you can walk in *relentless* faith no matter what trouble comes your way.

Read Scripture:

Philippians 4:1

Prayer:

Father God, I come to you now, and as an act of my will, I yield my will over to the Holy Spirit who is my help and who guides me into all truth. Holy Spirit, as I give myself over to hear and study the Word of God, and as I meditate upon it and confess it out of my mouth, strengthen me inwardly to stay consistent and continually in God's will, which is his Word. I declare relentless faith in God's

---

* *Relentless*—firmly, often unreasonably immovable in purpose or will.

Word, standing fast and immovable in all that God says and all that he has for me. In Jesus' name, I pray. Amen.

Notes:

_____

_____

_____

_____

_____

_____

_____

_____

_____

Wednesday, Day 4

(354) What seemed impossible for the Israelites was not too hard for God. With God on their side, they passed through the Red Sea and went to the other side, and their enemies who went after them to destroy them were destroyed instead. Don't *waver* in your faith, but always stand strong, believing and confessing that you are going to make it to the other side of the problem that you are facing. Take your eyes off your problem and off your enemies, and look to God and his strength. Follow his lead, and he will defeat your enemies for you as you continue to move ahead. Confess that you are going to the other side.

Read Scripture:

Hebrews 11:29

Prayer:

Father God, I thank you for the heroes of faith who did not waver in their faith in you, but believed that you would do for them what you said that you would do. I hold on to my faith in you, God,

---

* *Waver*—to move back and forth in an unsteady way; or to become unsteady because of weakness, emotion, tiredness, etc.

as the Author and the Finisher of my faith. I do not abandon or give up my rights as your child, but I confess with my mouth and believe in my heart that I am going to the other side of this problem that is before me. And that on the other side, I claim my victory in the mighty name of Jesus Christ. Amen.

Notes:

_____

_____

_____

_____

_____

_____

_____

_____

Thursday, Day 5

(355) One of the saddest things to hear a born-again Christian say when they are going through difficulty is this; "It's just the hand that life dealt to me." That statement is of someone who seems to have already been *defeated* and who has accepted it, embraced it, and has given up all hope. Whatever hand the devil tries to deal to you, remember that you already have the winning hand. Let your confession be, "I will not be defeated by this, and I will not quit." "I have the victory through Jesus Christ, my Lord!"

Read Scripture:

1 Corinthians 15:57

Prayer:

Heavenly Father, I come to you, giving you thanks and praise for your Word, which is truth. I confess with my mouth that Jesus is my Lord, and through him, I conquer defeat and stand in victory over all forces of darkness. Any hand the enemy tries to deal to me, I have already obtained the winning hand, and victory is mine. I do not embrace or accept defeat, and I will not quit because Jesus is the

---

* *Defeated*—conquered and destroyed.

Greater One who lives on the inside of me. He always causes me to triumph over all the power of the enemy. I am more than a conqueror through Christ Jesus. Amen.

Notes:

_____

_____

_____

_____

_____

_____

_____

_____

_____

Friday, Day 6

(356) When David defeated Goliath, Joshua fought the battle of Jericho, and Daniel faced the lions in the lion's den, they all had one thing in common. They had put their trust in God, and they were strong in the Lord. They took courage not in their own strength, but in their God's mighty strength. God was with them, and God is with you. So do not be *dismayed* because you do not have to face this alone. God is on your side, and with him, you can face anything.

Read Scripture:

2 Chronicles 32:7

Prayer:

Heavenly Father, I thank you that I can find encouragement and strength in your Word, which tells me that I am not facing any battles or hard circumstances on my own and that you are with me by my side in every hard time, including unwelcome attacks that come against me. I am not alarmed or moved from my place of peace in you because you are the Greater One that is with me. I am not

---

* *Dismayed*—experiencing or showing feelings of alarmed concern or being upset, worried, agitated, because of some unwelcome situation or occurrence.

intimidated by the outcome because, God, you are for me and not against me. I put my trust in you. In Jesus' name. Amen.

Notes:

_____

_____

_____

_____

_____

_____

_____

_____

_____

Saturday, Day 7

(357) Set your heart right each day by coming to God, giving him thanks for at least one thing he has done for you or he has given you. A thankful heart will always lead you to worship him for who he is to you. He is the one who is there for you no matter what. He will never leave you nor forsake you, and he is never far from you. After you spend time worshipping him, pray for your family, your friends, your pastor, all the saints, and leaders of the government. If you do not know what to say, then just ask God to bless them. Once you have unselfishly put others before you, then bring your requests to him and wait *expectantly* for him to manifest the answer to all of your prayers. He hears and he answers.

Read Scripture:

Psalm 5:3

Prayer:

Father God, I come before you today, giving you thanks for another day. Thank you that today is a day of promise and covenant. Thank you for my family and my friends. Bless them, keep them

---

* *Expectantly*—one who waits earnestly or fervently for something to happen.

from all harm, and bless their day. I ask you to strengthen my pastor today, and bless him and his family and meet their needs. I pray for all government leaders today: the president, the vice president, the congress, the senate, and the local government. I ask for your laborers to be sent to them and make their hearts receptive and responsive to the gospel of truth. Jesus, draw them to a right relationship with you through your saving grace. Help our leaders to put you first place, God, and to make right decisions based upon seeking you, first and foremost. Give them godly guidance and wisdom in all things. Father, I now lay all of my cares and needs before you, thanking you for being a good God who meets every one of my needs according to your riches and glory in Christ Jesus. Thank you for hearing all of my prayers as I expectantly wait on you to manifest the answers to each of them. In Jesus' name. Amen.

Notes:

_____

_____

_____

_____

_____

_____

_____

_____

_____

Sunday, Day 1

(358) I think that we can all agree when I say that no one enjoys hearing someone *boast* about themselves. When God begins to grow you in character, he is doing this so that you can rightly handle his greater glory. A mature Christian will not *boast in himself because he knows that he is nothing without him and that there is no boasting in the presence of God. You are growing and going from glory to glory.

Read Scripture:

1 Corinthians 1:29

Prayer:

Father God, I come before you now, asking for your forgiveness for the times where I have been boastful about the things that I have accomplished or done. I realize that it is prideful, and I repent for the sin of pride. I thank you for your forgiveness as I receive it now. Holy Spirit, I need you, and I am asking you to continue to teach me about humility and giving honor to God in everything that I do

---

* *Boast*—to speak with exaggeration and excessive pride, especially about oneself.

so that I may grow in character and go from glory to glory. In Jesus' name, I pray. Amen.

Notes:

_____

_____

_____

_____

_____

_____

_____

_____

_____

Monday, Day 2

(359) Reflect on all of the wonderful things that God has done for you. As it comes to your mind, just take a few minutes, lift your hands, and tell him thank you. Thank him for doing what you could not do for yourself. Thank him for his *loving-kindness** toward you, your children, and your children's children. God has done marvelous things for you, and he deserves to be thanked and praised.

Read Scripture:

Psalm 107:31

Prayer:

Heavenly Father, I come before you now without asking for anything. Today, I just want to tell you thank you for all that you have done for me. As I reflect on my walk with you, I think about your goodness, your kindness, and your faithfulness toward me. Thank you for all the wonderful things that you have done for me and my family, and for taking care of us like the good Father that you are. I lift my hands to you today and praise you for you are worthy of

---

* *Loving-kindness*—tender kindness motivated by or expressing affection.

all the praise, the glory, and the honor that is due your magnificent name. Amen.

Notes:

_____

_____

_____

_____

_____

_____

_____

_____

_____

Tuesday, Day 3

(360) We have all heard someone say, "It's my way or the highway." One may think that his way is the best way or that it's the only way until they realize they were wrong. God desires the best for you because he is a good God. Be willing to give up doing things your own way, which may seem good to you, and *accept* that God's way is better. The benefits of obeying his ways far outweigh doing it in our strength and having it our way.

Read Scripture:

Proverbs 14:12

Prayer:

Heavenly Father, I come to you now, asking you to forgive me for seeing things one way, which is not always best for me. Thank you for your forgiveness as I receive it now. Holy Spirit, I need you, and I am asking you to take the lead as I willingly surrender my will to you today. Guide me, direct me, and show me God's best for me so that I can live in his perfect will for my life. Thank you, Father, that you are a good God, and you desire to give me the best. I receive

---

*   *Accept*—to receive willingly and to agree to take.

all that you have for me by doing it your way, and I relinquish doing things independent from you. In Jesus' name, I pray. Amen.

Notes:

_____

_____

_____

_____

_____

_____

_____

_____

_____

Wednesday, Day 4

(361) Anger is a natural human emotion, but when it is not controlled, it can be destructive and can bring serious damage to relationships. Because it increases blood flow and adrenaline, it can cause high blood pressure, affecting your physical health. Anger is not a bad thing if you know how to express your feelings and when you find a solution to the problem that caused it in the first place. It's perfectly normal to feel angry when you've been mistreated or wronged. Anger becomes a problem when you express it in a way that harms yourself or others. *Suppressing* anger can also have damaging effects. One must take ownership of their anger by first taking a time out, stepping back, and waiting it out until you are not fuming; then you can calmly confront others by talking it out or by expressing your feelings and listening to the other person as well. Take time to research and find some coping skills that will help you handle your anger instead of letting anger sit and rest on your lap.

Read Scripture:

Ecclesiastes 7:9

---

* *Suppressing*—to keep it in and not expressing, or choke back and be silent about it.

Prayer:

Heavenly Father, I come before you now with more of an understanding about anger and how it can affect my life when it is not handled correctly. Thank you that you have given to me the Holy Spirit who is my help. Holy Spirit, I am asking you to teach me how to respond in situations where anger is stirred within me. Help me not to suppress the anger, but teach me how to confront it by talking it out with the person that I am angry at. Holy Spirit, as I research the resources that are available to me on how to better cope with anger, I trust you to always lead me to what is true and beneficial for me. Thank you, Holy Spirit, that I do not have to fear dealing with uncontrolled anger because you are with me to help every step of the way so that anger does not sit and rest on my lap, but is confronted and dealt with in healthy ways. In Jesus' name, I pray. Amen.

Notes:

_____

_____

_____

_____

_____

_____

_____

_____

_____

Thursday, Day 5

(362) In order for God to fulfill his will for our life, we must come to an understanding of what his will for us is. Faith is the reality of God's will based on the revealing of his Word. Because God is very watchful over his Word and he attends to it, he is awake, and alert, and he *hastens* to perform it, accomplish it, do it, and fulfill it, we must be in total agreement with his Word. In order to know what God's will is for you, then it is vitally important to study God's Word, or the Bible, so that God can reveal himself to you, making known his will for you in a very personal way. When you begin to get revelation of what God's will is for your life, then you can begin to live according to it, knowing that he will accomplish it in your life.

Read Scripture:

Jeremiah 1:12

Prayer:

Father God, I come to you now, thanking you for your Word, which is your will for my life. In your Word is every promise that

---

* *Hasten*—to cause to happen quickly. To speed up or accelerate, move, or act swiftly.

you have given to me as your child. Holy Spirit, I need you. I am asking you to give me a greater desire and hunger for God's Word to know and understand what God says in his Word for me personally. Holy Spirit, as I take and make time to read, study, and meditate on God's Word, teach me how to study in depth. Give me revelation and wisdom to carry it out and execute it in my own life so that God can perform, accomplish, and fulfill every single promise that he has for me. In Jesus' name, I pray. Amen.

Notes:

_____

_____

_____

_____

_____

_____

_____

_____

_____

Friday, Day 6

(363) God is in every detail of your life, and his hand is upon you. So much so that he has *planned* your future, and the plans that he has for you are good and promising. It is something you can look forward to. Even if there seems to be no one else rooting for you or cheering you on, take heart because God is always on your side.

Read Scriptures:

Psalm 139:5

Prayer:

Heavenly Father, thank you that you've gone into my future to prepare the way, and in kindness, you follow behind me to spare me from the harm of my past. With your hand of love upon my life, you impart a blessing to me. And I thank you that every day, I can look forward to your goodness toward me. In Jesus' name. Amen.

---

* *Planned*—a proposed or intended course of action or blueprint.

Notes:

Saturday, Day 7

(364) Do you remember hearing the story about the three little piggies growing up? Two of the three little piggies were *lazy.*† One built his house out of straw, the other built his out of sticks, but the third was wise and took the time and energy to build his out of bricks. The Big Bad Wolf huffed and puffed and blew the straw house down, but the little piggy escaped and ran to the house of the piggy that had built his house out of sticks. The Big Bad Wolf came, and he huffed and puffed and blew that stick house down, but the two little piggies escaped and ran to the third little piggy's house which was built out of brick. The Big Bad Wolf came, and he huffed and puffed, and he huffed and puffed again and again; but because the house was built with bricks, it was so strong that he could not blow it down. The Big Bad Wolf then tried to crawl down through the chimney with the intention of catching the three little piggies to eat them for dinner, but instead, the three little piggies put a pot of boiling water under the chimney. The wolf fell right in, and the three little piggies ate him for dinner. The moral of the story is this: a life built upon Jesus Christ will stand firm in the end times against all attacks of the enemy, also known as the wolf Satan.

---

† *Lazy*—lax, inactive, and not willing to work. Idle, negligent, sluggish, and slothful. If someone is lazy, they do not want to work or make any effort to do anything.

Luke 6:46–48 says, What good does it do for you to say I am your Lord and Master if what I teach you is not put into practice? Let me describe the one who truly follows me and does what I say. He is like a man who chooses the right place to build a house and then lays a deep and secure foundation. When the storms and floods rage against that house, it continues to stand strong and unshaken through the tempest, for it has been wisely built on the right foundation."

We can learn from the third little piggy about taking the time to build our lives on the teachings of Jesus Christ. The Bible has answers to every problem that man faces. There are godly solutions found in scriptures for us, but we need to seek them out. There are no shortcuts, and laziness is unacceptable. In the end, when the storms of life beat down on your house, all will see the kind of foundation your house and life was built on. Make time daily to come to God in his presence, always giving him thanks, and worship him with your whole heart. Spend time studying his Word, which is his perfect will for you. In doing this, your life will be built on the foundation of Jesus Christ and will stand firm, strong, and relentless through every test, trial, and storm that comes to beat upon your home. When your life is built upon Jesus, the Cornerstone, nothing you go through and no one can move you from that secure place in him.

Read Scripture:

Luke 6:48

Prayer:

Heavenly Father, I come to you this day, admitting that my heart has been pricked or pierced, causing me to feel sorrow and remorse for being negligent and slothful when it comes to serving you wholeheartedly. Forgive me for allowing laziness to set in and pull me away from your presence and my intimate time with you. In godly sorrow, I ask you to forgive me for not making the effort to spend time with you in order to get to know you and learn from you the things that are vital to my life. I thank you for your forgiveness as I receive it now.

Holy Spirit, you are my help. As an act of my will, I submit my life to you, and I yield myself to your guidance. Thank you, Holy Spirit, that you always lead me on the path of righteousness for his name's sake. Holy Spirit, I cannot do this without you. I give you my hand, and I am asking you to lead me into the green pastures where I can feed on God's Word and where my soul can be restored. Renew the joy of my salvation in his presence where I can always find fullness of joy. Reveal to me the secrets of God's kingdom. Give me revelation knowledge and understanding as I study the Word of God, and show me how to apply his Word to my life. Give me stoutness of heart, uncompromising strength in my inward man, and the desire for more of God's presence as he draws me with his loving-kindness that I would decrease, and he would increase in me so that I would live for him, and he would live through me. All of this I ask in the precious name of Jesus Christ. Amen.

Notes:

_____

_____

_____

_____

_____

_____

_____

_____

_____

Sunday, Day 1

(365) For those who have traveled out of the country, we know that you have to have a passport to cross over from one country to another; and without it, you will not be allowed to enter that country. If you ask people if they want to go to heaven, a high majority of them will say "yes" or "I hope so." No one can come to the Father, who is in heaven, except they enter through a union with Jesus first. Heaven is the *destination* of every believer who has accepted Jesus Christ as their Savior, and he is the only accepted passport for anyone to get into heaven. Are you ready for *destination heaven?

Read Scripture:

John 14:6

Romans 10:9–10 says, If you shalt confess with thy mouth the Lord Jesus, and shalt believe in your heart that God hath raised him from the dead, thou shalt be saved. For with the heart man believeth unto righteousness; and with the mouth confession is made unto salvation."

---

* *Destination*—the place to which a person or thing travels or is sent to.

Prayer of Salvation:

I believe that Jesus Christ is the Son of God and that he died for all of my sins. I believe that on the third day, he rose from the dead and is seated at the right hand of God the Father. I am a sinner in need of forgiveness for everything that I have done, so I come to you, God, asking you to forgive me for all of my sin. Right now, I receive the forgiveness that was paid for by Jesus Christ, and I now ask Jesus to come into my heart and be my Lord and Savior. Today, I receive my pardon and salvation through Jesus Christ; and because of this union that I now have with him, I am assured of my destination, which is heaven, where I will be with the Father forever for I am a child of the Most High God. Amen!

Notes:

_____

_____

_____

_____

_____

_____

_____

_____

_____

ABOUT THE AUTHOR

Laurie Deanna Fisher is a native of Colorado and presently resides in Aurora, Colorado, with her husband of twelve years, Glenn Fisher. She has a blended family of six children, eighteen grandchildren, and four great-grandchildren. Laurie received Jesus Christ as her personal Lord and Savior in 1984, when she was twenty-three years old. This decision has changed her life immensely, and she has found great fulfillment in serving the body of Christ in many capacities. Laurie and her husband have pastored a church for three and a half years in Denver, Colorado, and have also traveled to the nation of India and have been involved in prison ministries for several years. Laurie's love for the Word of God inspired her to attend Bible College where she has received her Bachelor of Arts in Biblical Theology degree from the Minnesota Graduate School of Theology.

In March of 2018, Laurie has published a book called, *When Trouble Comes*, a thought-provoking work that tackles the challenges that people face in different aspects in life and how the Lord guides mankind in times of need, and that God does not desert his children in times of trouble and perplexing circumstances, but he has an amazing plan for each person.

Currently, Laurie serves as her husband's caregiver who suffered a stroke on Father's Day in 2016, which left him paralyzed on his left side. Despite this life-changing occurrence, Laurie and her husband continue in their faith in God and enjoy praying for others who need encouragement or healing in their bodies, mind, or soul all for the glory of God.